THE ORIGIN AND OF THE SIK CHAPELTOWN ROAD LEEDS 7

Satwant Kaur Rait
with
Harbhajan Singh Rait

2007

First published in Great Britain in 2007 by
SK RAIT
23 Vesper Rise
Leeds LS5 3NJ

Cpoyright © Satwant Kaur Rait & Harbhajan Singh Rait 2007

The rights of Satwant Kaur Rait and Harbhajan Singh Rait to be identified as the authors of this work has been asserted by them in accordance with the Copyright, Designs and Patents Act 1998

A catalogue record for this book is
available from the British Library

Paperback ISBN-13 978-0-9555085-0-9

All rights reserved. No part of this publication may be reproduced, transmitted, or stored in a retrieval system, in any form or by any means, without permission in writing from SK Rait.

Typset and printed by Peepal Tree Press Ltd, Leeds, UK

Dedicated to the many
Sikh Volunteers who have
worked for the long-term
benefit of the Sikh community
in Leeds

Contents

Introduction	7
Research Methods used in the study	11
Acknowledgements	17

Chapter 1:
    A Background to the Life of Sikhs in Leeds — 19

Chapter 2:
    The Origin and Development of the Sikh Temple — 28

Chapter 3:
    The Sikh Centre — 59

Chapter 4:
    The Constitution — 77

Chapter 5:
    Religious Activities of the Sikh Temple — 87

Chapter 6:
    The Educational Role of the *Gurdwara* — 106

Chapter 7:
    The Social and Political Role of the Sikh Temple — 119

Conclusion	138
Bibliography	146
Appendix 1: The Constitutions	148
Appendix 2: Executive Committees	191
Appendix 3: Biographical Sketches	237
Appendix 4: Glossary	259
About the Authors	271

Introduction

My keenness to contribute to the Sikh community and its heritage in Leeds led me to begin writing the history of the Sikh Temple, Leeds 7, in May 2005, after the success of my previous book on Sikh women in England. The main aim of this study is to give a historical perspective to the origin and development of the Sikh Temple from its very beginnings in an attempt to preserve our local Sikh heritage. It covers the background of the Sikh settlers in Leeds and provides a chronicled historical account of the three *Gurdwara* (Sikh place of worship) buildings here and of the Sikh Centre. It also analyses the religious role of the *Gurdwara* and the other educational, social and political activities which take place in the *Gurdwara*. The role of volunteers has always been significant in the running and management of the *Gurdwara* and their contributions are highlighted here. I felt it was necessary to name these volunteers in order to give them credit for their services and to keep their memory alive in years to come. This does not infringe confidentiality and privacy, as it has always been the policy of management committees to display the names of the newly-elected committee members after every general election. However, certain events in the community linked with the development of the *Gurdwara* have also been discussed without mention being made of the names of the people involved simply because these were outside the remit of this research. All the factors which have influenced the development of the *Gurdwara* either directly or indirectly, are mentioned.

The value and importance of preserving our local heritage have not up to now been recognised within the Sikh community for reasons of lack of time, expertise and resources. The first generation of Sikhs in Britain was occupied in building *gurdwaras* and the second generation in consolidating and maximising their numbers and during this process the requirement of preserving the records lost its impetus. This problem first came to my notice when someone from the Heritage Unit approached me to ask if it was possible to access records kept by *gurdwaras* in Leeds. I tried to check the catalogue in the Local History sections of Leeds Libraries and Leeds Archives and found that there were few records of such a nature and these were mainly topics covered by the local newspapers, the *Yorkshire Post* and the *Yorkshire Evening Post*. The Sikh Temple in Chapeltown was approached for access to the records kept by them, but this met with a poor response. As a librarian by profession, I have always felt that it is important to preserve records and decided that I would try to do something myself.

My research focuses on the origin and development of the Sikh Temple, the first *Gurdwara* established in Yorkshire and created jointly by Yorkshire Sikhs. It is now almost fifty years since this idea was conceived. A *gurdwara* is highly significant in the lives of Sikhs, as their lives revolve around it. For Sikhs it is not only a place of worship but also a centre for many other activities. The research I have done shows the continuity of Sikh religious traditions from their beginning in an alien culture and reflects the vigour and creativity of Sikhs.

There are a number of books available on the Sikh religion and religious traditions as well as on *gurdwaras* which have historical significance, such as the Golden Temple, Amritsar. However, there is a lack of original material written on the operative traditions of *gurdwaras* and what happens inside a *gurdwara*. It is rare to find any literature available on local places of Sikh worship and how these developed. Studies are scarce, partly because of the lack of documented information available from *gurdwaras* and partly as the result of the fear of a backlash from the community. Since the Second World War, Britain has become a multicultural society accommodating many cultures and faith communities. It is important to understand the different aspects of living faiths and how religion and religious faiths impact on people's lives. So far, nothing has been written on the history of *gurdwaras* in Leeds. This study is the first to relate not only the history of the original Sikh Temple in Leeds, but also to give an insight into the activities that have taken place in the *Gurdwara* and how they were managed. It will, I hope, contribute towards a more sophisticated understanding of the rich and dynamic Sikh religious values and the part played by *gurdwaras*.

Gurdwaras maintain records and the most common ones are the minutes of meetings, accounts and membership lists. However, members do not always think of preserving these records and finding the right places in which to store them, such as for example, the Local History section of a library, the local Archives, or perhaps a suitable corner of their own *gurdwara*. During my research period at the Sikh Temple, I was surprised to find many valuable papers under rubble and wet sand, as renovation work was being carried out on the old building, including in the room where the records were kept. One informant said that he had destroyed the records he had had in his possession because of a lack of space in which to keep them in his house.

This discovery led me to believe that there would be definite gaps and this assumption became true as the research proceeded and I did my best to fill some of the gaps through memories. In order to bridge these gaps, I made a strenuous effort to look for information before writing this book. I do not by any means claim that my work is comprehensive but it is surely a start in the right direction. I collected information through fieldwork from May 2005 to August 2006. My sources of information were minutes of meetings, interviews with knowledgeable people and the memories of early Sikh pioneers. There was also a thesis produced by a local Sikh, Sewa Singh Kalsi, on *The evolution of the Sikh community in Britain*. This research focused on the significance of caste among the Sikh community in Leeds and how it became an influential factor in the lives of Sikhs and their institutions. It was useful for me to read about his observations of the period during which he was active in the Sikh Temple.

The information collected could be presented in various ways but I chose to restrict it to a purely historical account describing the creation of the Sikh Temple in Leeds, and I hope that this, the first detailed book on this subject, will be an asset for the Sikh community, future researchers, the Leeds Archives, local and oral history units and other public and academic libraries. It should be stimulating for those working with multi-faith communities and should be a valuable addition to multi-faith literature. The book is aimed mainly at the Sikh community of Leeds, but may also be beneficial for the Sikh community in general and those members of the indigenous community who are interested in multi-faith questions. This is by no means an academic thesis and in order to make a simple, easy-to-read book, efforts have been made to avoid jargon, complicated vocabulary and unnecessary references from other source materials, in an attempt to maintain a natural flow.

Panjabi terms are used in the text, as the use of such terminology is natural and gives authenticity to a document so closely associated with the Sikh community. The terms are transcribed, but not formally transliterated because of the difficulty of adding diacritical marks on the computer keyboard. Panjabi words are given in italics and their meanings given in English within brackets. A glossary of Panjabi terms is provided at the end of the text. To avoid confusion, it is also important to explain the spelling of the words Punjab, Punjabi and Panjabi, which are used frequently in the text. Punjab is the name of the state and spelt with a 'u'. The culture, traditions and values of the Punjab are also spelt 'Punjabi', with a 'u', but the language of the Sikhs is spelt 'Panjabi', with an 'a'. Another point to note is that Sikh names may be transcribed into English with different spellings due to the inconsistent use of vowels in English language, for instance Gurmeet and Gurmit, are the same name with different spellings transcribed into English. Thus two Sikhs may spell the same name differently. I have tried to follow the approved and most accepted forms of spelling.

Research Methods Used in the Study

The main purpose of this study is to preserve the local heritage of the Leeds Sikh community by documenting the history of the Sikh Temple. This has been a challenging project as the *Gurdwara*'s records are not easily available. A number of different approaches have been used to collect the information. My husband took part in the collection of data from various sources. I tried to get written or documented information where possible. I used my own observation and experience and also I interviewed a number of informants. The identity of the informants was not always disclosed and their names were not mentioned. My husband approached Sikhs who had held responsible positions in the community and convinced them of the genuineness of my enquiries. Many of these men would have been unwilling to discuss the affairs of the *Gurdwara* with a woman and his participation in some of the interviews which I conducted was therefore of great importance in putting such men at their ease. Much information was acquired by talking to people at parties, functions and other such gatherings. Community gossip was another source, and, although not always reliable, it often gave leads to further investigation. Most of the information is substantiated by written evidence.

The information for this study was collected through unstructured interviews. Informal, conversational interviews on a one-to-one basis were held with the people who had been or are involved with the *Gurdwara*. This approach was preferred by many and ensured that they were not inhibited and could talk freely. This gave me a lot of information, though it was time-consuming as I often had to make several telephone calls to make appointments with the respondents. Most interviews were conducted in Panjabi, the language with which interviewees felt most comfortable, using general prompts and questions. They were given a choice of venue and those used were my house, their own homes or the *gurdwaras* they normally attended. They volunteered the information and no pressure of any kind was exerted upon them. They were asked to talk about their experiences or to share any information they had about the Sikh Temple. I listened to them patiently, without interrupting, in order to maintain the flow of their conversation. I made some notes at the time of the interviews, as they felt uneasy about recording their conversation on tape. These notes were mainly of names and dates, which were transferred onto a computer soon after the interview. A guide questionnaire was prepared to take some of their personal details, including their address and telephone number for future contact. Initially I would approach the people, introduce myself to them, explain the purpose of this research and finally ask if they were willing to participate. Appointments were made with willing subjects who were prepared to talk. An attempt was made to involve all those who had taken part in and contributed to the creation of this *Gurdwara*. Contacts were made with all the people I could locate, though it was difficult to track down some members as they had moved away from Leeds or had died. The families of people who had died were contacted wherever possible. These interviews proved very useful in eliciting their experiences and details of who else was involved. Some of them gave me records that they had kept in their possession. The interviews were a useful source of photographs and documented information, which proved valuable especially where gaps existed. I promised, and have maintained, strict confidentiality where necessary throughout the entire process.

For years for which records are missing the only other reliable source is the memory of the participants. There are often two basic problems associated with memories, that is to say, bias and inaccuracy. Most memories are biased in favour of the narrator and often lack objectivity. They are not always accurate simply because it is often difficult to recall things perfectly after the lapse of many years. Indeed, I found that it was almost impossible for anyone to remember everything in sequence even if they had a good memory. However, these memories were a good indicator of what had happened and proved useful in leading to further research. I tried to keep a balance by interviewing as many contemporaries as I could find and then tried to assess the accuracy of what they had all said.

Participants did not favour group discussions, as they did not want to take part in these, owing to the sensitive nature of the subject matter.

One group meeting was organized, but it was not attended by many people and proved unproductive.

Communication within the Sikh community takes place in Panjabi and this is the language used in *Gurdwara* meetings. The main documents produced by the *Gurdwara*, such as the proceedings of meetings, minutes and reports, are written in Panjabi using *Gurmukhi* script. In order to undertake such research and understand what was happening in the *Gurdwara*, knowledge of the Panjabi language is essential. I was in an advantageous position as it is my mother tongue and I read, write and speak Panjabi fluently. This has made it easy for me to read and understand the documentary material. I have had no difficulty in grasping the subtleties of meaning, which could have a considerable impact on drawing conclusions. It is also important for any researcher to understand the culture, religion and religious traditions of the community he or she is researching. I was brought up in a Sikh family for whom the way of life was dictated by Sikh religious values. My primary education was in a *Khalsa* (religious) school, which embedded religious values in me at an early age and gave me an insight into religious traditions. Thus my background and education have helped me to understand the way things were happening in the *Gurdwara*. I have lived within the Sikh community in Leeds for thirty-eight years and during these years I have acquired a great deal of knowledge about the local Sikh community and what has been happening in the *Gurdwara*. My husband knows many local Sikhs and that was helpful in tracing many participants. I also gathered information through chance conversations in the *langar* hall (where communal food is served) which were related to the *Gurdwara* committee members, and this proved invaluable for my research. I always like to keep up with developments taking place in the Sikh community and try to attend the Sunday *diwan* (congregation) if I am in Leeds.

My language skills and background have made it possible for me to become a participant observer, an approach most commonly used in social sciences research. Direct observation is obviously the core technique used in participant observation. This approach offers a direct experience of the community's behaviour in a variety of situations. I attended annual general meetings and other meetings open to general members of the *Gurdwara* regularly. My husband and I regularly attend the *Gurdwara* and we have observed its activities closely ever since I decided to do this research. We have participated in many programmes and events organised by the Sikh Temple. During my research period I spent most of my weekends in the *Gurdwara*. This brought me into direct contact with many men, women and young Sikhs enabling me to listen to their views. Thus, I gained an insight into the behaviour pattern of the Sikh community and their leaders over the years. I participated in the celebration of community festivals in the *Gurdwara* and in other festivals and events taking place outside the *Gurdwara*. This also gave me the opportunity to gather information that helped me, in some cases, to judge the adequacy of my account. This was done through 'total participation'; becoming an inconspicuous member of the group.

The minutes are the only written records of the discussions and decisions made by Executive Committees and Minute books are strictly guarded and not made public. It is possible to use minutes as a guide if one accepts the fact that they may be biased. The Sikh Temple has three registers, which contain the minutes of meetings from 1976 onwards. The first register covers from 22.8.76 to 21.8.82 and has 350 pages; the second covers the period from 18.9.82 to 9.5.99 and has 518 pages and the third was started on 23.5.99 and is still in use. I found that the quality of the minutes varied from month to month depending on the minute takers. The minutes of 17th July 1982 suggested that minutes should be concise and should not be written in a way that brings friction in the long term, indicating that minutes ought to be written with caution. The minutes also stated that in May 1982 the committee decided to burn unnecessary records lying in the General Secretary's cabinet. There was no explanation of what these unnecessary records were and what they contained, but I found that records prior to August 1976 were completely missing from the records kept by the *Gurdwara*. This confirmed my view that there would be gaps, but the recollections of pioneer Sikhs and the written information given by them played a significant role in supplying the missing details.

It was fortunate that I had conducted a feasibility study before putting in an application for the research grant. During this period, I collected a lot of information including documents and photographs, which proved extremely useful, and had a brief sight of the minute books. Later I encountered difficulties in accessing these minutes, which made it impossible to verify the accuracy of some of the information given in the book. Sadly, information sharing for a research project like mine does not always work in harmony with the policies of committees, which frequently result in information blockage.

A study of this nature often creates difficulties for researchers. This particular project is closely associated with the Sikh community and their place of worship. Faith groups are often sensitive towards their religions and the image of their religious institutions, and researchers can be vulnerable if not aware of this. It is also difficult for the faith communities to accept the reality of many situations especially where facts and accounts are not favourable towards themselves. I found too that there was a poor response to written publicity. Sikh communities prefer oral traditions and they are better in conversation and meetings rather than in recording or responding by writing.

The Sikh belief is that women have an equal status in Sikh society and that they are treated equally. In many areas they do indeed enjoy more than equal status but in others they are marginalized or ignored. I was often annoyed and upset by evidence of the limited social role of Sikh women and by the expectations placed on them in the Sikh community, as well as by the failure of some men to credit me with the seriousness I thought my study deserved. There were also other attitudes and responses that occasionally impinged on the process of data collection. Talking with responsible and serious-minded men is a valuable source of information collection and, unfortunately, in a traditional Sikh community, a woman is not permitted to take part in such conversations. As I have already explained, there were times during my period of research when only the presence of my husband allowed me to gain the information I was looking for, and this I found, and continue to find, difficult to accept.

Again, Sikh *Gurus* strictly condemn caste. However, in spite of their condemnation, caste plays a significant role in Sikh society. Caste loyalty is often placed above many other good causes and such an approach to decision-making is an embarrassment for the Sikh community. Thus, caste bias was another barrier. It can be seen therefore, that this was a challenging study for me, as a Sikh woman, to conduct, but despite these problems I endeavoured to remain unbiased and focused on my task and I hope that the entire Sikh community will benefit from my work.

Acknowledgements

This project on the origin and development of the Sikh Temple, Leeds 7 has been funded by a Local Heritage Initiative (LHI) grant. The Local Heritage Initiative is a national grant scheme that helps local groups to investigate, explain and care for their local landscape, landmarks, traditions and culture. The Heritage Lottery Fund (HLF) provides the grant but the scheme was formerly administered by the Countryside Agency with additional funding from Nationwide Building Society. The research for this project was undertaken between May 2005 and August 2006 with the support of the LHI and I acknowledge that without their financial help this research would never have taken place.

A study like this is never accomplished by one person working alone. As most of the information was collected through fieldwork, I would like to thank all those who provided invaluable support and information for the completion of this research. I am particularly indebted to the pioneer Sikhs for their cooperation and help. Among those who deserve special mention are Daljit Singh Sond, Gurmeet Singh Nahal, Bhajan Singh Reehal, Piara Singh Chaggar, Kirpal Singh Duggal, Resham Singh Gill, Sohan Singh Seehra and Sarwan Singh Dandi. They helped me by relating their experiences and sharing their memories with me, and offering me access to any records they had in their possession. I am also grateful to the families of some of the pioneer Sikhs who readily offered me information, such as the daughter of Atma Singh Sood living in Northamptonshire and Sarwan Singh Cheema in Newcastle. Their kindness and hospitality will never be forgotten.

The research was made possible through the support I received from some individual members of the then serving Management Committee of the Sikh Temple. I have no hesitation in mentioning the names of these individuals, especially the President of the Sikh Temple, Nirmal Singh Sangha, and Bikrampal Singh, known as 'Raja', who helped me in good faith. They encouraged me to carry out this research and made special efforts to assist me in spite of the split in the Management Committee over supporting this project. This difference of opinion made it very difficult for me to access the minute books of committee meetings and I often had to rely on the memory of those people prepared to support me. I am completely at a loss for the words to thank them for the trust they placed in me. I am grateful for the help I received from Jatinder Singh Mehmi, Sukhraj Singh Gill, Baljinder Kaur Toor and Sarbjit Kaur concerning the project they have been doing with Sikh youths. It was good to know that the younger generation of Sikhs is more appreciative of what I was doing and of why I have been putting so much effort into this research. There are many more informants who shared their ideas and views with me, especially Ajit Singh Nijjar and Ujjal Singh Ryatt. I acknowledge their honesty, frankness and cooperation. They not only gave their valuable time to me but also directed me to other individuals who could offer me useful information and without whose help I would not have been able to give an overview of the whole situation. My expressions of gratitude for their assistance hardly suffice but unfortunately I cannot name them for the reasons of confidentiality. I am also grateful to those previous presidents of the Sikh Temple who spared time for me in spite of their busy schedules and voluntarily gave me personal information for the biographical sketches given in Appendix 3. A few did not want to be mentioned for personal reasons and their wishes have been respected.

I would like to express my sincere gratitude to Sue Gamblen, who is a Business Development Manager for Leeds Social Services, for sharing her views with me about the *Baba* Dal Day Centre and to Brett Harrison (Consultant Archivist) who acted as an editorial assistant and took a great deal of interest in this document. I offer my gratitude to the volunteers who offered to read the draft of this book and made constructive suggestions, namely, Dr Greta Rait, the Reverend Graham Brownlee, Regional Minister of the Yorkshire Baptist Association, and Robert Beard and Gillian Murray from the Churches Regional Commission for Yorkshire and the Humber. My thanks go also to my friend Susan Dolamore, who has diligently checked and corrected the final version of my text. It goes without saying that my family was extremely helpful at all times. My husband, especially, gave me all the help and advice I needed to complete this research. I needed his assistance desperately in many situations and I am pleased to give him credit for the part he has played in bringing this work to fruition by adding his name as supporting author.

Chapter 1
Background

1. 0 Introduction

Sikhs originate mainly from the Punjab, a state in northern India where they form the majority. They have a strong sense of being a separate community, based on a distinct religion (Sikhism). They are proud of their culture, traditions and language. Sikhs are adventurous by nature and they have a tendency to migrate whensoever they find any opportunity. The Leeds Sikh community is a mixture of direct migrants from the Punjab and secondary migrants from East Africa. A few Sikhs are from Malaysia and Singapore and lately there have been some asylum seekers from Afghanistan. The population of Sikhs in Leeds is about 7,586 (Census 2001) and at present their religious needs are met by seven *gurdwaras* (places of worship). Four *gurdwaras* are situated on Chapeltown Road, Leeds 7, one on Harehills Lane, Leeds 7, one in Beeston in Leeds 11 and one on Tong Road, Leeds 12. The history of *gurdwaras* in Leeds began with the Sikh Temple, Leeds 7, which was the first *gurdwara*, established in 1959.

2. 0 Sikhism

Sikhism is the name given to the religion and faith of the Sikhs. It became a socio-spiritual phenomenon in Punjab. Over the years, it acquired its own customs, traditions and ceremonies. The word Sikh is derived from the Pali *sikha* or Sanskrit *sisya*, meaning the disciple. A Sikh is a disciple of the ten *Gurus* (from *Guru* Nanak to *Guru* Gobind Singh) believing in the teachings of *Sri Guru Granth Sahib* (the Holy Scripture of Sikhs) and does not believe in any other religious doctrine. The *Guru Granth Sahib* is the Sikh's ultimate *Guru* (guide). Sikhs are monotheists and believe that there is only one God, who is beyond time and beyond the circle of death and rebirth. He is immortal, omniscient and omnipresent. He is the abstract principle of truth. Sikhism accepts the theory of *karma* (taking responsibility for one's actions) and transmigration of souls from one life to another, until their ultimate union with God.

Sikhism was founded in the fifteenth century in northern India. *Guru* Nanak, the founder, decided to crusade against fanaticism and intolerance. He raised his voice against the meaningless rituals and discriminations against the lower castes and women which were then prevalent in the society. It is a simple and practical religion, which was founded to promote gender and caste equality, human dignity and the maintenance of honest living. Sikhism has some unique characteristics, which are based on the ethics of *kirt karo* (honest living), *wand chhako* (share what you earn with the less fortunate) and *naam japo* (recite the name of the Lord). The code of conduct called the Sikh *Rahit Maryada* guides the Sikhs in leading their daily life, the performance of religious duties, the importance of the *gurdwara*, reading the Holy book and living and working in accordance with the principles of *gurmat* (according to the guidelines given by *Gurus*).

Sikh *Gurus* regarded the world as real and meaningful. The idea of *mukti* (transmigration of soul and its union with God) was given a new concept of striving for a moral and spiritual mode of living. Sikhism advocated full participation in life and it established the primacy of the householder's life. In fact normal family life became the medium of spiritual training and expression. The Sikh *Gurus* made *seva* (voluntary service) a prerequisite to spiritual development. They repeatedly emphasised that *haumen* (individualism or self-centredness) is at the root of the problems from which the individual and society suffer. They stressed that one should free oneself from the evil manifestations of *haumen*, i.e. lust, anger, greed, attachment and pride. Sikhs are advised to abstain from *halal* (meat slaughtered by the process of slow and ritual killing), intoxicants, adultery and polygamy. It is important to mention Sikh identity, Sikh traditions, celebrations, and Sikh places of worship, in order to understand the contents of this book.

3. 0 Sikh Identity

Sikhs were given their identity by the tenth *Guru*, Gobind Singh. He created the initiation ceremony and the Sikh symbols. In order to become a complete Sikh, one has to undergo an initiation ceremony and keep the Sikh symbols (the five *K's*), which give a unique and easily recognised external identity. A Sikh is not born a Sikh, but acquires that status by following Sikh teachings and undergoing the specifically religious rite of *amrit chhakna* or initiation. Formal initiation into the Sikh faith is traditionally one of the most important and sacred ceremonies of Sikhism and it is open to both men and women. Taking *amrit* is an expression of full commitment to religion for a Sikh. The initiation ceremony is seen as the way to spiritual development, when coupled with adherence to the ethical principles of Sikhism.

There are three distinct terms used for a Sikh and it is important to define them in order to make a clear distinction, i.e. *amritdhari* (baptised), *sehajdhari* (clean-shaven), *kesadhari* (uncut hair and turbaned). An initiated Sikh is called *amritdhari* and Sikhs consider as *amritdhari* a complete Sikh who not only keeps the Sikh identity but also attempts to follow the Sikh way of life as well as accepting the doctrines of Sikhism. There are also *sehajdhari* Sikhs, who believe in the teachings of *Gurus*, but are not initiated and do not maintain an external identity by wearing or using the outward symbols of Sikhism. There are also Sikhs who keep a beard, uncut hair and wear a turban but are not initiated. They are referred as *kesadhari* Sikhs. It is believed by some Sikhs that *amritdharis* are the only genuine Sikhs and the other two categories are not true Sikhs.

3. 1 The five *K's*

Initiated Sikhs wear the five articles of faith commonly known as 'the five *K's*' - all beginning with the letter 'K'. The symbols are *kes* (uncut hair), *kangha* (comb), *kirpan* (dagger), *kachha* (undergarment) and *kara* (steel bangle). *Kes* is symbolic of an acceptance of God's will and considered to be a sign of spiritual and moral strength. The *kangha* is a symbol of personal care and cleanliness, orderly spirituality and discipline of the mind. The *kirpan* is a symbol of freedom from oppression and servility. It signifies dignity and self-respect. Its obvious meaning is of self-defence and individual freedom. The *kachha* is a symbol of chastity. This also signifies modesty, moral restraint and continence. The *kara* is a symbol of responsibility and allegiance to God. It is worn on the right wrist, reminding Sikhs that God is eternal with no beginning and no end.

4.0 Sikh Traditions

Sikh traditions emphasize Sikh ethics mentioned earlier, i.e. *kirt karo* (earning your living through honest and approved means), *wand chhako* (sharing with less fortunate) and *naam japo* (to recite the name of God). In addition, there are other important traditions such as equality, *seva* (voluntary service), to accompany *sangat* (congregation), *langar* (communal food), *pangat* (sitting in a row to take *langar*), and above all *bhana manana* (accepting the will of God).

Seva is highly valued in the Sikh religion. The ideal of a true Sikh is to look beyond the self and to serve one's fellow beings. Sikhs take great pride in doing *seva* in *gurdwaras*, undertaking community work and contributing towards other humane causes. *Wand chhakna* includes giving money to the needy and sharing food with the poor and hungry. Sikh religious traditions recommend giving *daswandh* (one tenth of earnings to charitable causes). Sikh families regularly donate money towards *langar*, the maintenance of *gurdwaras*, charities and other humane causes. The practice of *langar* (communal food) is important in Sikhism and offers everyone a free meal in a *gurdwara*. It is essential for *langar* takers to sit in a *pangat* (row) without any distinction between caste, creed, religion or social status, which lays the foundation for equality. *Langar* has become a unique and integral part of Sikh life. Sikhism also gives importance to congregation, a strong sense of fellowship, and belonging to the community. *Guru* Nanak encouraged a congregational style of spirituality; keeping shrines open to people of all castes and creeds without any discrimination. This is one of the reasons why the *gurdwara* is so important for Sikhs. Sikhs are also advised to carry out *sangat* (to sit in the company of good people) believing that sitting in the *sangat* with other devotees helps to develop good qualities and purify the mind. Sikh belief in *kirt karo* (earning your living through honest and approved means) puts an emphasis on a strong work ethos and *bhana manana* (accepting the will of God) means believing that everything happens according to the will of God and it should be accepted without complaining. One should remain the same in happiness and in grief.

Equality is a key concept in the Sikh religion with regard to caste, class and gender. The teachings of Sikhism categorically reject using the caste system as a pretext for promoting inequality. *Guru* Gobind Singh, the tenth *Guru* of Sikhs declared caste to be a hindrance to the brotherhood of the *Khalsa* and to ensure equality, he instituted the practice of adding 'Singh' to the names of all Sikh males and 'Kaur' to the names of Sikh females. This is significant for Sikhs as these names bring them within the fold of *Khalsa Panth* (Sikh brotherhood). The Sikh religion also promotes a classless society, giving more importance to virtue than wealth. The status of an individual should be determined by deeds or merits and not by class position. The Sikh concept of equality applies to both men and women in secular and religious life. Sikhism advocates sex equality and accords women an equal place in society.

5. 0 Sikh Celebrations

Sikhs have many religious occasions and festivals to celebrate. They celebrate the anniversaries of their *Gurus*, called *gurpurabs*. Gurdwaras celebrate *gurpurabs* elaborately, commemorating the births and deaths of the *Gurus* and important events in their lives. Some are celebrated more than others. The most important seem to be the martyrdom of *Guru* Arjun Dev (May or June), the birthday of *Guru* Nanak (November), the martyrdom of *Guru* Tegh Bahadur (November-December), and the birthday of *Guru* Gobind Singh (December-January). Additional anniversaries are celebrated by other *gurdwaras* but for many years the Sikh Temple has celebrated only the *gurpurabs* mentioned above.

All *gurpurab* ceremonies start with *akhandpath* (continuous recitation of the entire *Guru Granth Sahib*), which normally begins on Friday morning and finishes on Sunday morning. *Granthis* (readers of the Holy book) work in relays and the recitation takes approximately forty-eight hours. On the first day of each lunar month (when the sun enters the new Zodiac sign), *sangrand* is celebrated in *gurdwaras*. It is observed with a special service organized in *gurdwaras* and the new month is announced with the reading of the relevant portion, '*Barahmaha*' (hymns relating to twelve months), from the *Guru Granth Sahib*. Many *gurdwaras* start s*adharanpath* (the ordinary recitation of *Guru Granth Sahib*) on this day and hold *bhog* (the finishing ceremony) on the next *sangrand*.

There are many festivals celebrated by Sikhs. The most important Sikh festival is *Vaisakhi,* widely celebrated by Sikhs all over the world. It is the spring harvest festival in India and has particular importance in the Punjab. Sikhs celebrate this day to mark the birth of *Khalsa Panth,* which gave them a distinct identity and code of conduct. Initiation ceremonies are widely held in *gurdwaras. Akhandpath* is performed and *langar* is served for all three days. *Nagar kirtans,* religious processions, are carried out in many cities of Britain by the Sikh *sangat* (congregation). There are also other popular Indian festivals and some of these are celebrated by Sikhs. The Sikh *Gurus* gave these festivals an added religious interpretation. *Diwali,* the festival of lights, is the popular festival of Hindus. Sikhs celebrate this festival as their sixth *Guru* Hargobind was released from Gwalior Jail on this day. On his release, he went to the city of Amritsar where he was given a tumultuous welcome. The festival of *Lohri* falls on *makar sangrand,* around mid January and Sikhs celebrate it if a boy is born or a son gets married. In the Punjab, it is celebrated in homes, but in England it is celebrated in *gurdwaras* where a special *diwan* (religious programme) is held on this day. *Maghi* also falls in January and is named after *Magh,* an Indian lunar month. It is normally celebrated in a *gurdwara* and not at home. It is connected with the battle of Mukatsar where *Guru* Gobind Singh found forty men from Majha (a region of Punjab) who deserted him during the siege of Anandpur. Their women-folk were so ashamed of them that they would not let them enter their homes. The men then returned to reinforce the *Guru's* small army, and died fighting for him. The *Guru* was deeply moved and tore up the paper on which they had written their *betaba* (disclaimer), in front of *Bhai* Maha Singh (one of the *gursikh* fighting the battle) as a sign of forgiveness and reconciliation. He embraced each one of them, as they lay dead or dying, and called them the saved ones. This *mela* (festival) of *Maghi* is celebrated in their memory at Mukatsar and many Sikhs go there.

6. 0 *Gurdwara*

Faith is sustained through places of worship. The place of Sikh worship is called a *gurdwara* which literally means 'the doorway to God'. It is also called a *gurughar* meaning house of the Lord and Sikh temple

(Sikh place of worship). It is an essential institution for Sikhs because of the congregational nature of the religion and the importance given to the *sangat* (congregation) by the Sikh *Gurus*. Sikh *Gurus* gave the *sangat* a status higher than that of a *Guru*. The *gurdwara* is central to the lives of Sikhs as all the life cycle rites such as birth, naming and wedding ceremonies take place in a *gurdwara*. The last journey of death also departs finally from a *gurdwara*. There are a number of other activities taking place all around the year. *Gurdwaras* promote the Sikh religion and Sikh traditions. The essential characteristic of a *gurdwara* is that a copy of the *Guru Granth Sahib* is always kept in the main hall. This is the highest spiritual authority for Sikhs and they are instructed to follow the *shabad* (words) and teachings of their Sikh scripture. Sikhs treat their Holy book as a living *Guru*. There are other ways of promoting Sikh teachings, which often form part of daily and weekly prayers such as *kirtan* (hymn-singing) and *viakhia* (explaining the original text in simple Panjabi). The *Guru Granth Sahib* is written in *ragas* (verse form) and the hymns from this Holy book are sung in *kirtan*. *Gurdwaras* provide exceptional facilities. *Langar* (communal food) is served in almost all *gurdwaras* as part of Sikh religious traditions and also accommodation is offered to those visiting a *gurdwara*, free of any charge. Most *gurdwaras* offer religion and language teaching and maintain a library for its members. A *gurdwara* is therefore, a multipurpose institution for Sikhs. It binds them together religiously and socially and becomes a unifying force in a crisis. Donation from the *sangat* is the main source of the *gurdwara* income. The Sikh *sangat* generally donates generously. In addition, Sikh *sevadars* (volunteers) offer their services voluntarily and with dedication to run and manage *gurdwaras*. Management committees are elected democratically every year just after *Vaisakhi*. The executive committee is formed from within this committee, which takes the responsible positions of management. The committees are fully accountable to the *sangat* for their deeds and actions while in office through general and extraordinary meetings.

The language of communication for Sikhs is Panjabi and the script used in writing is *Gurmukhi*. *Guru* Angad Dev simplified and codified the *Gurmukhi* script. The Holy Sikh scripture *Guru Granth Sahib* and other original religious literature is written in Panjabi. Sikhs attach great importance to the Panjabi language and Panjabi teaching has become an integral part of *gurdwara* activities.

7. 0 Sikh life cycle rites and ceremonies

The life cycle rites of birth, naming, marriage and death have a special significance for the Sikh community and are closely associated with religion. These ceremonies are performed in the *gurdwara* in the presence of close family, relatives and friends.

Religion forms an integral part of Sikh life, from birth until death. The birth of any child, boy or girl, should be taken as a blessing from God. When a child is born, a naming ceremony called *naamkaran* is held in the *gurdwara* a few weeks after the birth. Nearly all children receive their name in this traditional manner. After a prayer from the family, the name of the child is taken from the first letter of the *vak* (the first word of the passage of the *Guru Granth Sahib* read after its random opening) from the left-hand page. Parents will then decide upon a name beginning with this first letter and the *granthi* will announce it publicly, adding Kaur for a girl and Singh for a boy.

The Sikh marriage ceremony is known as *anand karaj* (*anand* meaning bliss and *karaj* meaning ceremony). In Sikhism, marriage is not viewed simply as a social and civil contract, but is seen as a spiritual state, since family life is central to the Sikh way of life. The marriage ceremony takes place in the *gurdwara* before midday and involves *lavan* (the recitation of four stanzas from the *Guru Granth Sahib*) in the presence of the bride, the bridegroom and their relatives and friends. This religious ceremony is performed for all Sikh weddings.

Death is a part of the natural life cycle. At death, Sikhs cremate the dead body. The cremation ceremony is a family occasion. The dead body is washed and clothed by family members who ensure that the symbols of the faith are worn. The coffin is brought home and the family members pray for the soul. The coffin is then taken to the *gurdwara* where other acquaintances and friends pray for the deceased's soul. From the *gurd-*

wara, it proceeds to the crematorium. At the crematorium, the *granthi* (Sikh priest) leads the mourners in the reading of hymns. Everybody goes back to the *gurdwara* after the funeral where the reading of *Guru Granth Sahib* is completed and *langar* is served to all the mourners. The sharing of food at this time is particularly meaningful. It symbolizes the continuity of social life and normal activities. The *granthi* also accompanies the family when they take ashes and bones for consigning in running water. At first Sikhs in Leeds had a problem with consigning ashes, as there was no permanent place for this. They used to go around to find a quiet place near running water to consign the ashes, but eventually they acquired a permanent place on the river Aire on Kirkstall Road, with the help of Leeds City Council who worked closely with a Sikh Councillor, Ujjal Singh Ryatt.

In general it can be said that religion or at least religious observance has continued to play a dominant part in the lives of Sikhs since their migration to this country. They go to their *gurdwara* regularly. Their lives revolve around the *gurdwara* as all life cycle rites and religious festivals take place there and it also plays a significant role in their social and political life.

Chapter 2

The Sikh Temple
The Origin and Development of the Sikh Temple Leeds 7

1.0 Introduction

A *gurdwara* is a fundamental Sikh institution, which plays a central role in the life of the Sikh community. There is a long tradition of building *gurdwaras* among the Sikhs as all life cycle rites are conducted in them and they play a significant role in bringing the community together. The congregational nature of the Sikh religion also makes their place of worship highly significant for the community. These are the main reasons that building a *gurdwara* becomes one of the priorities for Sikhs in a new place of settlement. Sikhs began to migrate to Britain in the 1940s. By the 1950s there were only a small number of Sikhs in Leeds; this is supported by the source *Sikh Temples in the UK* (1976), which stated that there were roughly fifty individuals altogether. They formed a small community mainly of males and met to pray in one another's homes. Those who could play the harmonium and do *shabad kirtan* (hymn singing) did so whenever they had the opportunity. Sikhs normally shared their accommodation and those sharing the houses would join in. At first, meetings took place in three houses, namely, at Gurmeet Singh Nahal's house which was shared by his cousin, Sarwan Singh Cheema, and a lodger, Surain Singh Bhambra, who had come from Kenya for a short visit, at Daljit Singh Sond's home where a talented singer and harmonium player, Tirath Ram Sharma, came to stay as a lodger in 1949, and at the house of Tehal Singh, a devout Sikh, who possessed a copy of the *Guru Granth Sahib* where a regular weekly *diwan* was held.

Gurmeet Singh Nahal told me that, in the absence of a *gurdwara*, Sikhs began to meet on a weekly basis at his house at 53 Caledonia Road, Leeds 7. Surain Singh Bhamra played the harmonium as a hobby. He used to sing *shabads* (hymns) and did *kirtan* (hymn singing with harmonium). Between four and six men, including Inder Singh Ryatt, Kirpal

Singh Duggal, Bhajan Singh Reehal, Sarwan Singh Cheema and Teja Singh, attended regularly. Religious and social gatherings were also held at Tehal Singh's house at 23 Amberley Grove, Leeds 7, on Sundays, *sangrand* (the first day of the month according to the Indian calendar) and *Vaisakhi* (the day of the birth of the *Khalsa*, a term used for baptised Sikhs, created by the tenth *Guru* Gobind Singh) until the establishment of the *Gurdwara*. Sarwan Singh Bahra was very good at reading the *Guru Granth Sahib*. Tehal Singh's son, Sampuran Singh, informed me that this began in 1955 initially for the family only but soon attracted other Sikhs, namely, Balwant Singh Birdi, Piara Singh Chaggar, Mota Singh Bhamra, Harbans Singh Bhamra and Sarwan Singh Bahra. These religious gatherings brought the men closer together and before 1958 much background work was done unconsciously in these informal meetings in thinking about the need for a place of worship.

Sikhs began to feel the real need for a communal place for social gathering on the occasion of the death of Charan Das, a foundry worker at Catton Foundries in Leeds and originally from the village of Tahli in the district of Jalandhar. There was nowhere for his friends to sit together and mourn his death. After his death, Ajit Singh Sandhu, Dalip Singh Sohel, Narotam Dev Mishra, Dharam Singh Sagoo, Sohan Singh Virdee, Pritam Singh Dhiman and Resham Singh Gill met to play cards at Sandhu's house at 18 Kingston Road, Leeds 2 and Narotam Dev raised the point that they needed a place where they could all get together. Dalip Singh Sohel worked with Kirpal Singh Duggal and the next day he spoke to him about this suggestion. In response, Kirpal Singh Duggal said that he would join them if something sensible and beneficial for the whole Sikh community could be done. He made the suggestion that they should think about having a *gurdwara*, which would meet both religious and social needs. Surain Singh met Bhajan Singh Reehal whom he knew from East Africa and during their conversation he also suggested having a *gurdwara*. It is one thing to think and talk about a project and another to put it into action, yet it seems certain that from these casual conversations and the motivation of a few individuals, the idea to build the first *gurdwara* in Leeds was conceived and developed. Thus the history of *gurdwaras* in Leeds began with the enthusiasm and foresightedness of a small number of devout Sikhs who were keen to maintain and continue their religious traditions bearing in mind the future needs of Sikh families in an alien culture.

In April 1957, an ad-hoc committee was formed which also took the responsibility of organizing important functions and *gurpurabs* (anniversary celebrations of *Gurus*). Sikhs celebrated *gurpurabs* and functions in hired public buildings and the most important *gurpurab* was the *Vaisakhi* (birth of *Khalsa*) celebrated in 1958 in the Civic Theatre on Cookridge Street in Leeds, and attended by almost 150 Sikhs from all over Yorkshire. Tirath Ram Sharma, Resham Singh Gill (both from Leeds) and *ragis* (hymn singers) from London were invited; Santokh Singh Partakh, Joginder Singh Sodhi and a *ragan* (female hymn singer), Surinder Kaur, performed the *kirtan*. The significance of this *gurpurab* lies in the fact that it was one particular aspect of the Sikh tradition which became the main focus of Sikh corporate group identity in Leeds. This also brought Sikhs living in other parts of the Yorkshire in touch with Leeds Sikhs. This togetherness formed the basis for the first *Gurdwara* bought jointly by Yorkshire Sikhs in 1959.

1.1 The first *Gurdwara* building

A formal meeting was arranged on 2nd February 1958 to pursue the idea of having a place for a *gurdwara*. It was held at 21 Cobden Place, Leeds 2, the house of Dalip Singh Sohel. Friends informed other members who attended this meeting. Dalip Singh Sohel contacted Balwant Singh Birdi who was living at 2 Florence Road, Leeds 12 and invited him to the meeting. Narotam Dev Mishra, who had a market stall in Barnsley, rang Daljit Singh Sond. This meeting was recorded and from then on a minute book has been kept for recording the business conducted at future meetings. Inder Singh Ryatt chaired this first meeting and it was agreed unanimously that they would form an association in order to buy a *gurdwara* building. This was named as the United Sikh Association and for the time being the correspondence address given was 39 Cobden Place Leeds 2 (Inder Singh Ryatt's house). The names proposed for the Executive Committee were Balwant Singh Birdi, Sohan Singh Virdi, Ajit Singh Sandhu, Atma Singh Sood, Narotam Dev Mishra, Daljit Singh

Sond, G. S. Chaudhary (his full name was not given in the minutes), Pritam Singh Dhiman and Mohinder Singh Nyota. The next meeting scheduled on 9th February 1958 did not proceed due to the lack of a quorum. It was postponed until 16th February 1958, to be held at 21 Cobden Place, Leeds 2. At this meeting, the Executive Committee was elected and its members were Balwant Singh Birdi, known as Mistry (President), Narotam Dev Mishra (Vice-President), Kirpal Singh Duggal (General Secretary), Daljit Singh Sond (Secretary), Inder Singh Ryatt and G. S. Chaudhary (Finance Secretaries) and Dalip Singh Sohel and Sarwan Singh (Auditors). The involvement of these individuals belonging to different castes as indicated by their surnames suggests that in the early years of settlement, all Sikhs irrespective of their caste, class and sect worked together for the common cause of having a place of worship. Non-Sikhs also participated and one was elected to the Executive Committee. One informant said that 'We lived and worked together and the question of caste and religion never arose'. In the words of another informant, 'We had love and understanding and thought for the good of our community.' Their main source of inspiration was to maintain religious traditions and Punjabi values. Punjabi values are a fusion of the values of Hindus, Muslims and Sikhs who lived together in the Punjab and many such values formed an inseparable part of the Sikh traditions.

The next meeting was held on 2nd March 1958 at the house of Gurmej Singh (111 Great Horton Road, Bradford). In this meeting it was confirmed that the Sikh community of Bradford would fully support the proposal of having a building for a *gurdwara* whether it was sited in Leeds or Bradford. It was unanimously agreed that Gurmej Singh would be the nominated person for collecting donations in Bradford for a *gurdwara* building.

The Ordinary General Meeting of 9th March 1958 which was held at 18 Kensington Road, Leeds 2, at the house of Ajit Singh Sandhu decided a) the date for celebrating *Vaisakhi* which was fixed for 20th April 1958; b) to buy a printing machine; c) to approve unanimously the draft on the rules and regulations to run the *Gurdwara*; d) to present the accounts.

The *Vaisakhi* festival of 1958 was celebrated in the Leeds Civic Theatre building. There was a large gathering and Sikhs enjoyed getting together on this important festival of the birth of *Khalsa*. This *gurpurab* was highly significant for the Sikh community as it was symbolic of Sikh identity. Hari Singh, Pargat Singh and Sarwan Singh from the village of Lalian donated the harmonium and *tabla* (drums) and Ajit Singh of Mohaddipur village donated a copy of the *Guru Granth Sahib*. At this time Sikhs were gradually establishing themselves in this new cultural environment and their continuing engagement with their religious traditions and their generous financial contributions were forming the basis for a *gurdwara*.

It is important to mention that all the meetings took place in committee members' houses in rotation before they acquired the *Gurdwara* building and they provided refreshments voluntarily. The election of Executive Committees was held annually. (The names of the committee members for the years 1957 to 2005 are given in Appendix 2.) The meeting held on 29th June 1958 was an important meeting for the further development of the *Gurdwara*. The committee fully endorsed the idea of buying a building. In order to raise funds for this, a committee was formed to collect donations and its members were Gurbaksh Singh Rai, Sarwan Singh Kang, Sohan Singh Virdi, Sarwan Singh Cheema, Daljit Singh Sond, Narotam Dev, Karam Singh, Gurmej Singh Sahota, Resham Singh Gill, Piara Singh Chaggar, Tehal Singh, Kirpal Singh Duggal, Sarwan Singh Bahra and Kartar Singh. These members were drawn from Leeds, Bradford and Doncaster, thus demonstrating the commitment from across Yorkshire.

It was decided to celebrate four *gurpurabs* annually, that is to say, *Vaisakhi*, *Guru* Nanak Dev and *Guru* Gobind Singh's birthdays and the martyrdom of *Guru* Arjun Dev. Two *gurpurabs* were to be held in Bradford and two in Leeds. The *gurpurab* of *Guru* Nanak's birthday was celebrated on 14th December 1958 in Bradford Co-operative Hall on Thornton Road. The *prakash* (opening ceremony) of the *Guru Granth Sahib* was done on the stage and guest speakers were invited. *Guru* Gobind Singh's birthday was celebrated in Leeds and the *Dhadi Jatha* (a group of bards who sings religious warrior songs) of Pritam Singh was invited. The *Vaisakhi* of 1959 was celebrated at the Civic Theatre in Leeds. The responsibility of *sadharan path* (recitation of *Guru Granth Sahib*) was given to *Bhai* (word used to show respect) Hari Singh. All those involved did almost all the work voluntarily though the committee decided to pay the religious singers and *pathis* (reciters of the *Guru Granth Sahib*). As mentioned in the minutes, a fee of £2 was paid to *Pandit* Tirath Ram Sharma (a local harmonium player and singer) and £15 to the *Dhadi Jatha*. They were also given money donated directly by the *sangat* (congregation). *Bhai* Hari Singh was paid £7/5/- (£7.25p) for the *sadharan path* on *Vaisakh*i. This was the first time that payments were made.

The maintenance of accurate accounts became essential, as the source of income was mainly from donations. In the meeting held on 4th January 1959, the main agenda item was the accounts and how to present them. Ranbir Singh, who was auditor that year demonstrated the correct procedure of presenting accounts and suggested that proper receipts should be given. It was stated in the minutes that accounts for that year were presented and passed unanimously. This procedure was followed in the years to come.

Sikhs from all over Yorkshire celebrated *gurpurabs* together and this united approach proved useful in establishing their own place of worship. Sikhs were prepared financially to commit to a *gurdwara* building. In the meeting held on 12th April 1959 it was agreed unanimously that a small house should be bought to serve as a *gurdwara*. The responsibility for finding and buying such a house was originally given to Inder Singh Ryatt and later passed on to Sohan Singh Dhiman and Sohan Singh Virdi. Balwant Singh Birdi was given full authority to negotiate the price for the *gurdwara* building. A *Gurdwara* membership fee of £1 was introduced. A group of *jathedars* (group leaders) was appointed on 10th May 1959 for the purpose of collecting the membership fee from house to house. Sardara Singh, Gurmej Singh and Balbir Singh Basi for Bradford, Piara Singh Chaggar, Sarwan Singh Bahra, Resham Singh, Karam Singh, Ranjit Singh, Lashkar Singh Azad, Sohan Singh Dhiman and Inder Singh Ryatt for Leeds, and Gurbaksh Singh Rai for Doncaster were appointed to collect these fees.

The committee for 1959-60 was elected on 21st June 1959 at the Annual General Meeting held in the R.A.O.B. (Royal Antediluvian Order of Buffaloes) Club on North Street, Leeds. The meeting held on 5th July 1959 failed to constitute a quorum but those present insisted on having the meeting. The decision was taken by a vote and there were only two votes against, so following the majority view the meeting went ahead. The new draft of the Constitution was read in the meeting and it was unanimously agreed that it should be printed. It was also agreed that a corner through-terraced house at 3 Savile Road, Chapeltown Leeds 7, should be bought and Inder Singh Ryatt, Sohan Singh Virdi, Balwant Singh Birdi, Lashkar Singh Azad, Ranjit Singh Sahota and Kirpal Singh Duggal were recommended for the negotiation of this purchase. There was a legal requirement to appoint a trustee to buy the building for the *Gurdwara*, so Tirath Singh, the son of Balwant Singh Birdi, was appointed trustee during the meeting of 2nd August 1959 and the house was bought on 29th September 1959. The membership list of the United Sikh Association for 1959-60 suggested that there were one hundred and two members in Yorkshire including four Hindus, one Muslim and one white Briton. Of these, seventy-six lived in Leeds, twenty-three in Bradford, two in Doncaster and one in Dewsbury. Seventy-four out of seventy-six lived within walking distance of Chapeltown Road. The fact that the majority lived in Leeds and was concentrated around the areas of Chapeltown Road was the most influential factor in deciding the location and site for the first *Gurdwara* in Leeds. Neither the minutes nor the Registry of Deeds mentioned the price paid by Sikhs to buy this house. One of the founder members said that it was bought in 1958 for £1,250 but the amount quoted

3 Savile Road

by informants differed, ranging from £1,250 to £2,000. Another informant suggested £1,600 and seemed to be definite about the price paid for this building. The cost of the building was funded entirely by donations from Sikhs living across Yorkshire, especially in Leeds, Bradford and Doncaster.

Residential Distribution	
Leeds 7	41
Leeds 2	27
Leeds 8	6
Other areas	2

An examination of the history of buying the first building for a *gurdwara* highlights the significance of the Sikh religious concepts of donation (money given for any good cause) and *seva* (voluntary service) in which Sikhs take great pride. The membership of the United Sikh Association, the unity of Sikh volunteers and the representation on the Executive Committees reflect the true Sikh spirit of brotherhood crossing caste, class and status barriers. The Constitution allowed membership to any person irrespective of caste, creed, colour, religion or nationality (Constitution, 1959:2) and this was also obvious from the membership list. The Executive Committees worked towards achieving the aims and objectives outlined in the Constitution.

The first meeting that took place at 3 Savile Road, Leeds 7, the newly-bought house which would serve as the *Gurdwara*, was the Executive Committee meeting held on 11th October 1959. At this meeting they discussed getting the plan approved to make a large hall by removing walls and to carpet the hall as soon as possible. A current account was opened at the Midland Bank branch on North Street and three signatories (President, General Secretary and Treasurer) were appointed. Sohan Singh Virdi was given the responsibility of registering the Society as a religious institution. Atma Singh Sood's name was proposed and accepted by the Executive Committee to take the responsibility for buying a table, a dozen chairs and a cabinet to be used in the library reading-room. A decision was taken to start adult classes in the *Gurdwara*. Also discussed at this meeting was non-attendance in meetings. It was suggested in the minutes that letters would be sent to committee members who failed to attend meetings, requesting their reasons for non-attendance, and if they could not attend regularly they would be replaced. Jagat Singh Channa was appointed as caretaker and he was given a room in the *Gurdwara* to live in. He became the first *granthi* (priest) and worked on a voluntary basis. An informant said that Tehal Singh donated a copy of the *Guru Granth Sahib* to the *Gurdwara*. Sarwan Singh paid for another copy of the *Guru Granth Sahib* to be placed in the *Gurdwara*. With this extra copy, the facility was offered for the benefit of the general *sangat* so that it would be possible to borrow the copy of the *Guru Granth Sahib* for home use by donating £1/5/- (£1.25p) and all these offerings would go to the *Gurdwara* fund. The only condition imposed was that a family member must collect the *Granth Sahib* personally from the *Gurdwara* to ensure that the Holy Scripture was treated with respect and the family knew the whole procedure.

The *gurpurab* of *Guru* Nanak's birthday was celebrated in Leeds Civic Hall on Cookridge Street on 6th December 1959 and *Guru* Gobind Singh's birthday was celebrated in the Co-operative Hall, Bradford, on 17th January 1960. Well-known hymn singers were invited from Birmingham and London. *Langar* (communal food) was served. It was decided to celebrate *Vaisakhi* in Bradford and Balwant Singh Akali was given the *path* (liturgical reading of scriptural writings) responsibility for this festival.

As time went on Sikhs began to think of doing more as a community than just celebrating *gurpurabs* only as they had done in the past. They thought about other activities such as establishing a library and adult classes. The appointment of a *granthi* and plans to adapt the house for the needs of the *Gurdwara* were steps forward in establishing themselves. They tried to organize the *Gurdwara* activities around meeting their immediate needs. Activities in the *Gurdwara* began to expand and this required more *sevadars* (volunteers). More *sevadars* were selected and the responsibilities, such as serving *langar*, giving receipts for donations and receiving visitors to the *Gurdwara* were shared. The expenditure in the *Gurdwara* also grew with the increased activities and it became necessary to raise funds. A discussion was held on enrolling new members and collecting a membership fee. This responsibility was given to Piara Singh Chaggar, Jaswant Singh Bhamra, Sohan Singh Virdi, Balwant Singh Birdi, Balwant Singh Akali, Sarwan Singh Cheema, Kartar Singh, Resham Singh Gill, Atma Singh Sood and Dalip Singh Sohel.

The new committee for 1960-61 was elected on 3rd May 1960 and Jagat Singh Channa was re-elected as *granthi* of the *Gurdwara*. In August, Ranbir Singh wished to resign as Literature Secretary but he was persuaded to stay on. Harbhajan Singh was co-opted as a member. It was necessary at this time to maximize the use of human resources and this was achieved through mutual consent.

It was a wonderful achievement for Sikhs to own a building to use as a *gurdwara*. The Society formed to buy the *Gurdwara* building was later registered as a religious institution in April 1960 and the news of this registration was given to the committee at the meeting held on 1st May 1960. It was agreed that 'The Sikh Temple' should be added within brackets along with the United Sikh Association, and a board saying 'The Sikh Temple' should be displayed. There was a suggestion that an *akhandpath* (continuous recitation of *Guru* Granth Sahib in forty-eight hours) for the opening ceremony of the *Gurdwara* should be held. Up to then, they had concentrated on celebrating *gurpurabs* by hiring civic buildings. Having bought a house for use as the *Gurdwara*, they became keen to make the *Gurdwara* a prestigious place for the Sikh community. They painted the *Gurdwara* building and repaired the outside gates. The kitchen was made useable by installing gas cookers and putting in chairs and tables to sit at for taking *langar* (communal food). Serving *langar* in the *Gurdwara* is an integral part of the Sikh religious traditions, but initially it was difficult to maintain this tradition due to lack of resources. *Langar* was served only if someone volunteered to do this. It was decided to set up a study circle and to make use of the *Gurdwara* for other purposes, such as allowing groups like the Indian Workers Association to hold meetings. Mastan Singh, a printing student and caretaker, was given responsibility to report on any meeting held in the *Gurdwara*. There was a discussion about making an application to get permission to register marriages in the *Gurdwara*. Religious education was organized for children in the *Gurdwara* and the *Gurdwara* foundation paid for stationery. A Sikh ethic on alcohol was introduced and anyone consuming alcohol was not allowed into the *Gurdwara*. A public telephone was installed in the *Gurdwara* in order to make it easy for anyone to make a call in case of emergency. It is clearly noticeable that Sikhs gradually began to introduce many other important activities, such as religious education, registration of marriages and taking steps to ensure that Sikh values were maintained.

1. 2 Church Building

The size of the Sikh community grew rapidly in the 1960s. Between 1959 and 1962 a considerable number of Sikh families came from India and East Africa to live in Leeds. It is important to mention the pattern of migration and settlement of the Sikh community in Leeds. The Sikh community seems to have been divided into two main groups, that is to say, direct migrants from India mainly from the Punjab and those who came from East Africa. Direct migrants in general came from two districts in the Punjab, Jalandhar and Hoshiarpur, because of pressure on land, dense populations and scarcity of industrial employment. Sikh migration to Britain began in the late 1950s in response to the shortage of unskilled workers in the post-war reconstruction and subsequent expansion of the British economy. The main influx came in the early 1960s with the fear of future restrictive legislation for immigration to Britain. The process of chain migration also played its part. Owing to the unskilled nature of the work available, Sikh migrants came from different backgrounds and castes. The majority of these were *Jats* (land-owners), with a small minority of other castes such as *Ramgarhias* (artisans), *Khatris* (traders), *Bhatras* (palm-readers and astrologers), *Ravidasis* (untouchables), *Jhirs* (water-carriers), *Nais* (barbers) and *Julahas* (weavers). It was their first move from a rural to an urban industrialized area. They were mainly traditionalists, having very little experience of bureaucratic ways.

East African Sikhs were experienced migrants who came to the UK in the 1960s mainly influenced by the policy of Africanization in the newly independent colonies of Kenya, Uganda and Tanzania. They were part of an established community in East Africa and had acquired mainstream skills (e.g. language, education, familiarity with urban institutions and bureaucratic processes). In contrast with direct migrants they belonged predominantly to the *Ramgarhia* caste.

With the arrival of Sikh women and children from the Punjab and East Africa, who generally came in family units, the lifestyle of Sikh families in 1960s and 1970s changed. The presence of family units enhanced the life cycle rites and ceremonies, which became increasingly adapted to more traditional values. Migration also affected the settlement. There were one hundred and forty-five registered members by 1962, as noted in the *Gurdwara* membership register, and of these one hundred and thirty lived in Leeds. Out of that one hundred and thirty, seventy-three lived in Leeds 7, twenty lived in Leeds 8 and the rest lived in Leeds 6 (sixteen), Leeds 11 (seven), Leeds 12 (six), Leeds 2 (six) and Leeds 1 (two). The majority had settled in Chapeltown and Harehills and this residential distribution of Sikhs stemmed from the tendency towards buying houses near relatives and friends. The reasons given by Sikh migrants in a survey conducted by the author in 2000-2001 (Rait 2005: 4) were that the houses in this area were cheap and spacious, it was easy to get to work and into town and families wanted to live close to each other. However, the number given on the *Gurdwara* membership list reflects only the number of Sikhs who were registered. The number of Sikhs living in Leeds must undoubtedly have been greater than the listed members.

The first *Gurdwara* building on Savile Road soon became too small to accommodate the growing size of the Sikh *sangat*. This concern was taken on board and it was agreed at the meeting held on 8th October 1961 that the Church building at 281A Chapeltown Road should be bought and this responsibility was given to Tehal Singh, Sardara Singh, Balwant Singh Birdi, Piara Singh Chaggar and Bhajan Singh Reehal. The minutes indicate that the November 1961

The Church building

meeting decided to part-exchange the existing *Gurdwara* building with the person from whom this church was to be bought. Four trustees, Balwant Singh Birdi of 30 Mexborough Street, Atma Singh Sood of 34 Wellclose Mount, Tehal Singh of 80 Roundhay Road and Lashkar Singh Azad of 58 Rosebank Road were appointed to register the building as a *gurdwara*. If any trustee left for any reason then another was to be elected in the General Meeting. The trustees were responsible for any expenditure on the *Gurdwara* building. In order to share the work two committees were formed, one for repair and the other for collecting the donations. As a result, the premises at 281A Chapeltown Road, Leeds 7 were bought. This was a disused church in a dilapidated state, which had been bought previously by the owner of Warsaw Stores, a Polish businessman. The Council had declined his request to use this building for commercial purposes. One informant said that this man knew that the Sikhs were looking for a bigger building and had told Resham Singh Gill that they could have this building by contacting Rothenberg Property Agents. Resham Singh Gill and Atma Singh Sood collected the keys for other members to view the building. The committee members gave their approval and the trustees signed the deed on behalf of the Association. One Founder member said that the agreement was to sell the building of the first *Gurdwara* in part-exchange for £2,000 with the remaining sum of £2,000 to be paid over three years. One informant, suggesting that the first building was sold for £1,800 and the church building was bought for £3,800, rejected the notion of part-exchange. Another informant said that the house on 3 Savile Road was bought for £1,250 and sold for £1,600. The pamphlet distributed on the three-hundredth anniversary of *Vaisakhi* quoted the buying price as £2,700 and the selling price of the first building as £1,600 and another informant gave the selling price as £1,700. In his book, *The evolution of a Sikh community in Britain,* Kalsi mentioned that this building was bought for £2,700 (Kalsi: 1992). Another informant said that they had had to pay £3,100 in addition to the deposit of £2,000. These figures are based on recall and there is no documented evidence in the form of minutes or any other record held by the *Gurdwara*. One informant tried to get in touch with the legal firm who helped in buying this property but found that the firm was no longer in existence.

The most reliable source was the *Yorkshire Evening Post*, which reported on the opening of this *Gurdwara* and stated that it had been converted from the former Newton Park Union Church in Chapeltown Road, Leeds. The church had been closed shortly after the war, had served for a time as the Royal Air Force (RAF) Association Club and was then bought from the Polish community for £2,000 by the United Sikh Association of Yorkshire. The Association spent a further £1,500 on the repair and reconstruction of this Sikh temple and when this was opened in April 1962 more than 600 Sikhs attended. Mastan Singh, a printing student living in the building, acted as a caretaker (*Yorkshire Evening Post*. May 30, 1962). Failing other sources, the Registry of Deeds at Wakefield was contacted and the figures quoted in the Deed indicated that £3,500 was paid for this church. It was bought from S. Mirski, a Polish businessman, through the Walcote Investment Company Limited, whose registered office was situated at 153 Chapeltown Road. This matches with the information given in the *Yorkshire Evening Post* if £1,500 is taken out as the sum given in part-exchange. The *Gurdwara* building was insured for between £10,000 and £20,000 in June 1962.

The *Gurdwara* was opened in April 1962 after extensive renovations. The Salvation Army Band played in front of the *Gurdwara* building at the opening ceremony. This *Gurdwara* was to serve the Indian Communities of Bradford, Dewsbury, Doncaster and Huddersfield. The *Gurdwara* was initially registered as, 'The United Sikh Association (Sikh Temple) Yorks', based on a suggestion made by Ranjit Singh Sahota. One informant said

The Salvation Army Band

that the suggestion of registering it as an Association went against the wishes of many, though this was still done. Later, it was renamed 'The Sikh Temple' in order to obtain charitable status.

The repair committee was responsible for renovating the building and the renovation work started in February 1962. The Sikh community donated generously to renovate this derelict building and made extensive alterations in order to convert it into a proper *gurdwara* with a *Darbar* hall (where the Holy book is kept), *Langar* hall, kitchen, library and school for Sikh children to learn Panjabi. One informant said that Gurbaksh Singh Rai from Doncaster contributed significantly in raising funds for the *Gurdwara* as he had a van, which was used for collecting donations. Balwant Singh Birdi, Piara Singh Chaggar, Kirpal Singh Duggal, Resham Singh Gill, Daljit Singh Sond, Tehal Singh, Lashkar Singh Phull and Sarwan Singh Cheema also played a major role in collecting the donations. One informant said that Dhesi Contractors and Harry, Sons & Co. allowed the *Gurdwara* the use of their trucks and drivers to clear the church and volunteers offered free labour. As volunteers did most of the work, it was mainly carried out in the evenings and weekends. One informant quoted the names of these volunteers: Sohan Singh Seehra, Sadhu Singh Bhandari, Piara Singh Chaggar, Mota Singh Bhamra, Harbans Singh Bhamra, Hazara Singh Ghatora, Jagat Singh Channa, Vir Singh Rayit, *Giani* Kesar Singh Reehal, Sarwan Singh Cheema, Gurmeet Singh Cheema, Tehal Singh, Niranjan Singh, Akali Balwant Singh and Daljit Singh Sond. A great deal of hard labour and money went into restoring the building. Two pioneer Sikhs said that Mrs Balwant Kaur, the wife of Balwant Singh Birdi, cooked for twenty-five to thirty volunteers at the weekends and brought water from her home to be used in the *Gurdwara*. Gurbachan Kaur, wife of Daljit Singh Sond and sister-in-law of Balwant Kaur, helped her occasionally. It was the passion and zeal of the Sikh community that made them take a continued interest in building this *Gurdwara*. It seems obvious that these Sikhs were united and worked together, for the common cause of creating their place of worship.

The main concerns of the Sikh community were to adapt this building to the standard required for the *Gurdwara* and to pay the remaining balance of the purchasing cost, which had to be paid within three years. The *Gurdwara* management committees were very careful about any spending over these three years and concentrated on paying back the rest of the amount. Once that balance was cleared, renovations and the extension of the *Gurdwara* building became the main priorities.

The repairs and alterations in the building became the responsibility of Balwant Singh Birdi. He donated money for low-voltage supplies, which replaced the old lighting system, and two gas lamps. It was also decided that the upper hall should be partitioned and Sohan Singh Seehra undertook this work. The gutters and pipes were cleaned. Central heating was installed. It was decided that an immersion heater should be bought to heat water for washing dishes in the *Gurdwara*. They decided also to buy gas cookers, two more gas lamps, one electric fire and a safe for the *Gurdwara*. The fans, toilet and fire extinguishers were fixed and the bills were paid. The *Gurdwara* roof needed attention. The builders, Thorpe and Dobson, did the repair work on the tower, basement windows and inner staircase. The cellar under the kitchen was repaired and a fence was put around the *Gurdwara*. Two security gates were installed for security reasons, with a metal fence at the front and sides of the *Gurdwara*. The gallery of the main hall was opened temporarily to extend the library rooms and the builders were asked to do this. Windows were replaced and fans and floodlights were fixed in the main hall. A geyser was installed in the cellar to heat water. The electric heaters were repaired and connected to one switch in order to avoid frequent repairs.

Balwant Singh Birdi, Piara Singh Chaggar and Bhajan Singh Reehal supervised the building work. Niranjan Singh Seehra and Piara Singh Chaggar were given the responsibility of taking the steps necessary to prevent damp coming from the back wall of the *Gurdwara*. The newly-built rooms were wired and carpets were fitted in the extension. Niranjan Singh Seehra who quoted £1,000 and £50 extra for doing any additional work, did the paintwork on the basis of having given the best quotation. All this work enhanced the look of the building and the extension gave much needed space to accommodate the growing Sikh *sangat*.

Some repairs remained unfinished due to lack of resources. As stated in the minutes, the committee formed in 1970-1971 made a concerted effort to complete the unfinished tasks of the previous three years, that is to say, the repair of the roof and of the damp from the back walls, putting heater guards and a heater near the shoe racks, making a dais for *Nishan Sahib* and fixing the clock. The problem of car parking was resolved by having a car park space near the *Gurdwara*.

The concerted efforts of pioneer Sikhs and dedicated volunteers created a Sikh place of worship in which they could take pride. By 1965 they had paid off the loan taken to buy this building. After paying the loan they concentrated on the repairs and on the development of other activities in the *Gurdwara*. However, the Sikh community, which had stood united in the early period of settlement in Leeds, began to show signs of division. The majority of direct migrants from India belonged to the *Jat* caste but with the arrival of East Africans who were predominantly *Ramgarhias* the scene changed. The East Africans were experienced migrants who had considerable community and technical skills prior to migration, which they were able to use in Leeds. They dominated the *Gurdwara* management committees because of their experience and also because they were in the majority. *Jats* became a minority and it was difficult for them to accept minority status as they considered themselves superior, being landowners in the Punjab. They felt alienated and in order to address this concern, a suggestion of having proportionate representation was made, but met with little success. This feeling created unease in the community especially when the Ramgarhia Board was set up in 1968 at 138 Chapeltown Road and the *Bhatra biradari* (community) also established a *Bhatra* Sikh community centre in the same year at 6 Grange Terrace, Chapeltown, Leeds 7 in order to meet their social needs.

Caste began to play a dominant role in the lives of Sikhs in spite of the condemnation of caste by Sikh *Gurus*. By the mid-1970s the situation had become much more serious. Caste loyalties took precedence over religious loyalties and one personal dispute was turned into a caste dispute and became a court case in 1976. Some *Ramgarhias* held positions in the Ramgarhia Board and the *Gurdwara* simultaneously and this situation was strongly objected to by the members of other caste groups. The amendment of the Constitution in February 1977 'that all office bearers and trustees shall be *kesadhari* (uncut hair) Sikhs' further aggravated the situation. This amendment helped to assert Sikh identity but excluded clean-shaven Sikhs from taking powerful positions in the *Gurdwara*. Since most direct migrants, and notably the *Jats*, were clean-shaven, they felt discriminated against. A group of *Jat* Sikhs felt the need to organize their *biradari* to discuss the issues concerning the status of their *biradari* at the *Gurdwara* and the setting up of their *biradari* association and community centre. As a result, they were able to form a *Jat* Sikh association called the 'Indian Farmers Welfare Society, Leeds' in 1978. The formation of this organization was strongly supported by the *Jat* community. The formation of *Ramgarhia* and *Jat* organizations was a clear evidence of the polarization of the Sikh community along caste-lines. This caste rivalry had a strong impact on the future development of *gurdwaras* in Leeds.

3. 3 Extension

The year of 1976-77 was significant for the extension of the *Gurdwara* building. A new development took place. The minutes indicate that in October 1976, Leeds Corporation offered an unconditional grant of £17,000 and two acres of land behind the Chapeltown Post Office on Roundhay Road in Chapeltown to the Sikh community to build a new purpose-built *gurdwara*. This grant had to be spent before the end of April. In order to get the land, the outline plan had to be passed and this process normally took one year. Considering the circumstances, the committee decided at the meeting of 24th October 1976 to extend the current *Gurdwara* building and avail themselves of the offer of a grant. This was the first time that a grant from the Council had been offered to the *Gurdwara*.

Sikhs wanted to organize and expand many other *gurdwara*-related activities for which an extension to the *Gurdwara* building was felt appropriate. This responsibility was given to the Building Sub-committee which was formed of four trustees and nine committee members.

The contract for the extension for £29,922 was given to Tomlinson & Company and the installation of gas central heating was contracted for £5,880. The new architects, Hind & Partnership, who were approved by the City Council, were engaged.

The extension work began on 24th November 1976 and the foundation work was laid by *panj pyare* (ਪੰਜ ਪਿਆਰੇ-the five Loved Ones) *Baba* Khem Singh, Niranjan Singh Seehra, Sarwan Singh Cheema, Gurdev Singh Kahar and Gurcharan Singh. The total expenditure on the extension was £30,547.99, which was paid from the Council grant and from *Gurdwara* funds. The Building Sub-committee reported that the expenditure on the extension had exceeded the budget because of the extra work done on lights and radiators not originally in the plan. The volunteers who did most of the building work were Amar Singh Sohanpal, Kartar Singh, Jatan Singh, Mohinder Singh, Niranjan Singh Seehra, Balwant Singh Birdi and Chetan Singh Marwaha. It was expected that the extension work would be completed by 26th August 1977.

Preparations began for the ceremony for the opening of the extension. It was decided by the Committee on 31st October 1976 that the Rt. Hon. Merlyn Rees, Home Secretary, would be contacted, to ask him to undertake the opening ceremony. In case of his non-availability, the Lord Mayor of Leeds would be invited. The plans changed later due to the non-availability of the Home Secretary and it was suggested that *Sant Baba* Puran Singh (a holy man who spread the message of *Gurus* in East Africa) would perform the opening ceremony, with Councillor Hudson unveiling the plaque on 27th November 1977 on the *gurpurab* of *Guru* Nanak's birthday. According to the minutes of 13th November 1977, it was also decided that honorary membership of the *Gurdwara* would be given to *Sant Baba* Puran Singh, the Lord Mayor of Leeds, and to J. J. Pearlman (the *Gurdwara*'s solicitor). *Sant Baba* Puran Singh performed the opening ceremony and Councillor Hudson unveiled the plaque on 27th November 1977. The Lord Mayor, *Babaji* (respectful word used for Puran Singh), and the solicitor of the *Gurdwara* were given their honorary membership. The Lord Mayor and the *Gurdwara* architect were also honoured with engraved trays. Many guests from all walks of life were invited to attend this occasion, indicating how Sikhs were trying to promote an understanding of their religious beliefs with the wider community.

The Building Sub-committee met on 2nd July 1978 once again to consider the land offered by the Council. It was 2,400 square metres and the condition laid down by the Council was that the *Gurdwara* should be built within a year after the land was bought. It was estimated that the cost of building a new purpose-built *Gurdwara* would be £300,000. Keeping inflation in mind, it could go over £400,000. The committee also decided on 21st August 1978 to apply for a grant of £432,000 under the Inner City Programme for the construction of the *Gurdwara*. Bakhshish Singh Channa reported on 6th October 1978 that the application made to the Inner City Programme had been rejected on the grounds of its being too large an amount. This information was also published in the *Yorkshire Evening Post*. After the failure to obtain the grant, it was proposed that an Extraordinary General Meeting be called to discuss the land offered by the Council. As noted in the minutes, it was decided at the meeting of 29th June 1980 that this offer would not be accepted and this decision was based on the majority view taken by vote. This meant that Sikhs would have to manage with the present *Gurdwara* building.

A Building Sub-committee was formed on 24th September 1980 in order to manage building work. The upper room was partitioned. Provision to stack chairs and tables was also made. The building was rewired and partially cleaned including the gutters. The *Gurdwara* was partly painted, concrete was laid in the driveway, and the big hall and the roof were insulated. The clock tower and roof of the *Gurdwara* were repaired. New gutters and hand-dryers were fixed and the kitchen floor was levelled. The *Gurdwara* also received £1,000 from the Community Chest Fund (small grants available for community organizations) towards making improvements in the toilets.

The Building Chairman reported on 15th January 1981 that the plans were ready for the extension and these were displayed on the notice board. A meeting was held with the Planning Department in the *Gurdwara* on 12th January 1981 and it seemed from this meeting that permission would be given for the extension of the kitchen, basement and men's toilet. The estimated cost would be £34,000. The Building Chairman was asked to get a tender before the next general meeting. It was reported in the Executive Committee Meeting on 7th March 1981 that the extension plan had been divided into two phases. Phase 1 covered the extension to the cellar and dining room and phase 2 covered the extension to the men's toilet and the *Bhandari's* (caretaker's) room. The tenders sent by Roberts estimated the cost of Phase 1 at £20,500 and Phase 2 at £27,800. The Committee unanimously approved the estimate for Phase 1.

It was reported by the Building Sub-committee that the Council planning officer did not seem sympathetic to the plans submitted. His opinion was that the extension of the roof would obstruct the view and he suggested a slate, hipped roof. He also added that his office wanted written assurances that the car park would not be used. If the committee did not comply with these suggestions, the *Gurdwara* would not be able to put in any applications for a grant in future.

The amended plans were presented to the Council in the planning meeting of 13th November 1981 and were approved. It was decided that tenders would be invited after the official confirmation and details had been received. A report on tenders was presented at the General Meeting of 7th February 1982. According to the tender given by Garnet Johnson, the cost of Phase 1 would be £38,428 including £9,650 for plumbing and electrics, £2,500 for the basement and £26,778 for the extension. Roberts quoted £46,000 and J. Tomlinson Builders £37,295. According to the minutes, the suggestion was made that the extension work should be delayed. On 6th March 1982, there was a long discussion over why the work of the extension had been delayed and the reason given was that the majority thought that the *Gurdwara* building had constantly had to be extended over the years to accommodate the growing numbers of the Sikh community and that it was time to think about other alternatives such as building a purpose-built *gurdwara*.

This difference of opinion was a clear sign of the open split in the Sikh community. Until 1982, *Ramgarhias* dominated the management of the *Gurdwara* for the reasons given earlier and this dominance at the *Gurdwara* was bitterly resented by other Sikhs. There were other developments which also played a significant role, for instance the formation of the Indian Farmers' Welfare Association, a *Jat* caste-based association, and conflict over the grant from the City Council for Sikhs to build a community centre, which had been given to the Sikh Temple. This argument centred around the intention of the Council to offer the grant to the Sikh community as a whole and not to any individual organization. The Ramgarhia Board (RB) resented this decision and a letter was written to all the councillors of the City Council on 28th April 1983 pointing out that *Ramgarhias* represented 80% of the total Sikh population in Leeds.

The rift on the basis of caste grew which not only created tension in the Sikh community but also affected the atmosphere of the Sikh Temple. Another attempt was made in March 1984 to patch up differences. A committee of five members was set up to meet the RB in order to persuade them not to build another *gurdwara*. The RB responded by putting forward the following conditions: a) the RB intended to build a separate centre and no objections should be made to this, nor any attempt made to stop it; b) they would agree not to build a *gurdwara* on condition that the Sikh Temple donated half the money from the *Gurdwara* funds and half from the weekly offerings in order to fund the building of this centre; c) they would only use the RB as a *gurdwara* to raise funds for the *Ramgarhia* Sikh Centre. It was obvious that the RB would not open membership to or take members from other than their own caste, or allow members of other castes to serve on its management committee, even if the Sikh Temple agreed to their conditions.

Failing to patch up the differences, the minutes state that it was decided that the RB would be boycotted and a resolution was passed stating that ਜੋ ਸੰਸਥਾ ਸਿਖ ਪੰਥ ਏਕਤਾ ਲਈ ਇਸ ਗੁਰਦੁਵਾਰਾ ਸਾਹਿਬ ਨਾਲ ਸਹਿਮਤ ਨਹੀਂ ਹੈ ਇਸ ਗੁਰਦੁਵਾਰੇ ਦਾ ਕੋਈ ਵੀ ਅਹੁਦੇਦਾਰ ਉਸ ਸੰਸਥਾ ਨਾਲ ਅਪਣਾ ਸੰਬੰਧ ਨਹੀਂ ਰਖੇਗਾ (no committee member of this *Gurdwara* would maintain any relationship with an organization that did not agree on Sikh unity with this *Gurdwara*). Another resolution was passed unanimously in the Executive Committee meeting held on 8th April 1984 and was sent to the RB for information:

'The Sikh Temple, 281A Chapeltown Road, Leeds 7, is a representative body of all the Sikhs in Leeds and grants full rights to all the Sikhs in its administration. We, the Executive Committee members, recommend that all financial aid and grants for the welfare of the Sikhs should be made available only to this Sikh Temple incorporating the Sikh Centre'.

Undoubtedly, there was no scope left for reconciliation between the RB and the Sikh Temple. The 1980s witnessed the opening of other caste and sect-based *gurdwaras* in Leeds. In 1984, the *Ramgarhias* celebrated their first *Vaisakhi* festival on the plot of land acquired for building the *Ramgarhia* Sports Centre. On this occasion, the Sikh flag *Nishan Sahib* was hoisted, which meant that *Ramgarhias* wanted to establish their own identity and place of worship. The *Bhatras* officially opened *Gurdwara* Kalgidhar Sahib on 19th October 1986 at 138 Chapeltown Road. There was also a split among *Ramgarhias* over serving meat and alcohol at the Ramgarhia Board which resulted in the opening of another *Gurdwara*, *Guru* Nanak Nishkam Sevak Jatha, in December 1986 on Ladypit Lane, Leeds 11. Nishkam Sevak Jatha, the followers of *Baba* Puran Singh Karichowale, who are mainly *Ramgarhias*, are strictly *amritdharis* and are against the consumption of meat and alcohol. The *Ramgarhia* Sikh sports centre and *Ramgarhia Gurdwara* on 8-10 Chapeltown Road, Leeds 7 was officially opened on 6th May 1987. The *Namdhari sangat* broke away from the main *Gurdwara* and from the Ramgarhia Board because of their belief in the living *Guru* and they established their own *Gurdwara* at 61 Louis Street, Chapeltown Road, Leeds 7, which was opened on 21st July 1987. Quite recently a new *gurdwara* called Gurdwara Hargobind Sahibji was opened on 19th March 2006 in Potternewton Mansion on Harehills Lane, Leeds 7 mainly for the use of the *Bhatra* community.

1. 4 The New Purpose-Built *Gurdwara* Building

The rejection of the extension at the meeting of the 6th March 1982 made the Committee think about other alternatives. Councillor Mudie and Councillor Simmons came to the Sikh Temple indicating that they could buy the church building from the Sikh Temple and Sikhs could build a purpose-built *gurdwara* on the land opposite. The Council was willing to buy the present *Gurdwara* building for £25,000 and this sum might be increased to £60-70,000 after a survey, though nothing had yet been confirmed in writing.

There was land available across the road opposite to the present *Gurdwara* building, which the *Gurdwara* was prepared to buy. The Council made it very clear that after the construction of the Sikh community centre on Brandon Way, the new *Gurdwara* should be built within two years, otherwise, the Council would confiscate the land and the *Gurdwara* would have to pay the legal fees for its repurchase. The committee felt uneasy with this condition and negotiated with the Council to remove it. The Council withdrew the time limit condition but asserted that a *Gurdwara* must definitely be built.

Eventually a decision was made to buy 190 Chapeltown Road in February 1987 in order to construct the new building for the *Gurdwara*. The site of the new building was very important, as it was adjacent to the Sikh Centre, which provided facilities for social functions. Therefore, during weddings, the various religious and social activities could take place within one site. Gurdeep Singh Bhogal was asked to find out more about the Chapeltown Task Force grant. The decision to construct the new *Gurdwara* was passed in the General Meeting on 30th April 1989. Three architects prepared plans, which were submitted to the committee. According to the architect Pargat Singh Rayit, the building cost of a two-storey building with a covered area of 18,000 square feet would be £850,000 to £900,000. The architect's fee would be 10% of the total expenditure. Singh Partners quoted an approximate cost of £900,000 for constructing a two-storey building with a covered area of 21,500 square feet. The architect's fee would be 9% of the total expenditure, from which half of the fee would be donated to the *Gurdwara*. According to Moore Keighley Dales, the cost would be £990,000 for building a three-storey building with a covered area of 19,000 square feet. The architect's fee specified was 10.7% from which £6,000 would be donated to the *Gurdwara*.

The majority of committee members favoured Singh Partners, subject to the clarification of any conditions imposed on how to spend the donated money. It was agreed that the fees would be 8%, made up of an architect's fee of 3%, a construction engineer's fee of 3% and a quantity surveyor's fee of 2%. Of the architect's and construction engineer's fees, which were 6%, half would be donated to the *Gurdwara*. Dildar Singh from Singh Partners assured the committee that they would draw up the plan according to the *sangat*'s requirements. Soon afterwards, the architect died and the new architect asked for 5% and £38,000 in advance. This death further delayed any progress on this matter.

Later the building next door at 192 Chapeltown Road came up for sale and the Sikh Temple purchased it in December 1995. Two estimates for the cost of demolition were acquired, £1,500+VAT and £3,000+VAT. The project was also advertised in the paper and, as a result of the advertisement, Steven and Murphy stated that they would level the ground, cut the trees, and remove all the rubbish. They would not charge any money provided they were able to keep the stones. With the purchase of number 192, the size of the land in the possession of the Sikh Temple increased. The committee felt that they needed new plans and the *sangat* also wanted the *Gurdwara* built away from the main road and this had now been made possible by the purchase of the site of 192 Chapeltown Road. A new *Gurughar* (another Panjabi term for *Gurdwara*) Committee (building sub-committee) was formed to undertake the responsibility for the building work. One informant said that the Sikh Temple had enough money to start this project.

The minutes show that it was agreed in November 1996 that the *Gurdwara* building should be constructed on the sites of 190 and 192 Chapeltown Road. The fee for the architect, construction engineer and quality surveyor was £38,000 and they were asked to start work on the *Gurughar*

(*Gurdwara*) immediately. It was reckoned that the total expenditure of building the new *Gurughar* would be £928,786 and with the discount of £43,150 this remained at £885,636. In order to raise the money, it was decided to take a loan from the bank and to collect donations from Sikh homes. Donors would be requested to give at least £101 and those collecting donations could claim petrol expenses if they wished to do so. The names proposed for collecting the donations were Baldev Singh Duggal, Manohar Singh Bhakhar and Avtar Singh Toor on Sundays; Surinder Singh Bansal, Sarwan Singh Rai, Professor Bakhshish Singh and Nirmal Singh Sangha on Mondays; Bakhshish Singh and Nirmal Singh on Tuesdays; Hardeep Singh Ahluwalia, Kewal Singh and Joginder Singh on Wednesdays; Bakhshish Singh, Nirmal Singh Sangha and Inder Singh Ryatt on Thursdays. The committee members were asked to give an interest-free loan so that the *Gurdwara* could save on the interest.

In April 1997 work started with the aim of completing the structural shell for the building before winter set in. The *Yorkshire Evening Post* described the view of Sikh leaders that this purpose-built building would mark the start of a new era for the followers of the religion and would incorporate traditional features such as domes. It further added: 'The new temple will be three storeys high and include a main prayer hall for 500 people, a lower ground hall for smaller functions, a dining hall with accommodation for 250 people, catering facilities, a lift and a self-contained flat for the resident priest. The site will also incorporate a library, shop, creche, offices and space for coach and car parking' (*Yorkshire Evening Post*: 28.6.1997). The work on the temple was started by the then Lord Mayor, Councillor Linda Middleton, who led a turf-cutting ceremony to mark the start of the new project. The total cost of the project including refurbishing the *Gurdwara* was reckoned at around £1,000,000 and the Sikh community generously contributed money towards building the *Gurdwara*. The first phase of the *Gurughar* was completed in April 1998 at a cost of £568,000. The second phase was started and its estimated cost was £450,000. An emergency meeting was called to consider a bank loan of £1,000,000 and it was unanimously agreed at this meeting that an Extraordinary General Meeting should be called. It was decided that a loan of £325,000 should be borrowed from the bank. Other steps were also taken to raise funds. A series of *akhandpaths* were organised, which raised money to pay back the bank loan taken for the *Gurdwara* building. It was also decided that an appeal for donations for the building funds should be made at functions such as weddings. The Sikh *sangat* also showed an enormous capacity for donation to their religious institutions.

The opening ceremony of this purpose-built *Gurdwara* took place on the three-hundredth anniversary of the birth of the *Khalsa,* on *Vaisakhi* day in 1999. However, from the 21st March 1999, a continuous series of twenty *akhandpaths* began in celebration of this auspicious occasion. This day was celebrated in the *Gurdwara* with pomp and show. The *Gurdwara* was lit up in the evening and fireworks were displayed along with sweet stalls. It was a day of celebration and pride for the whole Sikh community of Leeds. The final cost of this building was £1.1 million and it took less than two years to build. Once again it was the concerted effort of the Sikh community that resulted in the creation of this unique purpose-built building in which they could take pride.

The new building incorporated many features such as a lift and better access for less able people, separate baby-changing and feeding rooms and facilities to hold conferences and seminars that the other *Gurdwara* building could not provide because of space limitations and the difficulties of further expansion.

The new purpose-built building of the *Gurdwara*

With a footprint of around 25,000 ft, the *Gurdwara* offered an open-plan *diwan* hall providing much needed space for the growing congregation. This hall can accommodate a congregation of five hundred and underneath on the ground floor is a *langar* hall for two hundred users. The main hall has air-conditioning with warm and cold air in the ceiling which cost over £24,000.

Finally, the major work on the *Gurughar* was completed though there were a few minor jobs left at the time of the opening ceremony, which were however, soon finished. Three members were appointed to look after the work of putting in the lights, painting and finishing the kitchen floor. A fridge and a freezer were bought for the kitchen and a mesh was fixed to kitchen windows in order to stop flies. It was felt necessary to install one more electric shower in the ladies' and men's sides, as there were problems at the time of large events and children's camps. It was also decided to convert the toilets adjoining the *giani's* room into a store. In the meanwhile, a lump sum of £50,000 was paid to the bank to reduce the bank loan. All this indicates the constant demand on the time of committee members and volunteers and on resources. One informant said that there was no problem about money but there were not enough volunteers to collect donations and do other jobs.

5.5 *Gurdwara* Car Parking Space

The land adjoining the *Gurdwara* went up for sale in 2002. An Extraordinary General Meeting was called on 6th October 2002 to consider the purchase of this land. After some discussion, it was unanimously agreed that this land should be purchased to solve the parking problems on Sundays and it was bought for £400,000. This land included a building which had been used by drug users, and the Department of the Environment inserted the condition that the building be demolished after the sale. The cost of demolition was £8,000. After this had been done, the land was levelled and road shells were laid before a temporary car park was made. The wall adjoining the Church of God was unsafe and it was pulled down. The wall near the road was also pulled down to match the new *Gurdwara* wall. A fence was put behind the car park to serve as a partition between the *Gurdwara* and the Church.

1. 6 The Disused Church Building

The church building of the old *Gurughar* (*gurdwara*) was declared a listed building. In April 2001, it was decided that a sub-committee should be formed to manage this building which included Professor Bakhshish Singh, Ujjal Singh Ryatt, Kalyan Singh, Nirmal Singh Sangha and the serving President of the new *Gurdwara*. It was decided to have the building surveyed and the survey cost was quoted at £800. The suggestion was that this should become a Sikh museum. Prof. Bakhshish Singh informed the committee that Parminder Singh Syan, a civil engineer, would prepare the plans and that an application for a grant should be made after the plans were approved. The Sub-committee pursued grant applications. The first application for a £¼ million grant from the Single Regeneration Budget (SRB) was rejected. The grant application made on 7th November 2003 to English Heritage and Leeds City Council was presented to the *Gurdwara* Executive Committee. The *Gurdwara* was successful in securing this grant of £110,000.

Parminder Singh Syan was invited to speak for the grant for the old *Gurughar* building (Church building). He informed the *Gurdwara* Committee that the grant of £110,000 to be given by Leeds City Council had to be spent on the work suggested by the surveyor in his report, which was also mentioned in the Grant Agreement. He also added if this grant was not used, it might be difficult to get any future grants. There was the possibility of getting a further £40-60,000 grant from English Heritage and £100,000 from Leeds City Council. His fee for this work would be £40,000 from which he would donate £30,000 to the *Gurdwara* and if value added tax was reclaimed then all that money could be spent on the *Gurdwara*. In the first phase, the ground floor and the area of 522 square metres would be made usable. In the following year the grant would not require to be matched with funding, which meant that the *Gurdwara* would not be obliged to provide an equivalent amount of money from its own resources. All members present were in favour of this grant but it was still necessary to seek consent from the general members because of the contribution from the *Gurdwara* funds. In the end it was decided that the work should be carried out. The building is at present being renovated and an informant told me that it will be used as a banqueting hall in future. This decision was made in order to keep social celebrations apart from the Sikh Temple. The adjoining building of the Sikh Centre will be used as a library, a Sikh museum and for other educational purposes. However, some members have reservations about using this place as a banqueting hall, suggesting that alcoholic drinks and meat should not be served in a place which was used as a *gurdwara* and where so many *paths* (recitation of *Granth Sahib*) were done.

1. 7 Conclusion

Sikhs take great pride in the current purpose-built building of the Sikh Temple. Sikhs of all castes have made contributions to the *Gurdwara* buildings from the very beginning. The foundations of this *Gurdwara* were laid on the principles of Sikhism and the concept of Sikh brotherhood, which are important to retain. It would be a great mistake to associate this *Gurdwara* with any particular caste and thus reflect caste bias in the management of the Sikh Temple. This is the oldest *Gurdwara* in Leeds and the second oldest *Gurdwara* in the United Kingdom. It is heavily used not only by local Sikhs but also by Sikhs from all over West Yorkshire. It has over four hundred members at present.

The Sikh community has worked very hard for the creation of their place of worship and it is in their favour that they have achieved what they desired. Over the last fifty years much went smoothly but now and again there were difficulties. Committees work in teams and occasionally there are personality clashes and personal animosities. They often solve their differences amicably by talking, negotiating or readjusting their views before circumstances go beyond control but occasionally such matters have gone beyond the boundaries of the *Gurdwara* and have become general knowledge in the public domain. This happened in 1963 when one committee member reported others to the police for threatening behaviour, and again in 1976 when there was a court case for affray.

It is essential to keep accurate accounts in *Gurdwaras*. *Gurdwaras* are generally funded by donations and the source of donations is the *sangat*, which makes committees accountable to them. Accounts are generally maintained carefully and often checked by auditors. Sometimes records may not seem satisfactory, not because of any deception but because of pressure of work. The auditor in 1959 demonstrated the correct procedure of presenting accounts and suggested that proper receipts should be kept and thereafter committees followed this procedure. Accounts have never been a major problem in the history of this *Gurdwara* except on one occasion. In 1999, there was some confusion over the accounts, which became a big issue and raised doubts in the minds of many. Since the completion of the new *Gurdwara* building there have been arguments over the accounts for certain years. The amount spent on the new *Gurdwara* building was huge and suggestions were made of money having been diverted simply because the accounts had been checked by a trustee rather than an external auditor. To resolve the matter, it was decided to get the accounts checked by an independent party. In the end, it was found that an administrative mistake had been made and the matter seemed to be resolved satisfactorily. One informant said that the procedures used in the Sikh Temple pre-empted any possibility of misuse of funds. However another interviewee suggested that though accounts might be accurate on paper, in reality it was possible that they were not. For instance, receipts for completed work are sometimes made available to auditors, so that the books can be balanced, before the work has in fact been finished.

Chapter 3
The Sikh Centre

1. 0 History

The main aim of establishing the Sikh Centre was to fulfil the social, cultural, educational and recreational needs of the Sikh community. The community was well established in Leeds by the end of the 1970s and Sikhs were in desperate need of a place where they could celebrate social and cultural functions, such as weddings, in a suitable, safe and secure environment.

Ramgarhia (artisans) and *Bhatra* (a caste of astrologers and *pathis*) Sikhs bought places to use as social centres in 1968. East African Sikhs considered it essential to build a purpose-built centre for the *Ramgarhias* when they arrived in large numbers in the early sixties (*Ramgarhia Sikh Bulletin* 1985). They bought a through-terraced house on 138 Chapeltown Road in 1968 to set up the Ramgarhia Board (RB) for social and cultural activities and made plans to build a community and sports centre in the near future, which was actually opened in 1987 at the Sheepscar intersection. *Bhatra* Sikhs opened the *Bhatra* Sikh Community Centre at 6 Grange Terrace, Chapeltown. These were both caste-based centres and other Sikhs who were in minority groups also felt the need for a common centre. The Indian Farmers Welfare (*Jat* caste-based) Association changed its name to the Indian Welfare Association (IWA) on 30th July 1981 in order to accommodate Sikhs other than *Jats*. It was intended to be a representative body of all Sikhs irrespective of caste. A grant was available under the Inner City Programme from the Council, which could be applied for by the Sikh community to build a community centre. Both associations (RB and IWA) became interested in this grant and applied for it. The Sikh Temple became involved only when, on 23rd September 1981, the members of the IWA reported that their association had applied for this grant and they asked the *Gurdwara* to support their application. The RB had also written a letter to the *Gurdwara* informing it that they were buying a new place in order to build a Sikh community and sports centre.

Both associations were competing with each other for this grant. An officer from Leeds City Council wrote to the *Gurdwara* stating that he wanted to discuss the applications made by the IWA and RB in an open meeting. The Council was keen to give this grant to the Sikh community as a whole rather than to any individual association or organization. It is indicated in the minutes that Mr Simmonds came from Leeds City Council on 28th November 1981 to discuss this with the *Gurdwara* Executive Committee and gave the impression that these two associations did not fit the criterion of being representative of the whole Sikh community.

The report prepared by the Council on the grant details was read. This grant of £50,000 was to create a social centre unconnected with religious matters for which £10,000 would be given in 1982 and £40,000 in 1983. This grant was substantial and the whole package was made up of £50,000 from the Inner City Programme and £50-60,000 from the Manpower Services Commission (MSC) to spend on wages. The running costs of the centre would be the responsibility of Sikhs. The Executive Committee considered this very carefully and in detail. They suggested a united joint committee knowing that the IWA represented the *Jat* community and the RB represented *Ramgarhias*. The Council was aware of the split within the Sikh community and once again reiterated that this grant was for the whole Sikh community and not for any individual group. On 12th December 1981, it was proposed that a meeting of the RB, IWA and *Bhatras* for Sikh unity should be called and four members from each organization were invited. The meeting took place on the 21st December 1981. Although there was no representation from the *Bhatra biradari,* they informed the *Gurdwara* that they would comply with any decision made by them. The IWA suggested that they would withdraw their grant application if the *Gurdwara* agreed to take responsibility for forming a joint committee. The General Secretary of the RB argued that their project had been going on for the last seventeen to eighteen months. In view of the growth of the Sikh community, they wanted to create a *gurdwara* and a Sikh Community and Sports Centre (SCSC) in the near future. He said that the Manpower Services Commission (MSC) was willing to give them the grant and there was also an offer of land, as they had plans for the SCSC. He argued further that the former name of the IWA was the Indian Farmers' Association whereas the former name of the RB was the *Ramgarhia* Sikh Centre. This matter was only brought to the *Gurdwara* because the Council was adamant that this grant must be given for the common use of the Sikh community.

Eventually, it was decided that the *Gurdwara* would take the responsibility and lead in this matter subject to the permission of the Sikh Temple members. This decision was conveyed to the Council in a meeting held in the Civic Hall on 23rd December 1981 and was also discussed in the General Meeting held on 27th December 1981. The Committee agreed unanimously at this meeting to build a united Sikh Centre and both the IWA and the RB were once again persuaded to support this. The RB had the land behind Roundhay Road post office at the Sheepscar intersection and they wanted to build a centre on that site. So eventually the Committee had a discussion with the IWA and agreed to write a letter to the Council stating that the *Gurdwara* Comittee would take responsibility for the Sikh centre, subject to the consent of the *Gurdwara* members. The Council replied that they wanted to meet the RB, the IWA and the *Gurdwara* Comittee again. Finally it was decided that the *Gurdwara* Committee would apply both for the land and the grant from the Council. The Council agreed to give the grant and appropriate land to the *Gurdwara* for building the centre. The *Gurdwara* made an application for the grant on 10th February 1982 and the Department of Environment replied on 6th April 1982 stating that the application for the grant had been accepted.

A sub-committee was established for the Sikh Centre, which was formed of Ajit Singh Nijjar, Buta Singh Mudhar, Niranjan Singh Seehra, Ajit Singh Bansal, Dr. Gurdev Singh, Paramjit Singh.Mudhar, Pritpal Singh Manku, Santokh Singh Dhillon, Malia Singh Rathor, Ranjit Singh Sahota, Gurdev Singh Dahele, Gurcharan Singh Kundi and Piara Singh Birdi. Kewal Singh Badesha became the treasurer. Gurdev Singh Dahele, Kewal Singh Badesha and Ajit Singh Nijjar became the named cheque signatories. Later these signatories were rejected and it was proposed that *Gurdwara* signatories should be used. It was also made clear that this sub-committee would work under the direction of the *Gurdwara*.

In September 1982 the committee received the information that there would be £50,000 from the Council and £100,000 from the MSC to be spent on labour. The MSC grant was increased from the original suggested sum because of inflation. In fact, the actual sum received for the Sikh Centre was £50,000 from the Council and £120,000 from the MSC (*Yorkshire Evening Post*, 6.1.1983). The committee was pleased and decided to write a letter of thanks to Leeds City Council. A separate account was opened and three signatories were appointed, two from the *Gurdwara* and one from the Council. The *Gurdwara* signatories were the serving President and the Chairman of the building committee. The occasion was celebrated by holding a thanksgiving *akhandpath*. Councillor Mudie and Mr. Simmonds were invited in order to thank them for their support.

The Sikh Centre received £170,000 (£50,000+ £120,000) and this money was added to a separate fund opened for the Sikh Centre. The cost of the land for the Sikh Centre on Brandon Way was £8,475 and a 10% deposit had to be paid. There were other estimated costs in addition to the cost of land, such as the architect and quality surveyor (£21,500), the structural engineer (£1,000), the electrical engineer (£500) and the heating engineer (£400). It was reckoned that £40,000 had to be raised from donations in order to meet these expenses and the costs of furniture and sports equipment. The *sangat* was encouraged to donate generously and a scheme of recording the names of donors of more than £250 on a Roll of Honour was introduced. The committee agreed that the *Gurdwara* would donate £20,000 to the Sikh Centre if the money was not raised by other means and the *Gurdwara* paid £20,000 as a donation.

It was suggested that the plan of the centre should include a multipurpose hall (65 ft x 55 ft) with a stage area of 26 ft x 15 ft, a reception area (18 ft x 12 ft), an old peoples' and children's room (18 ft x 18 ft), a kitchen (20 ft x15 ft) and a service and toilet area (20 ft x 18 ft). There were changing rooms for men and women, showers, a caretaker's room, a room for a youth leader and an office on the first floor (13 ft x 13 ft), a refreshment hall (74 ft x 16 ft) a second hall (52 ft x 19 ft) and a car park (95 ft x 77 ft) in the basement. The total area was 1.13 acres. As noted in the minutes of 8th December 1982, local architects Millard Design & Partners offered a more competitive tender than that of Amar Singh Egan who was based in Manchester. Their fee had been £5,450+VAT to work on stages A to F of the construction. The committee recommended engaging a local architect offering a cheaper quotation. Gian Singh Rayit quoted for wiring and gave an open offer that he would charge £200 less than the cheapest tender given in writing, and this came to £3,250 inclusive of VAT. As he was not given the work this suggests that someone else's estimate was less than £2,500, including labour and material.

Ajit Singh Nijjar who took a keen interest and played a major role in building the Sikh centre informed the committee that this project would be managed under the supervision of the City Council and the responsibility of ordering the material and making payments would be theirs. Work on the Sikh Centre began on 21st March 1983 and *Baba* Khem Singh Punn laid the

Foundation stone laid by Baba Khem Singh Punn

foundation stone. The first phase was completed in November 1983 and the full completion was expected by December 1985. Ajit Singh Nijjar, the Building Chairman and Ujjal Singh Ryatt, Assistant Building Chairman in 1984-85 took responsibility for the building work. An informant said that Buta Singh Mudhar supervised the day-to-day work. Any outstanding work would be carried out through agencies like the

National Association for Care and Resettlement of Offenders (NACRO) when the MSC grant finished. It was decided to celebrate *Guru* Nanak Dev's *gurpurab* in the Centre to mark its opening. *Guru* Nanak Dev's *gurpurab* was celebrated in the Sikh Centre on its completion on 31st October 1985. Ajit Singh Nijjar was re-elected as Building Chairman for 1985-1986. Mohinder Singh Virdee and Inder Singh Bahth became Assistant Building Chairmen to take care of the building work.

This Centre had the capacity to provide much-needed basic facilities for the Sikh community. It could accommodate up to four hundred people. It offered a number of activities and facilities. The main multipurpose hall was made available for weddings, reception parties and other social functions. The purpose-built kitchen adjoining the main hall could easily be used for catering for large gatherings. The main halls also offered sports facilities. Changing rooms were available. Other facilities offered were for the care of elderly Sikhs and the training programmes. The small rooms on the first floor were available for children's programmes and also offered facilities for small gatherings and study circles. It became necessary to appoint a caretaker to look after the Centre and Nichhattar Singh was appointed the first caretaker of the Sikh Centre on 15th March 1986. The contract for his job was drawn up soon after his appointment.

A Sub-committee for the Centre was formed in 1986-1987 to manage the Centre including Ajit Singh Nijjar, Kulwant Singh, Mohinderpal Singh Sarang, Tarlochan Singh Duggal, Gurdeep Singh Bhogal, Jaspal Singh, Kewal Singh, Paramjit Singh and Santokh Singh. This committee was concerned over the relationship between the *Gurdwara* and the Centre. Their boundaries had never been specified and the relationship remained unclear. This matter had arisen on several occasions. On 7th February 1987, a discussion was held on the following questions:

a) The membership.
b) The rights of the separate committee.
c) The relationship between Sikh Centre and *Gurdwara* - what would it be?

d) The status of the committee - will this committee be independent or attached to the *Gurdwara*?
e) The establishment of a separate committee for managing the Centre and also a Constitution for the Sikh Centre.
f) The importance of the Sikh Centre not becoming a club or a brewery.
g) The power of the separate committees - not be able to buy or sell property or apply for any loans.

The Committee discussed these points at great length as there were real issues to be resolved on the status of the Centre Committee and management of the Centre. The President suggested a separate committee for the Sikh Centre which would be responsible for its expenditure. Ajit Singh Nijjar agreed with the idea of a separate committee but also suggested separate membership for the Centre. Eventually it was decided that the Sikh Centre was part of the *Gurdwara* so two committees should be formed from *gurdwara* members, one for the *Gurdwara* and another for the Centre. An ad-hoc committee was formed which included Ajit Singh Nijjar, Manjit Singh Mehat, Kewal Singh Bhullar, Arminder Singh Saroa and Kulwant Singh Bhamra.

In 1987-1988 the Building and Sports Centre sub-committee was formed, including Kulwant Singh Bhamra (Chairman), Harbans Singh Dogra, Tara Singh, Dharam Singh and Gurdeep Singh Bhogal. The *Gurdwara* laid down the following conditions regarding the Sikh Centre Sub-committee:

1) Every member of the Sub-committee should already be a member of the *Gurdwara* Sahib.
2) Every member of the Sub-committee should be a paid-up member (£101) of the Sikh Centre.
3) The Committee should last for one year or for the same length of time as the *Gurdwara* committee.
4) Permission should not be given for political activities.
5) Programmes taking place in the Centre should be notified to the *Gurdwara*.

6) The *Gurdwara* Committee has the right to overturn the decisions made by the members of the Sikh Centre Sub-committee.

Further decisions were taken by the *Gurdwara* committee to the effect that:
a) On the Sub-committee of the Sikh Centre, there would be two members from the *Gurdwara* committee.
b) This Sub-committee would not merely be an advisory committee but should have full management responsibility for the Centre.
c) The formation of the Sub-committee would be the responsibility of the *Gurdwara*.

All these conditions reflected the intention of the *Gurdwara* to assert its supremacy. The *Gurdwara* was keen to control the activities and management of the Sikh Centre and therefore put forward such conditions to retain control. On the other hand, the Centre wished for autonomy and constant efforts were made to achieve this.

The Sikh Centre continued expanding its activities in spite of uncertainty over who controlled the management. Some new activities for the welfare of the Sikh community were introduced. Day care facilities for Sikh elders were started in June 1988 with funding from Social Services. Music classes were started in May 1989 on every Tuesday, and were also funded by Leeds City Council.

The expansion of activities in the Centre required a full-time caretaker to look after the Centre. On 6th May 1991 it was decided that the Council should be asked to fund and appoint a full-time caretaker and until this was arranged, the Centre should continue to be managed as before. Meanwhile Amar Singh and Inder Singh took responsibility for opening the Centre and the President took bookings. Gurcharan Singh Kundi was given the responsibility of liaising with the Education Department on the funding of the caretaker's post. He reported that the Education Department would not fund this post on the grounds that this Centre was not under the control of the Council or this Department. He also added that a suggestion had been made to start training classes, which might enable the Committee to claim the salary of a caretaker. In June 1991 Balbir Singh from Huddersfield was appointed as a caretaker on a weekly wage of £40 and a copy of the service conditions was given to him.

Once again, the management of the Centre and the status of the Centre's committee became an agenda item. The *Gurdwara* committee decided in April 1993 that:

a) The Sikh Centre's new committee would be in accordance with the *Gurdwara's* Constitution.
b) It would run the Sikh Centre for one year.
c) The *Gurdwara's* committee should not interfere in their work.
d) It would be independent.
e) It would conduct its own General Meetings and should submit its accounts to the *Gurdwara* committee before the Annual General Meeting.

However, these conditions were not approved at the general meeting. Ajit Singh Nijjar, Mohinderpal Singh Sarang, Pritpal Singh Manku and Gurdeep Singh Bhogal suggested that the Sikh Centre committee should remain for two years in the first instance. Sukhjinder Singh Hundal was unanimously appointed as a secretary and Amarjit Singh Uppal as treasurer in 1994. It was also agreed that the treasurer could authorize spending on an item of up to £200 without a committee meeting and up to £2,000 with the consultation and consent of the committee.

The Centre was used mainly for social functions and the use of alcoholic drinks at social gatherings was allowed in the Centre. In order to comply with licensing laws, the person booking the use of the Centre was made responsible for obtaining a licence. The use of the Centre increased and that made more demands on the *Gurdwara* kitchen for cooking the food. It was decided to use the Sikh Centre kitchen for cooking or warming food for weddings booked in the Sikh Centre. It was also decided that a second kitchen for the Sikh Centre should be created bearing in mind the situation which would occur when there were two functions booked on the same day. The site selected for the second kitchen was next to the store in the car park. The Committee applied for planning permission and tenders were invited.

The Sikh Centre was also used for educational purposes. It was decided in 1999 that Panjabi and religious classes in the Centre should be started. Panjabi classes were shifted from the old *Gurughar* to the Sikh Centre. Religious classes were held in the lower hall of the *Gurdwara* and as the number of children attending religious classes increased, it was suggested that those classes also be shifted to the Sikh Centre. This suggestion was not complied with as the rooms there were not large enough to accommodate the number of children attending this class.

The Sub-Committee formed in 2000-2001 for the Sikh Centre initially included one member from the *Gurdwara* Committee and Nirmal Singh Sangha represented the *Gurdwara* Committee. In May 2000, two members from the *Gurdwara* committee, namely, Hazara Singh Sindhar and Inder Singh Bahth, were voted onto the Sikh Centre committee. Balraj Singh Gill and Harbans Singh Saimbhi were co-opted. In September 2001, Inder Singh Bahth was appointed as a caretaker of the Sikh Centre on a weekly wage of £65. *Giani* Virender Singh looked after the Centre for three months when Inder Singh went to India on 22nd February 2002.

The records show that at this point the management of the Centre seemed unsatisfactory. In February 2003 some members of the Sikh Centre Sub-committee informed the *Gurdwara* Committee that the work of the Centre had not been carried out in consultation with the

Committee. Some members were making their own decisions without consulting the Sub-committee members. Accounts were not presented either to the *Gurdwara* committee or to the Sub-committee of the Centre. After a long discussion it was agreed to ask the treasurer of the Sikh Centre Committee to present the accounts until 31st March 2003, and Sarabjit Singh Toor, Harbans Singh Saimbhi and Kalyan Singh would check those before being passed to Chaudhary Accountants. The account books would be returned to the *Gurdwara* Committee, and would then be given to the new committee who would check the accounts again.

The Centre was heavily used in spite of its uninviting appearance. In order to improve this, the land was levelled and cleaned. A quotation was also invited for the levelling of the land adjoining the Sikh Centre and it was made available for users to sit outside in good weather. Gates were fixed between the Centre and the *Gurdwara* in order to stop people from wedding parties coming on to the *Gurdwara* premises and throwing or scattering any rubbish. The Sikh Centre was upgraded. Flameproof curtains were bought for the Centre costing £200. Soundproofing of the Sikh Centre was felt to be necessary as the noise during functions, especially wedding parties, disturbed *Gurdwara* programmes. The old chairs were replaced and a 'No Smoking' sign was put up in the Sikh Centre. It was decided that an architect would be asked to prepare plans for the use of the basement of the Sikh Centre for the *Khalsa* (religious) School. Expansion of the school, kitchen and stage was also considered.

The Sikh Centre was used for other than social functions such as the 'One world in a city' programme funded by a Council grant. The Centre made an unsuccessful grant application to the Department of Urban Development for substantial funding of £¼ million for a nursery, library and playroom for children, mainly for the use of single parents.

1. 1 Hiring Charges
Hiring charges were introduced soon after the completion of the Centre in order to raise funds to meet running and maintenance costs. The

Centre was furnished and carpeted. Tables, chairs, crockery, utensils, sports equipment and a sound system were bought in order to make the Centre functional. The following was the list of charges in 1986.

Hall, kitchen and gallery for 12 hours	£250
Hall	£150
Kitchen	£50
Upper gallery	£50
Utensils and crockery	£30
Gallery for half a day	£30

20% discount was given to the paid up members. Paid up members were those who had donated £100 or over to the building fund of the Centre. In 1991, the charges were fixed at £15 per hour and the amount was increased for the use of other facilities as follows:

Hall	£290
Kitchen	£80
Crockery	£20
Beer glasses	£10

A deposit of £100 was to be paid at the time of booking. Fifty per cent would be deducted from the deposit if bookings were cancelled more than two weeks before the event and no refund at all was to be given in case of cancellation less than two weeks before the event. The facilities of the Centre became popular with the community and the take-up was increased, especially for hiring crockery for parties held at home. In May 2000, a separate charge of £20 for hiring crockery included in a deposit of £50 was introduced. If all the crockery was returned safely £30 of this would be returned, otherwise breakages were charged for. The charges for booking the hall were also revised. The hiring charges for the hall were increased to £650. In order to book the hall, a deposit of £200 had to be paid in advance. A deduction of £50 per half hour was made if the hall was not vacated on time. The hall had to close by midnight. Bookings already made were charged at the old rates. The booking responsibility was that of the Secretary. The duty of the caretaker was to check the Centre after a party had finished and two committee members also checked the hall. The time for parties to end was also fixed, wedding parties by 5 pm and discos by 11 pm. The hall had to be closed by 6 pm after weddings.

2. 2 Services to elderly Sikhs

The principal aim of any *gurdwara* is to look after the welfare of the Sikh community. In line with this, the *Gurdwara* provided some services to elderly Sikhs by organizing excursions and outings from time to time. It was noted in the minute book that excursions for the elderly were arranged to Scarborough and to Blackpool to see the lights in 1985. A room was allocated to elderly Sikhs in the Sikh Centre where they could sit and socialize. It was equipped with television, video and hi-fi from a donation made by the Sarao family in June 1988. The family also donated £850 to improve the provisions for elderly Sikhs.

In 1988, day care facilities were offered to elderly Sikh males with supporting funding from Leeds Social Services Department. This funding was given under the Neighbourhood Network Project scheme, which provided money for local community organizations to develop preventative services. The main aim of funding was to provide culturally sensitive services to Sikh elders in order to maintain their quality of life while they were living at home, and to keep them in the community. The *Gurdwara* was given £20,000 to support the provision for elderly Sikh males and provided them with a room. This room given by the *Gurdwara* in the Sikh Centre was named as the Baba Dal Day Centre. The Deputy Lord Mayor of Leeds, Councillor Mr B. Kilgallon performed the official opening ceremony on 16th June 1988. The *Gurdwara* was to manage this service, which would be closely monitored by Social Services. The funding covered staff salaries and some contribution towards the cost of service delivery. The Social Services Department imposed some conditions on how to spend this money. One of the conditions was that the grant should be spent on the elderly. This service was funded for only three days a week. It was expected that part-time staff would be appointed and the appointments would follow the Council's recruitment and selection criteria and procedures. The other expectations were that activities to maintain the quality of life such as gentle exercises and healthy eating would be introduced. Social activities were to be organized so that the elderly could enjoy their life and create a social network. Home visits would be made and the elderly would be befriended in times of need. They should be provided with information responding to their needs, such as help in claiming benefits. In order to encourage elderly Sikhs to use this service they would be visited. Baba Dal would have its own management committee and separate bank account.

The Committee decided in 1992 to extend this service for the elderly to four days a week, Monday to Thursday, from 10.30 am to 3 pm, a total of 18 hours. The post of manager was advertised. Beant Singh became the first manager of the Baba Dal Day Centre. Darshan Kaur Channa was appointed as care assistant and assumed her duties from 6th September 1992, the temporary post of cook was given to Paramjit Kaur Dhand from April 1993 and Balbir Singh was appointed as cleaner. The service was well used and the numbers increased to between twenty-five and thirty users. Additional help was required for cooking and Santosh Kaur Ryatt was appointed. Service users had to make a minimal contribution. Users were charged thirty pence per session from 16th December 1991 and this was increased to fifty pence per session in April 1992. In June 2000 Beant Singh was given four weeks' notice as the committee was unhappy with his work and according to the minutes he had been found absent on many occasions. He sued the Centre for unfair dismissal and won the case.

Darshan Kaur Channa was appointed manager. In March 2002, she left her job and the decision to make another appointment was taken. It was a part-time post for 16 hours a week. Sukhchain Singh was appointed for a trial period of one month in April 2002 and a caretaker was appointed to replace the temporary caretaker. In April 2002 the following changes were made:

a) The opening hours of the day centre were fixed as 11 am to 3 pm, Monday to Thursday, and it would be closed on Friday.

b) No one was allowed to eat, drink alcohol or smoke in the room of the Baba Dal Day Centre.
c) If Baba Dal's members wished to eat then they could eat in the *Gurdwara langar* hall.
d) Permission was needed to celebrate any function in the Baba Dal's room.

The users of the Baba Dal Day Centre resented these changes and felt unhappy. In order to resolve the situation, a meeting was arranged by the Sikh Temple with the Baba Dal members on 20th May 2002. It was decided that Harpal Singh, Nirmal Singh Sangha, Professor Bakhshish Singh, Tejinderpal Singh Bal and Daljit Singh from the Sikh Temple would meet with them and report back to the *Gurdwara* Committee concerning their discussion. The Baba Dal members refused to attend this meeting in protest and the Committee decided that the decision made earlier would be applied temporarily for six months.

Some Baba Dal members were angered by this arrangement. They felt that their needs were not being met. They made several complaints to the Department of Social Services. Social Services found the services provided in the Centre to be unsatisfactory and were not in agreement with the fact that services were being developed on a religious basis. It was considered that the Sub-committee was failing to meet the service level agreement. Close monitoring by the Department also revealed that the suggested structure of the service was not in place either. This created tension and Social Services asked the Sub-committee to resolve this situation. However, the problems of the Baba Dal Centre were beyond remit of the Sub-committee and had to be tackled by the *Gurdwara* Committee. This Committee decided to have fresh talks with Baba Dal, suggesting that differences should be put aside.

Eventually the grant from Social Services was suspended in March 2003. Two of my informants told me that some of the users had had a meeting with Social Services and had suggested that the grant should be given to a new and independent committee organized by users. Social Services agreed and an independent committee was established. Ujjal

Singh Ryatt became the Chairman, Prem Singh Duggal, the Secretary and Bakhshish Singh, the Treasurer. This committee also included two user members, the serving President of the Sikh Temple and a local councillor. Social Services were invited to attend the meetings of this committee. This independent committee was accepted and recognized by the *Gurdwara* Committee.

The job of the manager was not advertised, though Pritpal Kaur Plaha was appointed for a month. Her contract was not extended as the feeling was that there was no need of a manager. The job of the cook was given to Surjit Kaur Bhogal who worked until July 2003 and then Paramjit Phull was appointed in her place. Her working hours are from 10 am to 2 pm, Monday to Friday. Users are charged £1.70 per day. The current grant is £21,000 and the Chairman, Secretary and Treasurer are cheque signatories. However, although an independent committee runs the day centre now, the services offered are still not developing to Social Services' expectations and also are not meeting the service level agreement. The day centre is predominantly for Sikh elders but it should nevertheless be open to any old people who live in the vicinity. Even though the Centre is based in part of the Sikh Temple, services should not be dominated by religion. Social Services also seem to be concerned about the lack of activities for elderly Sikhs, and of befriending and outreach programmes. The view of the independent committee is that they provide the services demanded by the users and religion is an inseparable part of their life.

2. 2 Sports Centre

Sikhs like to enjoy sport as a pastime. Sports activities were organized even before the opening of this Centre. The Sports Committee was first formed on 30th August 1970 and included Lashkar Singh Azad, Kirpal Singh Jutla, Gurcharan Singh Kundi, Sucha Singh Chahal and Sewa Singh Kalsi. Kirpal Singh Jutla was in charge of the committee which had responsibility for organizing sports activities and encouraging youths to participate.

In June 1982, a sub-committee for a Sikh Youth Club was formed to focus on youth activities including Gurdeep Singh Bhogal (Chairman), Paramjit Singh Mudhar, Paramjit Singh Bhogal, Kewal Singh Badesha, Pritpal Singh Manku, Ajit Singh Nijjar, Piara Singh Bains and the serving President and Secretary of the *Gurdwara*. The Sikh Youth Club was established as a result of an Inner City Grant of £500 in August 1982 to encourage young men to participate in sports. A further grant of £750 was received, which gave a boost to the club. Sports equipment was bought with this money. Such sports as snooker, table tennis, badminton, cricket, football and volleyball were organized free of charge. However, the activities of the Sikh Youth Club were hindered by problems of harassment on Chapeltown Road, which were difficult to stop. It was decided that activities would be organized in Scott Hall Middle School, though Elmhurst School and Earl Cowper School were also approached. In 1983, Paramjit Singh Bhogal resigned as Sports Secretary and Avtar Singh Aujula took his position. In 1984, it was decided that the same range of sports facilities would be offered free of charge in the Sports Club. This club was formed to use the facilities of the schools. Self-defence and Indian games such as Carrom Board were also introduced.

The Sikh Centre offered many sports facilities and activities, and over a period had bought its own sports equipment. Beant Singh was appointed to be in charge of weight training and he kept all the accounts. The annual fee for this was £5. Members were charged 30p and non-members had to pay £1 per session. Weight training operated three days a week on Mondays, Wednesdays and Fridays from 6 pm to 9 pm. The Sikh Lions Training Club met in the upper gallery of the Sikh Centre. A membership fee of £2 per annum plus 10p entry fee for members and 25p entry fee for non-members had been introduced for the youth club.

2. 3 Conclusion
The Sikh Temple undertook the responsibility for building the Sikh Centre to cater for the social needs of the Sikh community. The facilities of the Centre are currently very well used and it is a good source of income for the Sikh Temple. It has become a multipurpose centre

with the capacity to meet the basic social and recreational needs of the Sikh community. However, the relationship between the *Gurdwara* and the Centre has always remained unclear, which has affected the management of the Sikh Centre. The Centre has always struggled unsuccessfully over securing its autonomy.

The Sikh Centre may be a source of pride for the Sikh community and its site conveniently suited to them but it has not served the original aim of the grant. The Council gave the grant to build a centre which could be used by the whole community for other than religious purposes and especially for education and training. This purpose has not been fully achieved. One informant commented that they did not have a think tank at that time and they had made a strategic mistake by insisting that the Council allow them to add religion along with the social and educational aims. The Baba Dal Day Centre still forms part of the Sikh Centre. It is envisaged that there will be changes in the future with the restoration of the old *Gurughar* building and taking into account future strategic policies of Social Services to provide citywide services for Sikh elders by April 2007.

The *Gurdwara* committee members have so many responsibilities to cope with and it might be easier if other groups associated or linked with the *Gurdwara* were delegated to help them conduct their business using clearly specified policies and line management in order to deliver a more efficient and effective organization of work.

Chapter 4
The Constitution

The constitution within the context of a *gurdwara* is the set of rules by which a *gurdwara* is managed and it embodies the rights of the *sangat*. The rules and regulations to manage the first *Gurdwara* in Leeds were prepared when the decision was first taken to buy a house to serve as a *gurdwara*. The matter was discussed in the Ordinary General Meeting of 9th March 1958 where it was agreed that a Constitution should be drafted. The draft was prepared and was read and unanimously approved in the meeting held on 5th July 1959. The 'United Sikh Association, Yorks', printed this Constitution when Sikhs bought the first *Gurdwara* building on 3 Savile Road, Leeds 7, in the name of this society.

The Constitution was written in good English, easily comprehended. The style was jargon free. It met the requirements of the *Gurdwara* and was a remarkable achievement for the Sikhs who prepared it without much support from outside. It offered a comprehensive coverage of the subject and it was to the credit of the Sikhs involved that they from the very beginning followed set rules and procedures in running the *Gurdwara*. The uniqueness of this Constitution was that it reflected the Sikh principle of universal brotherhood by opening the *Gurdwara* membership to any person irrespective of caste, creed, colour, religion or nationality.

Soon after this, the composition of the Sikh community changed with the arrival of East African Sikhs and families from the Punjab between 1959 and 1962, which prompted the community to buy a bigger building for the *Gurdwara*. This change also affected the Constitution. These first amendments reflected the need for change as and when required and were discussed in the meeting held on 29th July 1962. They were as follows: that the *Gurdwara* be named 'The Sikh Temple'; that the elected members of the executive should number thirty instead of twenty-seven and should be elected in the *diwan* (congregation) and then these thirty members would elect the President and Secretary and other office bearers themselves; that the quorum to start a general meeting must be at least fifty, or one fifth of the total membership; that the clause related to visitors should be deleted. The suggestion was made that the amended version of the Constitution should be printed in both English and Panjabi.

The meeting held on 18th August 1963 focused on the trustees and the main agenda during the year revolved around the Constitution. A trustee should be a general member for at least three years and an executive member for a year. Trustees should be elected in an extraordinary general meeting. There should be seven trustees instead of five to serve the tenure of four years. The Chief Trustee should receive the minutes of the Executive Committee. Trustees should have the power to approve or reject any expenditure of over £100. Trustees could take a year out if they were going out of the country. This was further discussed at the meeting held on 28th June 1964. According to the Constitution there should be five trustees instead of four and the general members had the right to change any trustee after five years. The Executive Committee could nominate another trustee if any trustee left. It was also decided in the meeting of 9th August 1964 that two trustees would be selected in the general meeting and there should only be five trustees. In the case of a decision made by the Executive Committee being rejected, this had to be agreed by the Trustees Committee, twenty-seven general members and one third of the Executive Members.

It was agreed at the meeting held on 20th October 1963 that names should be put forward to the trustees for the nomination of the Management Committee one week prior to the annual general election and the trustees would select ten names. If there were fewer than ten names, extra names would be selected from the general membership. Trustees would also nominate seven members and ten members would be elected from the general membership and each member should have the support of five members. No member of the existing committee could volunteer or be nominated. If any serving committee member wished to serve again he or she required the support of twice the number of members.

Some further suggestions were made in the meeting held on 12th July

1964. The *Gurdwara* Executive Committee members were to be elected in the *sangat* in the General Meeting and this committee of twenty-seven members would elect the office bearers. Trustees could become office bearers but they had to resign from trusteeship. Only fully paid-up members could participate in the election.

In the beginning, executive members were decided with mutual consent but with the growth of the Sikh community, a proper procedure was required for electing executive committees. There was also the necessity of having more than one trustee to sign the deed and also to oversee the work of the Sikh Temple. Sikhs also wanted to register this organization with the Charity Commission and the main agenda item of the 7th March 1965 meeting was the amendment of the Constitution according to the suggestions made by the Charity Commission. The Constitution also covered the solution of certain problems encountered by executive committees such as the question of making information public or presenting it to the media, attendance at meetings and the fixing of election dates.

The name of the *Gurdwara* on the Constitution would be 'The Sikh Temple'. Twenty-three members would be elected from the general members in *sangat* and these elected members would nominate another four members making a total of twenty-seven members. The quorum should be forty-five for the General Meeting. The Executive Committee should approve any information given to the press. For emergency meetings, there should be at least five executive members. There should be three signatories for the chequebook, i.e. the President, Secretary and Treasurer. The Treasurer must deposit any money collected in the bank within two weeks. Clause 33, 'The *Granthi* shall make a reasonable charge for the goods deposited in the store-room by any person' should be deleted. One member of the Executive Committee should serve as storekeeper. Any member missing two meetings consecutively should be sent a letter by the secretary asking him to state his reason or reasons and encouraging him to attend meetings. Failure to attend a third meeting without giving a valid reason would result in his dismissal. It was unanimously agreed that the elections in future would be held on *Vaisakhi* starting from the year in question. Members could vote in that year's election without paying their membership fee. All these amendments and suggestions were unanimously accepted and it was decided that these suggested changes and amendments would be inserted in the revised Constitution to be printed shortly.

The Extraordinary General Meeting was held on 5th September 1965, soon after the Constitution was printed, to consider further amendments. The minutes state that the meeting held on 7th March 1965 had amended clause 23 to read 'the Executive Committee including General Secretary, President or Vice-President may unanimously grant such permission'. It was again replaced to read 'the General Secretary and the President may unanimously grant such permission'. The word 'committee' in clause 47 should read General Committee and it was also suggested that 'Issued by the General Committee, Sikh Temple, Leeds' should be written at the end rather than 'Signed by the Chairman'. An amendment slip to this affect was printed and attached to the Constitution. This revised Constitution reflected a transparent and open method of election.

A decision was taken on 9th April 1967 to form an election board of five members, including a trustee or trustees elected from the *sangat*, to take responsibility for the election of the Management Committee so as to ensure fairness according to the election procedures. At the most, thirty nominations should be taken from the *sangat* and this board would then select twenty-three members from these nominations. These twenty-three members would elect office bearers themselves. The first election board was made up of two elected members, *Giani* Kesar Singh and Piara Singh Chaggar, and three trustees, Balwant Singh Birdi, Gurbaksh Singh Rai and B. T. Singh. Balwant Singh Birdi had overall responsibility for the election held in 1967. Further changes were introduced in the following year. The new election board consisted of five members, including four trustees and one *gursikh* (a person who follows Sikh principles), *Giani* Kesar Singh, taking responsibility for the 1968-69 elections. It was decided that the Election Board would take twenty-three nominations to the management committee and the office bearers would be elected from persons nominated in the *sangat*. It is indicated in the minutes that the general members suggested not holding an election that year and allowing the same committee to serve for another year. This suggestion was accepted and the committee remained the same for the next year. This did not please all the general members and concerns were raised, with the suggestion that this new committee was unconstitutional. This led once again to changes being made in the *Gurdwara* Constitution and a sub-committee was formed with the remit to make suggestions to improve the *Gurdwara* management. It was once again decided on 19th October 1968 that the Constitution be printed in Panjabi though this did not happen.

The meeting held on 22nd February 1969 suggested further amendments in the Constitution, which were considered and passed unanimously in the Extraordinary General Meeting on 9th March 1969. These were, 1) The annual election must be held on the last Sunday of the month of April; 2) The participants could only take part in the election if they were paid-up members and they must have become members at least two weeks before the election date; 3) The election duties were to be carried out by the Board of five members consisting of four trustees and the retiring President from the out-going committee; 4) There should be nomination papers for the election and those who wanted to be nominated for the Executive Committee should fill them in and return them to the general secretary one week prior to the election; 5) There would be ballot papers with the names of the nominated candidates. Every member would get this ballot paper and voters would mark their choice and put them in the election box in the presence of the Board members; 6) Twenty-seven members would be elected on to the Executive Committee and four trustees would be ex-officio members; 7) The office bearers of the Executive Committee must have been members of the Executive Committee for at least two years; 8) There should be at least fifty signatures in order to call a general meeting; 9) Each member could only make one nomination; 10) The election box should be kept in front of the *Guru Granth Sahib*.

The election procedures were discussed again at the meeting held on 24th January 1970. It was decided that applications for general membership should be accepted from 25th January onwards and close at 7 pm on 12th April, fifteen days prior to the election on Sunday. The responsibility for the membership would be given to two trustees. The suggestion was made that no one should be present near the voting booth except the five Election Board members. The Election Board would check the ballot box before the election. The names on the ballot paper should be written alphabetically according to the Panjabi alphabet. Two children would be selected by the Election Board to read the election results. The tenure of the President, General Secretary and Treasurer should not last for more than two years. It was unanimously agreed that if the Management Committee failed for any reason to manage the *Gurdwara* satisfactorily then trustees would take over and hold a fresh election within four to six weeks. It was also agreed that if the quorum was not met in any general meeting then the next meeting should take place at the same venue and the same time four weeks later.

It is important to mention that these election procedures regularly drew the attention of the committees from 1967 to 1970 and a number of suggestions were made to resolve any possible difficulties, as is obvious from the minutes of the discussions held and eventually the amendments to the Constitution approved at an Extraordinary General Meeting held on 1st March 1970. These amendments were that, 1) The President, General Secretary and Treasurer of the *Gurdwara* Committee should not be elected for more than two years in the same position; 2) If for any reason the Management Committee failed to function satisfactorily, the management of the *Gurdwara* would be taken over by four trustees who would arrange for a new election to be held within four to six weeks; 3) If any general meeting could not take place because of the lack of a quorum, there would be another meeting at the same venue and at the same time four weeks later.

After all these discussions, a sub-committee was formed to revise the Constitution under the chairmanship of Pritam Singh, Q.C. (the official wording of the amendments is given in Appendix 1). The revised draft of the Constitution was presented on 27th February 1977 for the consideration of the committee.

The committee rejected one amendment, numbered 36a, b and c, concerning the suspension of any member and the right of the suspended member to appeal, on the grounds that this would make Executive Committees very powerful. Though these amendments were accepted unanimously on 3rd April 1977 the revised Constitution was not signed until 21st August 1983. The amendment that only turbaned Sikhs could be appointed to executive posts brought a significant change as this barred se*hajdhari* (clean-shaven) Sikhs from holding such powerful positions.

An extraordinary general meeting was held on 21st August 1983 to revise the Constitution with a view to getting charitable status for the *Gurdwara*. The suggested amendments were 1) To delete Clause 2b (iv) which dealt with establishing a school for teaching Panjabi language and literature, previously agreed on 3rd April 1977, as this was already covered by the aims and objectives of the *Gurdwara* (Passed unanimously); 2) To amend the clause on membership; 3) To amend Clause 15 so that two general meetings a year instead of four would be held (Passed unanimously); 4) That the statement regarding trustees (Clause 47) should be amended according to the direction of the Charity Commission and consideration should be given to their length of tenure. There was also concern about appointing one trustee every year and the expense thus incurred.

Many attempts were made at this point to amend the Constitution. Amendments were discussed and even agreed but the new version of the Constitution was not printed. A meeting was once again arranged on 1st June 1985 and another Extraordinary General Meeting was called on 6th October 1985 to consider the new Constitution in the light of the Charity Commission's requirements. The amendments were made (details can be found in Appendix 1). It was also suggested in the amended version that should any *amritdhari* committee member act *kurahit* (breach of the Sikh Code of Conduct) he should be dismissed from the committee. Once again, another meeting was held on 17th January 1988 to consider the constitutional amendments further. The final version of the Constitution was printed in English in 1988 (see Appendix 1) and this included the amendments passed up to 15 January 1988. This version is currently operational. It was decided to publish 2,000 copies each costing 6½ p and to be sold for 50p. A copy of the Constitution was also sent to the Charity Commission. However, once again, amendments to the Constitution were made on 3rd December 1989, to the effect that:

1) The Sikh Temple should be named Sri Gurdwara Sahib, Leeds.
2) The number of committee members should be reduced from twenty-seven to seventeen.
3) The tenure of the committee should be 2 years. This means that elections must be held every two years.
4) The President, General Secretary, Treasurer should only serve twice (*do miyad*) on the committee.

An Extraordinary Meeting was called in order to consider these amendments and all the amendments were passed unanimously except the second. The election procedure was discussed again at great length in 2002 and the conclusion was that the existing procedure given in the Constitution should be retained. Following this current procedure, nominations are taken for two weeks starting on *Vaisakhi* and stopping at 12 pm on the day of the General Meeting. If nominations exceed twenty-seven then elections must be held. If there are twenty-seven nominations then the committee will be formed under the supervision of the Trustee Board and the Committee should be announced within four weeks in the presence of the congregation. The name of the *Gurdwara* was also not changed and retained the original name.

In the year 2003-2004 nominations in the elections which took place on 25th May 2003 exceeded twenty-seven. Objections were raised over the violation of nomination procedures. It was suggested that *amritdharis* keeping *rahit maryada* should fill in the forms and the election procedure should be followed as outlined in the Constitution. This should be agreed at a general meeting. Nomination forms should be opened two weeks before the election in the presence of the President, General Secretary, three members and two trustees. The election would be carried out by two parties each having twenty-seven members who would be given their own *nishan* (symbol). The voter should mark the *nishan* he or she was voting for. Elections on a two-party basis were proposed on 27th April 2004 though this was not accepted. In the Extraordinary Annual General Meeting on 25th July 2004, it was approved that there should be twenty-seven nominations collectively or individually, the Management Committee could serve for two tenures and that committee members and trustees should be *amritdharis* and lead their life according to *rahit maryada*. It was also agreed that the existing election procedure given in the Constitution should be followed.

In the mid-1960s almost one-third of the Executive Committee members were clean-shaven, including one member of the Board of Trustees. No restriction was laid down about clean-shaven Sikhs holding official positions on the *Gurdwara* Management Committee until the amendments made to the Constitution in 1976. This amended version contained the clause stating that, 'All office bearers and trustees shall be *kesadhari* Sikhs'. This amendment was accepted on 3rd April 1977 and interpreted by some as a discriminatory clause which kept non-*kesadharis* out of the management committees. The thinking of Sikhs changed in 1984 when the Indian army attacked *Harimandir Sahib* and they felt that their religion was threatened. They became keen to keep their identity and many became initiated Sikhs. In December 1987 it was decided that the whole Committee should be constituted of initiated or *kesadhari* Sikhs and then this was changed to the President, Secretary, Treasurer, Religious Secretary and Public Relations Secretary being initiated Sikhs and other members being *kesadhari*. Later, this was changed again and Clause 6.5 of the 1988 Constitution stated that, 'The President, Secretary, Treasurer, Religious Secretary, Public Relations Secretary and Trustees and all members of the Executive Committee must be *amritdhari* Sikhs'. It is therefore assumed that only *amritdharis* should call themselves Sikhs. At present all the committee is constituted of *amritdharis*.

The Constitution concentrated on election and election procedures after the expansion of the Sikh community. From 1959 to 1962 committees were elected by mutual consent but it was decided at the meeting held on 29th July 1962 that the committee would be elected in the presence of the congregation. In October 1963 this became the joint responsibility of trustees and congregation and again in July 1964 it was suggested that the committee would be elected by the congregation in the General Meeting. It was also included in the revised constitution in 1965 that the committee members would be elected in the Annual

General Meeting. An election board was set up in 1967 to take the responsibility of ensuring fairness in conducting elections. In 1970 it was suggested that no one should be present near the voting booth except the Election Board members. The constitutional amendments considered on 17th January 1988 suggested that the procedure of the election should be proposed by the Executive Committee and presented for the approval at the Annual General Meeting and this was inserted in the Constitution printed in 1988. The election procedures were discussed at great length in 2002 and in 2004 but it was concluded that the existing procedures as outlined in the Constitution should be retained. It is, therefore, obvious that though the election and election procedures were often discussed it has never been possible to find an adequate solution to the satisfaction of everyone. Elections are supposed to be democratic and fair but procedures are not immune to malpractice. One informant said that the elections conducted under the auspices of the Charity Commission in 2004 were also found to be unsatisfactory on the grounds that almost all the information was in English and that the procedure practised seemed unfair, particularly regarding the presence of nominees near the election booth. It is important that there should be an independent election board which should take nominations. Election procedure should not be proposed by the committee and approved in an Annual General Meeting just before an election but should be properly laid down and recorded in the Constitution in order to avoid any confusion.

Trustees were another matter of discussion on several occasions, particularly concerning the election of one trustee every year. This problem has been resolved now. Many unsuccessful attempts were made to change the name of the Sikh Temple. The Constitution was amended in 1962 and it was decided then to get it printed in both Panjabi and English. It has often been suggested that it should be printed in Panjabi but this has never happened and even the present Constitution is in English. The basis of most of these amendments was that committees were experiencing difficulties and amendments were proposed or made to find a way around the problems, though changes were also made if the *sangat* was unhappy with certain clauses or procedures.

Chapter 5
The Religious Role of the Sikh Temple

The most important role of a *gurdwara* is to promote Sikh religion and religious activities. The Sikh Temple has taken many steps to promote Sikh religion and to continue and maintain Sikh traditions. Sikh priests generally recruited from the Punjab are instrumental in furthering this. They are called *granthis*, *gianis* or *bhais* and undertake the day-to-day work of the *gurdwaras*. The duties of a *granthi* are many and varied. A *granthi* opens the *gurdwara* in the morning and closes it at night, reads the Holy book and performs life rite ceremonies such as birth, naming, marriage and death. Some *granthis* teach Panjabi, religious education and *kirtan*. The job is a paid one and *granthis* also get money from families for performing life rite ceremonies. They work under the direction and supervision of management committees.

1. 1 Granthis & Gianis

Granthis play a crucial role in the running of a *gurdwara*. At the opening of the first *Gurdwara* in Leeds, Jagat Singh Channa was appointed as *granthi* and caretaker of the *Gurdwara* and worked on a voluntary basis. He was given accommodation in the *Gurdwara*. He resigned in May 1961 and his responsibility was given to Mastan Singh, a printing student. Vir Singh Rayat and *Giani* Sarwan Singh (two local Sikhs) helped by performing *shabad kirtan* every Sunday. Mastan Singh arranged religious education in the *Gurdwara* for children and the *Gurdwara* paid for stationery. In June 1962, Arjun Singh was given the responsibility of caretaker as Mastan Singh's family had come from India and it was difficult for him to continue to live in the *Gurdwara*.

It was decided that a paid *granthi* for the *Gurdwara* should be engaged and *Baba* Khem Singh was appointed on 17th March 1968. He was given £5 extra to teach religious education to children and also taught Panjabi. *Giani* Arjun Singh was the first full-time paid *granthi*, appointed on 24th April 1978 after lengthy negotiations. He had intended to go to Canada and the committee persuaded him to stay. However, a conflict arose over the *maryada* (Sikh religious tradition) followed by the *granthi*.

There are two *maryadas*, *Akal takht maryada* (*maryada* approved by *Akal takht* – the supreme Sikh authority) and the popular *sant maryada* (traditions practised by holy men or saints). According to the *sant maryada*, *dhup* (incense), *jyot* (lighting the flame with a cotton bud), *Japuji da path* (hymns generally recited in the morning) and *kumbh* (waterpot) are essential but *Akal takht maryada* does not need any of these in *akhandpath* ceremonies. An *akhandpath* was kept for a family from East Africa on 8th September 1979. On this occasion *Gianiji* followed *Akal takht Maryada* and this was not favoured by the general *sangat* of mainly East African Sikhs. The management committee asked *Gianiji* to follow *sant maryada* but *Gianiji* did not agree. A sub-committee was formed in September 1979 to talk to him. The sub-committee failed to persuade *Gianiji* to follow *sant maryada* and he was asked to resign. According to the minutes:

ਗਿਆਨੀ ਅਰਜਨ ਸਿੰਘ ਜੀ ਨੇ ਕਮੇਟੀ ਨਾਲ ਪੂਰਾ ਸਹਿਯੋਗ ਨਹੀਂ ਦਿੱਤਾ ਤੇ ਕਮੇਟੀ ਦੇ ਕੰਮਾ ਨਾਲ ਉਹ ਸਹਿਮਤ ਨਹੀਂ ਸਨ ਅਤੇ ਆਪਣੀ ਡਿਊਟੀ ਨੂੰ ਵੀ ਉਨਾਂ ਨੇ ਪੂਰੀ ਜ਼ੁੰਮੇਵਾਰੀ ਨਾਲ ਨਹੀਂ ਨਿਭਾਇਆ। ਇਸ ਲਈ ਉਨ੍ਹਾਂ ਨੂੰ ਉਨ੍ਹਾਂ ਦੇ ਸੇਵਾਪਦ ਤੋਂ ਹਟਾਇਆ। ਉਹਨਾਂ ਨੂੰ ਦੋ ਹਫਤੇ ਦੀ ਜਾਣ ਲਗਿਆਂ ਨੂੰ ਤਨਖਾਹ ਦਿੱਤੀ ਗਈ।

(He was made to resign on the basis that he was uncooperative and did not agree with the committee. He was irresponsible in performing his duties. He was paid two weeks salary before his departure.) He resigned on 24th October 1979.

In the absence of a *granthi*, Amarjit Singh was appointed mainly for *kirtan* shortly after the resignation of *Giani* Arjun Singh and it was decided on 30th July 1980 that Malia Singh Rathor (a pioneer Sikh) would take the responsibility for the morning and evening programmes of the *Gurdwara*. It was also decided that a contract for a year would be given to *ragis* and that they should be paid £20 each. Another *granthi* was appointed who also resigned on 7th November 1982 and the third *granthi*, Swaran Singh, continued until 31st December 1982.

The *maryada* incident of 1979 had prompted concern in many and it was decided in June 1983 that all *gurdwaras* in the North of England should meet. This meeting was held in the Sikh Temple on 31st July

1983 to decide on one common *maryada* to be followed by all *gurdwaras* in order to maintain consistency in the practice of the ceremony.

Giani Didar Singh was appointed for a trial period of two months on 27th August 1983. His duties were explained to him and he was told that if his work proved satisfactory, his contract would be extended. He was given a contract for a year on 24th September 1983. Soon afterwards, as stated in the minutes, it was felt that the attitude of the *Giani* had changed towards the *sangat* and Committee and he was asked to leave and the Committee gave him one month's notice.

Hari Singh Syan (a devoted volunteer) worked as a *granthi* in the absence of a *gurdwara granthi* and money paid to him was donated to the *Gurdwara*. In November 1984, it was decided to increase the wages of *granthis* as much as the stamp-free code allowed. They were also allowed to have four weeks paid leave to go to India and the *Gurdwara* would pay their airfare. In 1985 *Bhai* (a respectful word for *granthis*) Paramjit Singh and *Bhai* Darshan Singh were appointed *granthis* of the *Gurdwara* at a weekly wage of £30. The new contract was drafted and appropriate accommodation was arranged for *Bhai* Darshan Singh. They were asked to disclose their income from outside sources, to which they disagreed. The Committee decided unanimously that National Insurance contributions would not be paid for the *granthis* but an increase of £5 in the wages of each *granthi* was suggested for keeping the *Gurdwara* open all day. The *granthis* did not agree with the Committee decision and demanded:

a) That the *Gurdwara* should pay their National Insurance stamps.
b) That they be given an increase in pay.
c) That the *Gurdwara* should provide all the required food ingredients for *granthis*.

The Committee decided unanimously to relieve the *granthis* of their duties. *Bhai* Kuldip Singh and *Bhai* Baldev Singh requested that they should be given the opportunity to serve the *Gurdwara*. It was decided that the new appointees should be paid £35 weekly and that they should donate one third of their outside income to the *Gurdwara*. The *granthis* were given new contracts but they did not sign for a week and put forward their own conditions:

1. Weekly pay of £40 and £10 extra for vegetables.
2. The *Gurdwara* should pay the National Insurance stamps.
3. A reduction in duty hours to run from 6.30 am to 9 pm.

On 16th August 1987 it was decided that these *granthis* should be asked to leave, which they both did. Of the two other *granthis* appointed at this time, according to the minutes one was later sacked because of his controversial character and the other was asked to resign because of his behaviour and the complaints that had been received about him. For example:

a) He was not opening the *Gurdwara* until 8 am.
b) Fresh *prasad* was not made every day and sometimes the same *prasad* was used for two or three days.
c) The small kitchen used by *Gianiji* was kept dirty and untidy.
d) Utensils in which he cooked and ate were left unwashed.
e) Donated *romallas* were not cared for.
f) His controversial views on engagement, *langar* and beards were annoying to many in the *sangat*.

The post was advertised in the press. *Bhai* Jaswant Singh and *Bhai* Harbans Singh were appointed on a temporary basis in March 1990. *Giani* Jaswant Singh left on 20th May 1990 while *Bhai* Harbans Singh continued to work. The Committee decided that having one *granthi* was not enough for the work of the *Gurdwara* and that another *granthi* should be appointed. *Giani* Balbir Singh was appointed and it was unanimously agreed that *Giani* Harbans Singh and *Giani* Balbir Singh should be given £40 weekly pay and £5 extra for opening the *Gurdwara* every day. *Giani* Harbans Singh would give £10 to *Giani* Balbir Singh from the money donated at weddings. In September 1991 Varinder Singh was appointed as a *granthi* on a weekly wage of £45. It was left to the *granthis* as to how they would share the income earned by *kirtan*.

Professor Devinder Singh and Karamjit Singh were appointed on a weekly wage of £45 in June 1992. In July 1992, it was decided by the Committee that Professor Devinder Singh should be paid £54, Karamjit Singh £45 and *Giani* Harbans Singh £50. Their duties were allocated according to the previous contract and they were told that the committee reserved the right to alter the contract at any time.

A new *granthi*, Harpal Singh, was appointed in September 1996 because of the increased workload in the *Gurdwara*. He was given a salary of £130 from which £60 was to be donated to the *Gurdwara*. The actual salary of a *granthi* was fixed at £70 per week. Harpal Singh was told that he could stay until 15th May 1998 and by that time the committee would be able to judge his work in order to extend his stay. The Committee decided in July 1997 that *Bhai* Bakhshish Singh could work for the period that he was allowed to stay in England. When he went back to India, *Giani* Sant Singh was appointed as permanent *granthi*. In order to keep Harpal Singh, a visa extension was applied for. *Giani* Harpal Singh left on 12th March 2000. *Giani* Sant Singh also resigned in April 2001 and the reason for his resignation was that he wanted to work freelance with his *jatha* (group). Inder Singh also left and went to America. In November 2001 *Giani* Ram Singh was appointed for four weeks.

Giani Varinder Singh and Amrik Singh left in April 2002 and in their place, Tarlok Singh Delhiwala and his *jatha* of three were appointed for three months on a weekly wage of £45 each. In June 2002 *Giani* Manjit Singh was appointed on a temporary basis on a weekly wage of £60 and in July 2002 *Giani* Daljit Singh was appointed for four months on a weekly wage of £50. It was decided to keep him for another year. *Giani* Manjit Singh went on leave for a month and *Giani* Satnam Singh from the Sikh Centre served in his absence. It was decided by the Committee that service conditions and contracts should be signed by *granthis*. It should be noted that the information given here does not include all the *granthis* named in the minute book. Names have been omitted where full details were not available but the historical sequence has been respected.

The information extracted from the minutes indicates how *gianis* were appointed and shows their relationship with the committees and the problems faced on both sides. It is obvious that the views expressed were those of the serving committees. As it was not possible to collect the views of the *granthis* involved, and how they felt, it is difficult to comment on the accuracy of the facts. However, during my research I was able to interview two *gianis* (another word used for *granthis*) who shared with me the general difficulties they faced. In one interview, *Gianiji* expressed his feelings that committees were generally dominant and heavy-handed with *granthis* and made impossible for them to perform their duties as they thought right. He also added that most committee members did not seem to have a full understanding of all aspects of the Sikh religion, but they nevertheless had no hesitation in undermining *gianis* and their work. He considered that *gianis* are treated like servants rather than employees of the *Gurdwara*. In the second interview the *granthi* expressed the view that, 'There are high expectations of what we do but we are not given similar regard'.

It is the responsibility of Management Committees to appoint *granthis*. Since the post of a *granthi* is normally a paid one, it is expected that he will satisfy the Management Committee and the *sangat*. *Granthis* are generally appointed from the Punjab either on temporary or on short contracts. They do not seem to have job security and under such circumstances it is very difficult for them to perform well. It is natural that there will be a tendency to wish to earn as much as possible within that short period or to look for other alternatives. *Granthis* from the Punjab also find themselves in a very different climate and cultural environment. They have no knowledge of the community they are expected to serve and also what is expected of them. Both committees and *sangat* have high expectations of what *gianis* should do. *Gianis* find it impossible to meet such expectations in the work environment in which they are placed. Many *granthis* seem to have experienced unnecessary interference from committee members and feel that they have been limited in the performance of their role. An informant also commented that occasionally serving *granthis* have been harassed in order that relatives of committee members might be appointed and that such appointees have been favoured with more pay and facilities. *Granthis* also feel that they are expected to be present in the *Gurdwara* all the hours of the day and they are not given any time to themselves. It was suggested by *gianis* that they would prefer some kind of timetable, with time allocated for shopping and relaxing.

It has been observed that most of the problems have occurred when the principles of the Sikh religion have not been followed, either by committee members or *granthis*. However, there have been *granthis* who have managed to serve the *Gurdwara* for more than one year and have tried to adapt and perform well. Committees have also learnt from their experience and it is evident that they have made changes when and where necessary. It is important that *granthis* be sent information on the nature of the community and the job description before being appointed and they should be asked for certificates of character and qualifications. It is important too to appoint qualified *granthis* who are also fluent in English in order to fulfil the religious needs of the Sikh youths born and brought up in this country. Perhaps home-grown *granthis* may be in a better situation to settle down, to adjust and meet the expectations of *gurdwaras* and *sangat*.

1. 2 Fixing *path* fee

One of the main responsibilities of a *granthi* is to perform *sadharan path* (a recitation of the *Granth Sahib* with no fixed time-limit, generally managed by one *pathi*, a trained reciter of the *Granth Sahib*) and *akhand path* (a recitation of the *Granth Sahib* in forty-eight hours generally managed by five *pathis*). A fee is charged for reciting these *paths*, which is normally fixed by *gurdwaras*. This fee was fixed for the first time on 2nd October 1966 in order to maintain consistency. It was £25 for *akhand path* and £10 for *sadharan path*. The *path bhaintan* (fee) for s*adharan path* was increased to £15 and a *saropa* (*dastar*/turban) and for *akhand path* £30 and a *dastar* (turban) on 21st June 1969. In September 1976, the fee fixed for *akhand path* was £13 and a *dastar* for each of five *pathis* and £25 and a *dastar* for *sadharan path*. On 6th October 1978 it was decided to call a joint meeting inviting Huddersfield and Bradford *gurdwaras* to decide the *path di bhaintan di maryada* (the amount of donated money given to *granthis*). By August 1979 the fee had been further increased and fixed at £35 for *sadharan path* and £90 for *akhand path* to be divided within five *pathi*s. The weekly wage of *giani jatha* was fixed at £60. On 30th August 1980, it was fixed at £40 for *sadharan path* and £100 for *akhand path*. In 1986, the fee was increased for *akhand path* to £111 instead of £100 and for *sadharan path* to £45 instead of £40. In 1989, the fee for *akhand path* was further increased to £35 for each *pathi* and £65 for *sadharan path*. By 1997 it was £200 for *akhand path*, £100 for *sadharan path* and £125 for weekly *path*.

1. 3 Gurpurabs

The celebration of *gurpurabs* is the most important role of a *gurdwara*. Sikhs from the very beginning have maintained this tradition. Four main *gurpurabs* were celebrated every year, that is to say, *Vaisakhi* in April, the martyrdom of *Guru* Arjun Dev in June, *Guru* Nanak Dev's birthday in November and the birthday of *Guru* Gobind Singh in December. The active participation of growing numbers of Sikh *sevadars* had made the programmes very organized. *Gurpurabs* were always started with *akhand path* and *langar* (communal food) was served over all three days. Duties, for example, *path* (recitation of religious book), *langar* and *jore seva* (looking after shoes) were properly allocated. On these special occasions, hymn singers and speakers were invited from outside. For the first time in 1964, the initiation ceremony was held on *Vaisakhi*, and after that it took place at that time every year.

The *Vaisakhi* of 1965 was celebrated with pomp and show on 18th April. The *akhand path* was started on 16th April and the actual ceremony began with the *bhog* of the *path*. A band was arranged for the occasion of *Nishan Sahib* and the press was invited. Renowned hymn singers and speakers came from London, Birmingham and Huddersfield. Local *jathas* also contributed. Some leaflets in English on the Sikh religion were distributed to the public. The initiation ceremony was held and special ceremonial clothes for *panj pyares* (five Sikhs) were bought. It was decided to send a letter to the High Commission of India asking them to approach the British Broadcasting Corporation with a view to introducing a programme in Panjabi.

The decision was taken to celebrate the three-hundredth anniversary of *Guru* Gobind Singh in Leeds. A committee was formed on 9th July 1967 to help in organizing this function. *Guru* Gobind Singh's hymns were printed and distributed to the local organizations. Mrs Wyllam (a writer on Sikh religion) was invited on the *gurpurab* and she was honoured with *saropa*, £11 and a *panj granthi* (a religious book containing five prayers) in English. *Sant Baba* Udham Singh, a visiting religious saint, was honoured with £21 and a *dastar* at his departure. Visiting priests were also honoured from time to time. Serving *Gianis* were also honoured for their outstanding work, such as Man Singh who was given £51 and a *dastar* for his continuous *seva* and *Giani* Nahar Singh who was given £25.

Children were encouraged to participate in the celebration of *gurpurabs* for the first time in 1970. The martyrdom of *Guru* Arjun Dev was celebrated on the 14th June 1970 when artistic children were asked to display their artwork and they were awarded prizes. This was the first time that the *Gurdwara* celebrated extra *gurpurabs* in addition to the traditional four. The additional *gurpurabs* fell on the birthday of *Bhagat* Ravidas (a well-known saint belonging to the untouchable community called *chamars*), the birthday of *Guru* Amardas (the third Sikh *Guru*), the martyrdom of the S*ahibjadas* (young sons of the tenth Sikh *Guru*) and *Guru* Tegh Bahadur (ninth Sikh *Guru*) and *Shahid* (martyr) Nankana Sahib. The Sikh Temple also celebrated festivals and functions like *Diwali*, *Hola Mohalla* and Republic Day on 26th January. *Sangrand* (the first day of the solar month) *diwans* were also held every month. The *Namdhari Satguru* Jagjit Singh came to the *Gurdwara* and there was a big *samagam* (function) held in his honour. Many outside groups came to perform *kirtan*. The ladies' *satsang* was held every Saturday. The *Gurdwara* held thirteen *akhand paths*, eighteen *sadharan paths*, two initiation ceremonies (one by *Baba* Puran Singh Krichowale and another under *Giani* Gurcharan Singh and Avtar Singh from Delhi), twenty-five weddings, twenty-five engagements and thirty-six naming ceremonies in one year.

The *Gurdwara* organized seminars, *kavi darbars*, *gurmat camps* and *kirtan darbars* in order to raise awareness and create interest in the Panjabi language, literature and Sikh religion. A *kavi darbar* was organized on 11th November 1963 from 5 pm to 9 pm in the Sikh Temple and this was repeated on 19th June 1980 on Thursday from 6 pm to 8 pm and Punjabi poets came from all over the country. A seminar on Sikhism was organised on 28th-29th October 1978. The *Gurdwara* also paid £101 plus travelling expenses for the *kirtan darbar* on 19th March 1988.

The *rein swayi kirtan* (continuous *kirtan* during the night) was organised on 15th November 1969 on *Guru* Nanak's birthday and £250 worth of literature was distributed on this occasion. Other *rein swayi kirtans* took place on 26th August 1978 and again on 31st December 1997.

Many *gurdwaras* in the United Kingdom organize *gurmat* camps for Sikh children in the school holidays in order to give practical training in leading life according to the Sikh religion. It was decided to organize a *gurmat* camp from 31st July to 7th August 1987. The *Gurdwara* was willing to pay the expenses for the Sikh *gurmat* camp to be organized in August 2003. From time to time the *Gurdwara* spends money on Sikh religious literature for free distribution in order to raise awareness. Many parties of school children visit the Sikh Temple every year.

Leeds University Sikh students were given £50 to attend a Sikh student conference in London. In 1969 it was decided to spend at least £50 annually on publicity and religious preaching. In 1982 the Sikh Temple also supported the cause of *shigligar* (gypsies) and offered help in order to bring them into the Sikh fold.

1. 4 Initiation Ceremony

The initiation ceremony has a special significance for Sikhs and it is important for any Sikh to go through this ceremony in order to become a *sampuran* (complete) Sikh. It becomes obligatory to keep the five 'K's, i.e. *kes* (uncut hair), *kangha* (comb), *kaccha* (undergarment), *kara* (steel bangle), *kirpan* (dagger). For baptised Sikhs it is a requirement to keep the Sikh identity and wear Sikh symbols. They also have to observe do's and don'ts in order to respect Sikh beliefs. One of the most important parts of the initiation is to lead life according to the principles of Sikhism and, without that, initiation becomes a token gesture only. Above all they have to be kind, honest and truthful, with a belief in one God. Initiation ceremonies in Leeds first started in 1964 and took place on *Vaisakhi* day. Only one Sikh was initiated in 1964 and seven Sikhs were initiated in 1965. The initiation ceremony began to take place every year on *Vaisakhi*. The Committee decided in May 1965 to buy the things, like clothes and daggers, needed for five *pyares* (loved ones) to perform this ceremony. Eight Sikhs were initiated in 1966 and thirteen Sikhs were initiated in 1967. In April 1968 it was made obligatory for any Sikh undergoing this ceremony to make a donation of £1/5/- (£1.25p) and the *Gurdwara* in return would give them the *kirpan* (dagger) and *kangha* (comb).

The numbers undergoing this ceremony fluctuated every year. One Sikh was initiated in 1969, two in 1970, sixteen in 1971 and seven in 1972 according to the initiation records kept by the *Gurdwara*. Baba Puran Singh Kirocowale did *amrit prachar* (initiation) on 2nd October 1971 and thirty-one Sikhs, seventeen men and fourteen women, were baptised. On the *Vaisakhi* of 1978, eighteen Sikhs were baptised. For the first time in August 1979, the arrangements for the *amrit prachar* and initiation ceremony were put high on the agenda. Eight members were initiated on *Vaisakhi* 1987 and fourteen Sikhs were initiated on *Vaisakhi* 1988 and twenty-three Sikhs were initiated on *Vaisakhi* 1990. Eighteen Sikhs were initiated on *Vaisakhi* 1999.

The information available on the number of Sikhs initiated is inserted in this book in full knowledge of the fact that there are gaps, but it may be that these gaps are there because the ceremony might not have taken place in certain years because of a lack of participants or a lack of other resources. It has been helpful to have numbers to indicate the continuous interest of Sikhs in their traditions but it was difficult to get the information on how many were able to comply with the initiation obligations.

1. 5 Langar

Langar is a communal food prepared in the *Gurdwara* kitchen and eaten in *pangat* (row). It is a Sikh religious tradition introduced by the Sikh *Gurus* in order to create equality and understanding by sitting and eating together. The concept of *pangat* was to introduce equality by removing the barriers of caste, class and status. The *Gurdwara* either provides *Langar* or some one from the *sangat* offers to take this *seva*. Every *Gurdwara* follows this tradition, as it is an integral part of the Sikh religious service. *Langar* is made available at all times and every day in India to any needy person but here in Britain it is normally served on the days when religious programmes, such as *gurpurabs*

Preparation of Langar by volunteers

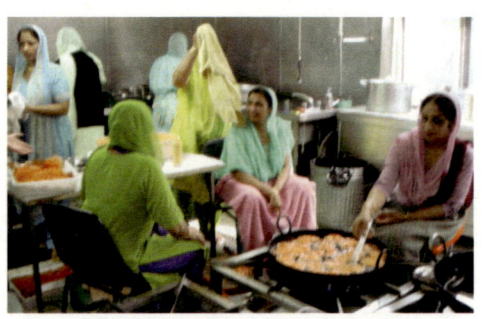

Jalebis prepared by volunteers

and regular weekend programmes, are held in *gurdwaras*. *Langar* was not made a part of regular Sunday services in Leeds when the *Gurdwara* was first opened. It was served only on *gurpurabs* over three days and also if some one offered to take this *seva*. Some crockery and utensils were bought for the *Gurdwara* kitchen. Akali Balwant Singh donated one dozen *thalis* (stainless steel plates) and it was decided that twelve dozen spoons would be bought for the *Gurdwara* kitchen. The *Gurdwara* bought fifty chairs to be used in the *langar* hall.

On 12th March 1980 it was decided to start a weekly *langar* on regular basis. More utensils were bought and all utensils were stamped with the *Gurdwara* stamp and stored in the storeroom and this responsibility was given to the named *sevadars*. The *langar* had to be prepared in accordance with the instructions of the *jathedars*. The order for one hundred *thalis* was given to Ralph H. Lawton, a Birmingham firm.

In August 1981, it was decided by the Management Committee that the Sunday *langar* should be stopped because of the growing expense over the building work, unless some one from the congregation wanted to take this *seva*. The *sangat* was disappointed and this decision was overturned. On 17th November 1982, the Committee decided to serve simple *langar* of *dal* and *phulka* (bean curry and *chapatis*) on *sangrand*.

Langar bhaintan (money fixed for *langar seva*) was increased from £125 to £150 for a single use and £225 for *akhand path* in March 2003. *Bibi* Saran Kaur was appointed in July 2003 for *langar seva* in the *Gurdwara* and paid £60 a week and £10 for cleaning.

1. 6 Rates to use the *Gurdwara's* kitchen

The returnable deposit of £5 was fixed for the hire of utensils from the *Gurdwara*. In May 1968 the timing for hiring was also fixed. Articles could only be hired on Fridays between 7.30 pm and 8.30 pm, to be returned on Sunday or Monday. Gas charges of £5 were introduced in July 1977 to be paid by those taking *langar seva* or preparing sweets for weddings or other occasions. On 30th July 1980 it was decided to increase gas charges to £10 for a day and also to introduce £5 for the use of crockery for weddings. This was increased to £15 for gas for a day and £20 for *akhand path*, £21 for Sunday *degh* (*prasad* made of butter, sugar and semolina or flour) and £11 for the *anand karaj degh* in October 1983. A further increase was made in 1989 to charge £21 for a day's gas and £35 for *akhand path*. In 1991 the charges were increased to £25 a day and £40 for *akhand path*. For the Sunday *degh*, the charge was £21 and for the *degh* for *anand karaj*, it was £11.

In England, the kitchen in a *gurdwara* is also used for social functions apart from preparing *langar*. It is normal practice for *gurdwaras* to charge for the private use of the kitchen to prepare food and sweets for weddings and parties. The charge for the use of the kitchen was £10 a day on 30th August 1980, £15 a day in 1983, £21 in 1989 and £40 in 1991. This was increased to £75 per day in July 2001. This included gas, electricity and water charges.

1. 7 Financial help to other *gurdwaras*, religious organizations and humane causes

It is a common tradition to give financial help to other *gurdwaras*. The Sikh Temple is the second oldest *gurdwara* in Britain and many other communities asked for donations when they first started building *gurdwaras*. *Gurdwara* Singh Sabha in London requested a donation in December 1966 and in response a donation of £11 was made. Balwant Singh Birdi, a well-known businessman and trustee, was disappointed at this decision and suggested being more generous in future. It was decided that donations of £251 each would be sent to the two *gurdwaras* in Bradford. The Armley Sikh Temple in Leeds requested help and £501 was donated twice. Requests for donations came from other newly-built *gurdwara*s. It was decided in July 1980 that the *Gurdwara* would contribute £101 towards a Building Fund for other *gurdwaras*. £500 was given to a *gurdwara* in Paris. An appeal was made to *sangat* for this and the money collected was topped up by the *Gurdwara* to stick to £500. £101 was given to the *Sri Guru* Nanak Sikh Temple, Grimsby, £101 to a *gurdwara* in Petersborough and £101 to the *gurdwara* in Austria. £500 went to the Hull *Gurdwara*. In December 1997, £501 was donated to the Fartown *Gurdwara* in Huddersfield and £501 to the Glasgow *Gurdwara*.

The *Gurdwara* supported the activities of the Sikh Youth Federation (a federation working for the welfare of the Sikh *panth* and political in nature). The meeting of the International Youth Federation was attended and £1,000 was donated to them from the *Gurdwara* fund. It was agreed at the General Meeting held on the 18th September 2005 that £3,200 would be donated. £51 was given to Hull University on occasion of the *Guru* Nanak memorial lectures. £51 was given to the Leeds University Sikh Students Association to organize a cultural and religious programme, which according to the minutes was very successful and much appreciated.

The Wolverhampton Turban Action Committee was given £101. In 1992, £101 was given to the Sikh *sangharash* and Sikh preaching Action Committee and £101 to *Sri Guru* Tegh Bahadur College, Dasua, Hoshiarpur, £101 to *Gurdwara* Har Rai Sahib in Pakistan, £151 to the Northern Ireland Sikh Association, and £501 to the Sikh Missionary Society in 1995 and £151 was given to the Punjab Women's Welfare Association in 1996. In 1996, a donation of £501 was given to the Nishkam Sikh Council based in Delhi. The *Gurdwara* also subscribed to the membership of the Sikh Network Association.

The *Gurdwara* has always donated money to humane causes and it was unanimously agreed to keep £100 aside to spend on charitable causes in 1970-1971. £11 was sent to the Royal Society for the Blind, £2.50p to the Friends of Old People's Committee and £51 for Cancer Research. In 1985, the Sikh Temple collected money for the Bradford Football Stadium disaster and £101 was sent. A sympathetic letter was written to the Lord Mayor of Bradford and the club manager. £2,000 was given to Sikh Human Rights in 1988 to support this project. £5 was given to the campaign to scrap the Nationality Bill, £31 to the Immigration Action Group, £100 to the Disabled Society. A cheque for £572 was also presented to the Lord Mayor for the disabled on 27th September 1981.

The money was also sent to the widows of deceased in the early days of settlement in this country as mentioned earlier. Recognition was given to the services rendered by *sevadars* (volunteers) in the earlier period by doing *path* (recitation of the Holy book) in their remembrance after death to pay respect for their contributions to the *Gurdwara*. This tradition still continues.

1. 7 Nagar Kirtan

Nagar kirtan is a religious procession, which passes through a city, or certain areas of a city, singing religious hymns in the praise of the Supreme power. The Sikh Temple was informed of the *nagar kirtan* on 24th April 1988 taking place in London. The Committee approved a grant to subsidise the coach expenses for those who wished to go. Those who were prepared to go had to pay £5 for the ticket and children under twelve were not allowed.

In 1990, Leeds *gurdwaras* decided to have *nagar kirtan* in their own city. All *gurdwaras* participated in this procession. In the first year, the *nagar kirtan* was started from *Guru* Nanak Nishkam Sevak Jatha, Leeds 11 and ended at 281a Chapeltown Road on *Guru* Nanak Dev's birthday. The expenses were borne by three *gurdwaras*, *langar* was prepared in the Sikh Centre and the responsibility for the arrangements was given to Paramjit Singh Mudhar. In 1991 a meeting was held to organise *nagar kirtan* and the members representing the Sikh Temple in this meeting were Prem Singh, Tarlok Singh, Professor Bakhshish Singh, Paramjit Singh and Manmohan Singh. Permission was given to spend £200 for the *palki* to be used in the *nagar kirtan* and it was also agreed to have *gatka* (martial game played with swords) for which £50 was sanctioned. In that year, *Nagar kirtan* started from the Leeds 12 *Gurdwara* and the ceremony ended at Ramgarhia Board. It stopped for a short while at the Town Hall where *langar* was served.

Nagar Kirtan

On 28th August 1992 Leeds *Gurdwara* Council drafted the next *nagar kirtan* programme outlining the uniform of the five *pyares* and the duties of *pathi Singhs*. However, there was a split over the colour of the *dastar*s as the Sikh Temple, Leeds 7 suggested *kesri* (saffron) and Niskam Jatha, Leeds 11 suggested white. This difference of opinion persisted in spite of attempts at reconciliation and in the end it was decided that the *nagar kirtan* would go ahead anyway. The date was fixed for 10th November 1992 on *Guru* Nanak Dev's birthday. The programme was announced on Radio Leeds and the community radio programme of the Leeds 12 *Gurdwara*. The route taken by the procession was agreed. Calendar Television, Sunrise radio and Awaz-e-Qaum were to cover the programme. It was also decided to have FM Radio involved at a cost of £625 for the coverage of the procession and Hardeep Singh Ahluwalia was given the responsibility of organizing this. It was decided that the Joint Committee formed for *nagar kirtan* would not be invited and that the balance of £70 left over from the previous *nagar kirtan* grant would be put into the *gurughar golak* (*Gurdwara* money box).

In November 1993 the arrangements for another *nagar kirtan* were made. Tarlok Singh, Paramjit Singh, Kewal Singh, Harpal Singh and Inderjit Singh were selected as *panj pyare*. *Chaur di seva* was given to Manmohan Singh and Surinder Singh. *Langar* and refreshment arrangements were delegated to Darshan Singh Cheema, Tarlok Singh and Kesar Singh Seehra. The *akhand path* duties were organized by Professor Bakhshish Singh. The duty of *tavya* (sitting behind the *Guru Granth Sahib*) was given to Balbir Singh and Hazara Singh, the float and *kirtani jatha* to Gian Singh and Surjit Singh, and decoration of the float to *Giani* Harbans Singh and Major Singh. The booking of a double-decker bus was the responsibility of Prem Singh Duggal, Manohar Singh, Hardeep Singh Ahluwalia and Amarjit Singh. The stage duty at Victoria Garden was given to Prem Singh Duggal and Hardeep Singh Ahluwalia. *Giani* Balbir Singh prepared *sevadara de bille* (volunteers' name cards) and Professor Bakhshish Singh prepared banners. The Committee decided to get half a page of information published in the vernacular paper *Des Pradesh*. Narinder Singh Matharu, a Sikh Lord Mayor from London, was honoured with a plate presented to him by Tarlok Singh, *Babu* Inder Singh, Pritpal Singh Manku, Kesar Singh Seehra and Professor Bakhshish Singh.

In December 1993, it was decided by the Committee that the *nagar kirtan* should take place on *Vaisakhi* rather than on *Guru* Nank Dev's birthday because of wintry weather. The *nagar kirtan* on *Vaisakhi* 1994 included *panj pyare* (five Sikhs) namely Tarlok Singh, Surinder Singh, Paramjit Singh, Narinder Singh and Kartar Singh. Professor Bakhshish Singh and Beant Singh undertook *chaubdara di seva*. The *prasad seva* was given to Kesar Singh and Hazara Singh, *Guru Maharaj Tavya seva* to Gurdev Singh, Balbir Singh and Gurcharan Singh and float *seva* to Manohar Singh Bhakhar, Tarlok Singh Toor and Hardeep Singh Ahluwalia. *Kirtan seva* was the responsibility of *Giani* Harbans Singh and *Giani* Malkiat Singh. The duties of refreshment were given to Tarlok Singh and Kesar Singh Seehra, bus arrangement to Nirmal Singh Sangha and banner and Victoria Garden stage to Professor Bakhshish Singh. The lecture on *Vaisakhi* became the joint duty of Bakhshish Singh and Harjit Singh and liaison with the press became the responsibility of Hardeep Singh Ahluwalia. Kuldip Singh made the video film.

The *nagar kirtan* of 1996 started from the Sikh Temple, proceeded to Kalgidhar *Gurdwara*, then to Ramgarhia Board and then reached Victoria Garden at 2 pm. Inderjit Singh from the Sikh Messenger was the guest speaker, speaking on the importance of *Vaisakhi*. Councillors and officers from the Leeds City Council were invited. The *panj pyare* were Surinder Singh Bansal, Kewal Singh Kular, Joginder Singh Patara, Kartar Singh Bhamra and Narinder Singh. The *langar sevadars* were Kesar Singh Seehra, Manohar Singh, Tarlok Singh and Gurmeet Singh. The float preparation was given to Manohar Singh Bhakhar and stage duty at Victoria Gardens was given to Ujjal Singh Ryatt and Baldev Singh Duggal. *Chaubdar* and *Nishan Sahib di seva* was given to Bakhshish Singh Kang and Beant Singh. Refreshment was served by the Sikh Centre committee and *prasad* on the float by Kesar Singh Seehra and Manohar Singh Bhakhar.

The arrangement for the 1997 *nagar kirtan* was that Ujjal Singh Ryatt was given the responsibility for hiring the bus or coach, the *langar seva* went to Kesar Singh Seehra and the float *seva* to K. D. Brothers (business partners dealing in car repairs). Manohar Singh organized the sound system for the *Gurdwara* and Professor Bakhshish Singh arranged for the spokesperson on *Vaisakhi*. It had become an annual event.

The *nagar kirtan* of 1999 was significant. It was the year of the three-hundredth anniversary of *Khalsa Panth* and was organized for Saturday 17th April 1999. The Committee decided to invite the Bishop of York and the leaders of the Conservatives, Liberals and Labour. It was also decided to make a special presentation on this three- hundredth anniversary and that this gift should be kept in the Civic Hall. Today Leeds Sikhs continue to celebrate this annual event with great pride and look forward to participating in it.

1. 8 Interfaith Activities

The *Gurdwara* has always taken an interest in interfaith activities and has been involved in local interfaith organizations. The *Gurdwara* has also hosted activities organized by such interfaith organizations. On 13th December 1981, the Interfaith Human Rights Service was held in the *Gurdwara*. Concord requested permission to hold a meeting on 'Buddha and the future', which was held in the *Gurdwara* on 14th April 1982. Concord was given free use of the hall for two hours. The multi-faith centre based at Elmhurst Middle School requested permission to hold a multi-faith meeting in the *Gurdwara* on the 18th-20th April 1986. In this meeting they wanted to highlight Sikh religion, and Inderjit Singh from London was invited to address the meeting. This was an important meeting for Sikhs to raise awareness of their religion in other faith communities because of the dreadful massacre which had taken place in India after the Golden Temple incident in 1984.

1. 9 Conclusion

Sikhs have always been keen to continue their religious traditions and to promote the Sikh religion. Free religious literature has been distributed from time to time. Other faith communities and school children have been welcomed in the Sikh Temple where Sikh traditions are explained to them. There are also other activities undertaken by the Sikh Temple, as mentioned above, which aim to spread a greater understanding of the Sikh religion and religious values.

Chapter 6
The Educational Role of the *Gurdwara*

Culture and language have strong links. Knowledge of one's mother tongue is vital to knowing, understanding and appreciating one's culture, history and heritage. An individual can only communicate and form bonds with his or her community through the medium of the mother tongue. When people migrate to other countries, they lose their natural cultural environment of growth. It becomes important to revitalize their religion, culture and traditions in the new country of settlement, especially in one with a different social structure and conflicting values. It often becomes the responsibility of parents, dedicated individuals and religious organizations to make some arrangements in the absence of official support.

1. 0 Panjabi Teaching
Sikhs speak Panjabi, which is written in the *Gurmukhi* script. Panjabi is not only a medium of their day-to-day communication but also the language of their religious scripture and literature. For a Sikh, the knowledge of Panjabi is essential, as the Sikh Holy Scripture is written in Panjabi and to understand the right and correct meaning one must have a thorough knowledge and understanding of the language. Knowledge of the Panjabi language helps Sikhs access the essentials of Sikh history, traditions, culture and religion. Panjabi teaching has always been a paramount responsibility of *gurdwaras* outside India.

Panjabi teaching was first started in the Sikh Temple in 1965 when Udham Singh Syan volunteered himself for teaching Panjabi. He outlined a full programme in order to run the Panjabi classes effectively and Panjabi teaching manuals were bought in multiple copies for the use of pupils attending Panjabi classes in the Sikh Temple.

The reform committee for the Panjabi school was formed to prepare a detailed report on the school on 28th June 1970 and consisted of Gurcharan Singh Kundi, Master Mohinder Singh, Gurdeep Singh Bhogal, *Baba* Khem Singh, Sewa Singh Kalsi, Sohan Singh Kalsi and Resham

Singh Gill. It was decided to start Panjabi classes twice a week and the *Gurdwara* would spend £4 to £6 extra a week on these classes. Gurcharan Singh Kundi suggested the appointment of two teachers, Gurdeep Singh Bhogal and *Bibi* Baljinder Kaur on a weekly wage of £3. His suggestion was based on the survey conducted in November 1971 which showed that there were between 100 and 125 children attending the Panjabi classes. Gurdeep Singh Bhogal taught the beginners and *Bibi* Baljinder Kaur took the advanced class. Children were of different ages and ability. Under the circumstances, it was difficult to give individual attention to the children and it was recommended that another teacher be appointed. By April 1977, the number had grown to 242 children, of whom 209 came regularly and, out of these, ten children could read Panjabi by themselves. In June 1977, Jagdish Singh Saundh presented a plan prepared by the Education Sub-Committee to improve the standard of teaching and discipline. It was decided to call a meeting with parents to introduce this programme but lack of parental support did nothing to move things forward.

Gurdeep Singh Bhogal, one of the schoolteachers was asked to prepare a report on the cost of running the Panjabi classes. He did so, and stated that the estimated cost of running the classes was £1,200. His report was accepted and classes began. By October 1977, the number of children had further increased. *Baba* Khem Singh was asked to help with the growing demand and his wage was increased because of the additional work.

An application for a grant to teach Panjabi was made in December 1978 to the Community Relations Council (CRC). As the Panjabi classes were not doing well, it was agreed in April 1979 to form a separate management committee for running these classes. In August 1979, it was decided to increase the rate of pay of the teachers teaching Panjabi in the *Gurdwara*.

My husband and I started Panjabi classes at Brudenell School, Leeds 6, as we were living in that area. We contacted the Education Department requesting the introduction of Panjabi language classes as there were many Sikh families living in the area and the Sikh Temple was not easily accessible for children living in Leeds 6. Leeds City Council Education Department gave us free use of a room in the school and the classes began on 3rd September 1979. We taught on a voluntary basis. Later Leeds City Council offered to pay us because of the popularity of the class and the number of children attending regularly. Jagdish Singh Saundh went to observe the classes from the *Gurdwara* and reported as stated in the minutes of 4th May 1980 that the Panjabi classes in Leeds 6 were run in a very professional manner and the number of children attending them had reached fifty (ਲੀਡਜ਼ ੬ ਦਾ ਸਕੂਲ ਬਹੁਤ ਹੀ ਸੁਹਣੇ ਢੰਗ ਨਾਲ ਚਲ ਰਿਹਾ ਹੈ ਤੇ ੫੦ ਤਕ ਬਚਿਆਂ ਦੀ ਗਿਣਤੀ ਪਹੁੰਚ ਚੁਕੀ ਹੈ). Mr. Saundh confirmed this statement to be true in his interview. Our efforts were very much appreciated by the parents of the children attending the classes though the *Gurdwara* hardly did anything to learn from our experience.

By September 1980, there were 102 children learning Panjabi in the Sikh Temple. There was a shortage of good teachers. The room where children were taught was too small and there was not enough furniture to accommodate the children. One teacher had to manage a class of fifty to sixty children and it was difficult to give them individual attention. It was suggested that some teaching aids, like a tape recorder, might be bought in order to make lessons interesting. Children under five were not admitted in order to make the classes manageable. Keeping in view the increased interest in learning Panjabi, it was suggested that an approach be made to the Leeds Council to ask them to introduce Panjabi in schools where Sikh pupils formed a majority within minority groups.

In August 1981, Gurdeep Singh Bhogal informed the Committee of the discussion with Education Advisory members regarding the teaching of Panjabi in schools. He said that from July 1981 there would be a legal obligation to teach the mother tongue in schools but that there were a few problems to overcome, including the availability of qualified teachers.

A fee and admission forms for learning Panjabi in the *Gurdwara* were introduced in 1982. Every child had to enrol and pay 10p as a fee. Classes were organized according to the ability and age of children and they had to take tests once or twice a year. Teachers were provided with boards, charts and cabinets. Parents were encouraged to take an interest in their children's progress and make comments and suggestions. Applications were made for grants available from the CRC and Inner City Programme. A selection board for the appointment of new teachers was formed in July 1982. Dr Kamaljit Ryatt resigned as the Education Secretary and Pritam Singh Sagoo took over this responsibility. It was further suggested in 1983 that children should be tested every three months and final tests should be once a year. The children who got first and second positions would be rewarded and given certificates. There was a suggestion that a computer and projector would be bought to make teaching modern and interesting.

Baljinder Kaur Ranu became the Education Secretary in 1987-1988. Soon after this she resigned and Manmohan Singh Brah was appointed in her place. The responsibility of monitoring the number of children, class divisions and overall improvement in the teaching of Panjabi was given to Nirmal Singh Sangha. The Committee was keen to make an improvement in the standard of Panjabi teaching by dividing classes according to ability. At this stage, there were fifty children taking lessons in Panjabi and they were divided into two classes, which were held on Saturdays and Sundays from 10 am to midday. The Committee also approved the publication of *Balbodh* - a Panjabi Primer. Five thousand copies were printed each costing 18p.

Two teachers Inderjit Kaur and Baljinder Kaur Ranu had been appointed to teach Panjabi. In order to improve and raise the standard of teaching, an additional teacher, *Bibi* Joginder Kaur, was appointed. There was hardly any noticeable improvement in this, despite there being three teachers, as there were occasional absences of teachers at the weekends because of family commitments. Various approaches were made to improve the standard, for instance, in February 1992 it was decided to ask for help from volunteers and in May 1992 the teachers' pay was increased to £5 per hour to give them an incentive. Over that year, the Panjabi school children and their parents participated in three religious programmes, *Vaisakhi*, *Sri Guru* Nanak Dev's birthday and *Sri Guru* Gobind Singh's birthday.

There were 170 children attending Panjabi classes in 1993, but the Committee was still concerned about the standard of teaching and took steps to improve it. They decided that the teachers appointed should be able to deliver a high standard of education. Qualifications and ability should be given preference during the selection. Teachers should be appointed initially on probation for three months. Children aged between five and fourteen should be admitted. A committee of three members, namely, Pritpal Singh Manku, Professor Bakhshish Singh and Nirmal Singh Sangha, two of whom were teachers by profession, was formed in January 1994 to assist the Education Secretary to improve the standard of Panjabi teaching.

In February 1995, *Bibi* Jaspal Kaur was asked to continue teaching on a paid basis. It was suggested in 1997 that the parents of school children attending Panjabi classes should be charged a fee of £40. Again mention was made of the problems of appointing good teachers and the lack of parental participation. Ujjal Singh Ryatt, then teacher in-charge of the Panjabi classes said in the General Meeting held on 30th June 2002 that he would look into the matter and report back to the Committee. He made suggestions for improving standards by setting targets and offering incentives to the children. Admission forms and the syllabus were printed. The school was named the Khalsa School and a uniform was introduced. It was decided that qualified teachers would be appointed and that volunteers would be recruited to help them. The number of children increased and it was suggested that the Panjabi school should be moved out of the Sikh Temple to the basement of the Sikh Centre and Nirmal Singh

Punjabi classes held on Sundays

Sangha and Sukhchain Singh Gill took on the responsibility of making plans for the school. There were also suggestions that a grant to extend the Sikh Centre for the Khalsa School might be applied for and that the children should be charged fees. At the time of writing this book, the classes are held in three rooms on the first floor of the Sikh Centre. As an informant told me, there are about fifty children in the school divided into three classes and taught by volunteers. The current teacher in-charge of the Panjabi school is Harpal Singh.

The teaching of Panjabi was high on the agenda for many years. Many efforts were made to improve the standard of teaching including appointing paid teachers, increasing the teachers' pay from time to time, the use of volunteers and creating incentives for the children. The lack of qualified and proficient teachers and lack of parental participation has hindered the achievement of this. In an interview with a Panjabi teacher I learnt that it was always too difficult to introduce new initiatives, as this required resources and the *Gurdwara* Committee did not like making demands. A volunteer added that the contributions of individuals were not appreciated.

2. 0 Religious education

Religious education is considered very important in order to pass on knowledge of the religion in which a child is born. Children are taught religious values and traditions in order to understand the Sikh way of life. This helps to create confidence and a firm sense of belonging. In order to promote and raise awareness of the Sikh religion *gurdwaras* have always given high priority to religious education by running classes, by offering practical experience of religious traditions and by distribution of free religious literature.

Religious education was first introduced in the Sikh Temple on 23rd March 1962. Mastan Singh, a printing student, was given the responsibility of doing the teaching and classes were held every Sunday evening from 6 pm to 7 pm. He performed his duties on a voluntary basis and the *Gurdwara* foundation paid for the stationery used by children. In 1965 multiple copies of elementary religious books were bought for the use of pupils attending classes in the *Gurdwara*. It became necessary to engage a paid *granthi* to take care of the *Gurdwara* and to give religious education to children. Daljit Singh Sond negotiated with Khem Singh from London. *Baba* Khem Singh was appointed as *granthi* on 21st January 1968 and the Committee decided on 17th March 1968 to pay him extra to give religious education to children. The programme of religious education was outlined in consultation with him and religious films were ordered from India to use as visual aids, in order to make the lessons more interesting and stimulating. Children were sent to *Baba* Khem Singh for religious education when they could read Panjabi. *Babaji* taught them the correct pronunciation of the *path* (recitation of *gurbani*). By April 1977, eleven children were attending religious education classes. The children were shown films on Sikh history and Sikhism with the help of *Giani* Gurbakhash Singh, who answered their questions. Amarjit Singh, a *kirtiniya* (hymn singer), was appointed in 1978 and he also agreed to give free teaching of *kirtan* (music) to children as part of their religious education.

The number of children attending religious education classes increased every year and there were forty-two children in the class in 1980. This convinced the Committee that children under five ought not to be admitted and fluency in reading Panjabi was made compulsory for attending the classes. This reduced the number and by September 1980 there were nine children left in the class who could read Panjabi. Two teachers, Gurcharan Singh Wahge and Harbans Singh Lall, taught them. The Religious Education Sub-committee was formed in 1982, consisting of Piara Singh Saimbhi, Harbans Singh Sagoo, Ajit Singh Bansal and Chamkaur Singh, in order to focus on and bring about any necessary changes in religious education. Classes were organized according to ability and a syllabus was prepared in 1984. English was introduced as the medium of instruction as it was considered that children born and brought up here could better grasp teaching in the language they knew. Sikh history was introduced as a part of religious heritage and Harjit Singh Ryatt taught Sikh history in English. A prize scheme was introduced in 1986 to encourage the children to do well. The children who passed Sikh history and religion were given certificates and those who got first, second and third positions were given prizes from £20 downwards according to their positions.

Namsimran (reciting the name of God) and *gurbani sikhia* (reading the Holy book) sessions were started on Sundays running from 6 pm to 7.30 pm, in November 1986. In 1987 religious education classes were started for children over thirteen and were taught by the *giani*. At this point the method of teaching adopted by the *giani* was traditional and certain young people felt that children should be taught using modern techniques. Jatinder Singh Mehmi, a twenty-year old Sikh, encouraged young people to get together to have discussions on the different aspects of Sikh religion. As a Sikh himself, he felt the need for Sikh youths to know their roots and heritage. In the beginning there were ad-hoc sessions attended by children over the age of twelve and the classes were held in the old *Gurughar*. Gradually the youngsters showed their interest and numbers increased. These classes were held every Sunday. Jatinder Singh Mehmi's approach was to equip youngsters with the knowledge of Sikh religion and religious values. There were open discussions on religious topics and his style made classes very popular. The popularity of this method of teaching attracted many children who were keen to attend his class. It became difficult for one person to meet the growing demand and, in March 1997, Mohinder Singh offered to work with Jatinder Singh Mehmi and shared the responsibility for running this class, which became more and more popular.

In 1998, a group keen on religious education met to discuss the strategy for the expansion of religious education. Baljinder Kaur Toor, as a mother, was very keen that children should be given religious education and she approached Balraj Singh Gill who suggested that his brother, Sukhraj Singh Gill, would be an appropriate person for this type of work. The first meeting was held by the group which included Baljinder Kaur Toor, Balraj Singh Gill, Sukhraj Singh Gill, Jatinder Singh Mehmi and an initiated Sikh, Bhagat Singh Kalar. All these participants had a vested interest in religious education for Sikh children either because of their teaching background or as a parent. They were all willing to work on a voluntary basis for future Sikh generations. Sukhraj Singh

Gill, who had spent a year in India studying the Sikh religion, became the lead person and took on this responsibility in 2002. Later Sarabjit Mehmi and Mrs Kalar joined this group. There was no grant available for this project. The funding came either from the *Gurdwara* or from parents.

The classes were advertised during *Vaisakhi* and enrolment started in October 2002. Classes began on 9th November 2002 with the help of committed Sikh volunteers. The strategy followed in these classes was based on giving confidence in making informed choices and decisions and life skills to children. The main aim of these classes was to give the children the knowledge of the basics of Sikh religion and of their own roots in a relaxed environment. The method of teaching followed was one of exploring and not of instructing or of imposing religious values. The whole idea was to give them a better foundation for making informed choices. This approach was implemented by having open debates on the Sikh identity and contemporary issues of the time and how they related to or affected Sikhs. The classes were divided by age and held every Friday from 6.30 pm to 8.30 pm in the lower hall of the *Gurdwara*. The number attending fluctuated from fifty-seven to two hundred and fifty, on average there were eighty to a hundred children depending on the weather and their other commitments.

The teaching moved away from the traditional methods of instruction towards the use of modern techniques such as computers, CDs and multimedia. Looking at the success of these classes, the *Gurdwara* was asked on 7th December 2002 to buy a projector to be used in religious teaching and sanctioned £2,000 for its purchase.

The teaching group felt it necessary to give children a real life experience of Sikh ways by organizing summer camps for children attending religious classes, hoping also to attract other children. This summer camp was called the Sikh Inspiration Camp, and was introduced in summer 2003. It was a day camp funded by the *Gurdwara*. The first *Gurmat* camp was held from 26th to 29th August 2003 and attended by more than two hundred children. The estimated cost was £3,000, which was met by the *Gurdwara* fund and every child contributed £10.

Every year a theme is selected on which the activities of the camp are based. So far it has covered a general introduction as to who and what Sikhs are (2003), the four-hundredth anniversary of the *prakash* (opening) *of Guru Granth Sahib* (2004), and *Ardas* - its history and meaning (2005) and the theme for this current year was marriage, death and initiation.

The Sikh inspirational class

The attendance was well beyond their expectations. So far, this group has held four successful Sikh camps, two *akhand paths* and several *kirtan darbars* and charity programmes. Every year the numbers in the school are increasing.

3. 0 Music Teaching

Kirtan is an essential part of *gurbani*. *Gurbani* is composed in *ragas*, which underlines the importance of music. Ladies' *satsang* was introduced in June 1969 and women met on Saturdays to do the *kirtan*. It was not only a social occasion but also an opportunity to learn to play the harmonium and sing devotional songs. *Baba* Khem Singh also encouraged and taught women music. Amarjit Singh, a *kirtiniya* (hymn singer) was appointed in 1978, and agreed to give free teaching of *kirtan* (music). One informant said that interested parents also encouraged their children to learn music and formed their own small groups. *Bibi* Gunvant Kaur, a qualified music teacher, started music classes in September 1991 in the Sikh Centre, funded by Leeds City Council. Ladies also learn from each other in the ladies' *satsang* held every Wednesday in the Sikh Temple.

4. 0 Library

The library has always been an integral part of any *gurdwara*. As soon as the first building for the *Gurdwara* was bought, a library became the main priority in order for members to keep in touch with what was happening in their country of origin and also to follow developments taking place here in Britain. It became the main source of religious books and of books to teach Panjabi and religious education to children. On 11th October 1959 Atma Singh Sood was allocated £20 to buy books for the library and was also given the responsibility of buying one big table, a dozen chairs and a cabinet for library use.

Books were issued to library members and to members of the United Sikh Association. Members had to show their membership cards at the time of borrowing library books. Books were issued for two weeks and in case of damage to a book, members had to pay the cost.

The use of the library increased, as it was the only source of vernacular books locally. Its increased use encouraged the Committee to think about forming rules and regulations. The following rules were drawn up and introduced on the 20th November 1960 in order to ensure that the library would run smoothly, effectively and efficiently:

1. Library books should only be issued to library members and the members of the United Sikh Association.
2. Each member is entitled to borrow one book at a time.
3. Membership cards should be produced at the time of borrowing books.
4. Books are issued for two weeks only.
5. The borrower should pay the cost of the book in case of damage.

The heavy use of library books justified buying new stock. £100 was sanctioned for the purchase of new books in order to increase and boost the existing stock. The budget of the library was increased to £30 in the meeting of 5th March 1961. An additional sum of £12 was given on 3rd July 1966 for further expansion and Harbans Singh Bhamra became the Librarian. The responsibility for book selection was given to the Librarian, Assistant Librarian, President, Vice-President and Secretary. The library also bought Panjabi teaching manuals and elementary religious books in multiple copies for the use of pupils attending Panjabi and religious classes held in the Sikh Temple. Documentary video films were added to the library stock. Subscriptions to two newspapers, one in Panjabi and another in Urdu, were taken out.

The library also stocked *kanghas* (combs) and *karas* (bangles) - two important 'K's provided for sale for the convenience of the *sangat*.

It was considered important that the library should be tidy and attractive. In order to improve the image of the library, a long table was bought for the use of children and the responsibility of making a cabinet for shelving library books was given to Resham Singh Gill. The library room was extended by removing a partition. Membership cards for the library were printed in 1965 and by May 1968 it had been decided that the *Gurdwara* library should remain open from midday to 12.30 pm every Sunday. Another volunteer offered his services to help the Literature Secretary to deal with the increased workload.

The stock needed to be revised and on 28th June 1970 Gurcharan Singh Kundi, Sohan Singh Kalsi and Resham Singh Gill were given the responsibility of checking the library stock thoroughly. Gurcharan Singh Kundi prepared lists for improving the library stock and £50 was sent to Bakhshish Singh Channa, who was then in India, so that he could buy books and parcel them up for the *Gurdwara*. That year £150 in total was spent on the library stock and bookshelves were made to stack the books.

Gurdeep Singh Bhogal reported on 21st April 1977 that there were 620 books in the library stock, out of which 85 were in English and 535 in Panjabi. The stock was constantly growing and it was suggested that a separate room in which to stack books should be found. Niranjan Singh Bansal who was librarian from 1979 to 1982 encouraged users to make maximum use of the library and requested members to care for borrowed books and return them on time. In September 1981 it was suggested that there were many hand-written Panjabi manuscripts in the British Museum Library in London for which either microprints could be bought or that the Leeds Libraries could be asked to get.

A librarian or literature secretary managed the normal work of the library. Over the years not a great deal of emphasis has been placed on the library as other more important things have become the priorities for the *Gurdwara*, such as establishing the Sikh Centre, building a new purpose-built building for the *Gurdwara* and buying land for car parking. Books have been left stacked in the cabinets and not much used. Sikhs were able to get a much better library service from Leeds Libraries after the reorganisation in 1974, when many books in Asian languages were bought by library services to serve the local Asian population. This will have reduced the workload of the *Gurdwara* library and saved its funds. Since the collection was started so early, I am sure that it must be a unique collection, though I have had no opportunity to view it. For the future, it is planned that the library will be housed in the Sikh Centre after its extension. It is also important for the Sikh Temple to preserve its records which can prove very useful for future generations to learn exact information about the *Gurdwara*.

5. 0 The *Gurdwara* Shop

The *Gurdwara* shop is based on the first floor in front of the main hall. The stock is spread out on three big tables and is open to the public on Sundays and during major functions. It stocks religious books, *gutkas* (collection of prayers), videocassettes, tapes, DVDs and CDs. It also sells *karas, kanghas* and daggers. A group of volunteers manages it and it is open to the public. The prices seem reasonable and profits made from sales go to the *Gurdwara*.

The *Gurdwara* Shop

6. 0 Conclusion

The teaching role of the *Gurdwara* is important in spreading the knowledge of Sikhism and equipping the younger generation of Sikhs to know their religion and roots. Many Sikh children are able to sing *shabads*, do *kirtan* and play instruments such as the harmonium and the *sitar*. They are able to understand beats and play *dholak* and *dholki*. Some children can recite *gurbani* and others can read and write Panjabi. The Sikh Temple, teachers, children and their parents deserve credit for such achievements.

Chapter 7
The Social and Political Role of the Sikh Temple

The *Gurdwara* is not only a place of worship but also contributes to social and political activities. It celebrates festivals and social occasions. It offers Sikhs a place to get together where they can get to know each other and exchange ideas. It is a source of information for the Sikh community. *Gurdwaras* always play a significant role in looking after the welfare of Sikhs and the Sikh *Panth* by involving themselves in politics if the need arises.

1. 0 Social Role
Gurdwara plays an important part in the social life of the Sikhs. Sikhs celebrate their life cycle rites and ceremonies in the *Gurdwara* which have an essential social part in them. Sikhs also celebrate festivals in the Sikh Temple and the Sikh Temple provides the venue for many other activities and host groups. In the beginning, the Sikh Temple also played a major role in resolving domestic disputes and helping in the times of need. It worked as a support agency for the Sikh community.

1. 1 Interpersonal relations
The Sikh Temple played an invaluable role in the earlier years of settlement in Britain in resolving domestic and marital disputes, giving financial help to the families of the deceased and solving problems which had arisen from borrowing money from family and friends. Sikhs were not keen to use the judicial facilities that existed in this country because of the language barrier, discrimination and a lack of knowledge but relied on their own traditional ways of solving disputes and problems. This began to change as the Sikh community settled and learned about the existing facilities.

From the beginning Sikhs have often helped one another in times of distress and need and the *Gurdwara* has played a major role in a collective response. Teja Singh died in 1958 of a brain haemorrhage and Gurmeet Singh Nahal paid for his funeral. Sikhs collected £335, which was sent to his family through the bank and this amount was noted in the minutes of the meeting held on 29th June 1958. An offering of money on the *path bhog* of Jeeva Singh was collected to send to his widow in India. It was decided initially that the money would be deposited in the bank and the bank would be instructed to transfer one hundred rupees every month to his family. However, on 21st April 1968, it was decided that all the money, amounting to £140, should be sent to his widow, so that she could complete the unfinished work on her house.

The President of the Sikh Temple was also given the power to deal with situations arising out of money having been borrowed from others. Borrowing money in times of need from relatives, friends and acquaintances was common practice in the past as banks and building societies were reluctant to give loans to Asians. Some people returned the borrowed money as promised and others failed to keep to their word, which caused unpleasant situations. Involvement in such affairs is indicative of the social role of the *Gurdwara* in diffusing difficult situations arising out of these conflicts of interest.

The *Gurdwara* was involved with domestic disputes and marital problems which were brought to the Committee in the early days when Sikhs were hesitant about using the judicial system of this country. They were keen to use their own traditional methods of resolving their problems. For instance, in 1965 a letter was received from a woman, who had come to join her husband, regarding her marital problems. The Committee decided to nominate *Giani* Kesar Singh, *Giani* Sarwan Singh, Piara Singh Chaggar and Sardara Singh so that they could contact her father-in-law to find out the details in order to resolve the matter. Her father-in-law did not respond so the Committee asked their solicitor to write him a letter telling him to meet them and that, if he failed to meet with the Committee, the solicitor would take legal action on behalf of his daughter-in-law. However, nothing more was heard from her and the case was filed.

The *Gurdwara* also supported another woman in fighting her deportation case. Appropriate help was given to other women who had been thrown out of their homes. The *Gurdwara* helped them by giving them some kind of part-time work. There have been numerous examples of cases in which the *Gurdwara* actively played a part in resolving marital problems by liaising with families and finding solutions suitable for both parties. The *Gurdwara* dealt with most cases in a just manner though occasional failures were also noted in the minutes of meetings because either of bias or of the rules being bent in favour of the family and relatives of committee members.

The *Gurdwara* could also punish Sikhs behaving improperly such as using abusive language or entering the Sikh Temple after drinking alcohol. These people were normally given a religious punishment called *dun* (ਠਠ), in which a task is given to be done without expecting any payment, for example, *joriyan di seva* (looking after the shoes of the congregation). It is like community service.

2. 2 Life cycle Rites
In England, it is common for Sikhs to conduct and celebrate life cycle ceremonies such as those for birth, marriage and death in *gurdwaras*. Religious ceremonies connected with life cycle rites are held in *gurdwaras*, but it has also become a common practice to combine and celebrate religious and social ceremonies there too. Most *gurdwaras* have community centres and halls adjacent to their premises and these are often used for social celebrations such as birthday and marriage celebrations.

1. 2. 1 Birth celebration
The birth of a child is considered a blessing from God. Sikhs celebrate the birth of their sons on a large scale by distributing *ladoos* (an Indian sweet) and holding big parties in halls or having *langar* in the *Gurdwara*, especially on the birth of their first son. The distribution of *ladoos* is considered to be essential on the birth of a son. Some Sikh women have become expert in making *ladoos* and they make them in the *Gurdwara* kitchen for the families who celebrate this occasion in the Sikh Temple. It has become a common tradition for many parents to celebrate birthdays in the Sikh Temple and invite their families, relatives and friends to celebrate these occasions together. It is becoming common to celebrate the eighteenth or twenty-first birthdays of daughters as well.

1. 2. 2 *Naamkaran*

Naamkaran is a naming ceremony, basically religious in nature. Every child is given a name from the first word of the *vak* (the hymn at the top of the left-hand page of the Sikh scripture opened at random) from the *Guru Granth Sahib*. Sikhs always get the first letter of the name from the *Gurdwara* and the parents then choose the full name beginning with that first letter, for example, from 'G' it can be Gurdeep, Gursharan, Gurbakhash or whatever the parents wish. Balwant Singh Birdi was given the responsibility for organizing *naamkaran* in the Sikh Temple. It was decided in 1969 that the children would be given a *romalla* (a square piece of cloth to cover the *Guru Granth Sahib*) as a *saropa* (honour) on this occasion and since then this tradition has been continued.

3. 3. 3 Marriage

The Sikh Temple contributes enormously to wedding arrangements. Many Sikh families meet in the *Gurdwara* for the first time and introduce their sons and daughters to each other. Many initial wedding ceremonies such as *rockna* (reserving the bridegroom) and engagement take place in the Sikh Temple. It is also a general practice to organize refreshments after *milni* (introduction of the families of the bride and bridegroom on the wedding day) in the *Gurdwara*. The bridegroom's party and the invited guests from the bride's side have a breakfast consisting of *samosas*, *bhajiya* (Indian savouries) and Indian sweets with tea made in the Indian way. Wedding parties can get help in organizing programmes and an extra pair of hands for cooking and cleaning if it is needed.

It was decided in 1959 that an application should be made to allow marriages to be registered in the Sikh Temple for the convenience of the Sikh community. Up until then, Sikhs had had to take time off from work to attend the local Registry office to register their marriage and there was also a language barrier. Akali Kesar Singh and Balwant Singh Birdi's names were put forward as Marriage Registrars on 10th May 1964.

The *Gurdwara* began registering marriages in 1965 and the first marriage to be registered in this *Gurdwara* was that of Ujjal Singh Ryatt on 17th

July 1965. Kesar Singh Reehal was appointed as the first Marriage Registrar. The second Registrar was *Baba* Khem Singh Punn who was appointed on 11th April 1971. Bakhshish Singh Channa and Piara Singh Saimbhi became Marriage Registrars on 21st August 1978. One of the current Marriage Registrars is Professor Bakhshish Singh who was appointed on 19th April 1986. Harbans Singh Shahid was also appointed on 17th June 1986 because of the increased workload. It is calculated that 1,401 marriages were registered in this *Gurdwara* between 17th July 1965 and 25th May 2003. Currently there are five Marriage Registrars, namely, Bakhshish Singh, Ujjal Singh Ryatt, Kalyan Singh, Kanwarpal Singh Gill and Amarjit Singh Uppal.

1. 2. 4 *Sagan*

The *Gurdwara* took the decision to put a restriction on anyone except the parents giving *sagans* (money given on auspicious occasions such as a wedding) during either engagement or marriage ceremonies held in the *Gurdwara* hall and stopped people throwing flower petals over the couple. It was also decided that only one *thal* (stainless steel platter full of *ladoos*, an Indian sweet) of *sagan* (ceremonial gift) should be brought to the *Gurdwara* for the engagement ceremony. This information was displayed on the notice board and also announced in the Sunday *diwan*. However, this rule is not currently followed and it is left to the family to decide what they want to do.

1. 2. 5 Funeral

Death is the final life cycle rite. When someone dies, relatives and friends are informed and appropriate arrangements are made for the funeral. On the funeral day, the *Gurdwara* plays an important part. The Sikh Temple prepares food for the family of the deceased and a communal meal is served to all those attending the funeral after the *bhog*, to mark the normality of life.

It is common knowledge that after the funeral there is *path bhog*, which is normally a *sadharan path* kept for the peace of the soul of the dead. After the *bhog*, there is a turban ceremony if the head of a family has died. On this occasion, relatives bring turban lengths to his successor, who is the eldest son. The son's in-laws normally bring the turban which is tied by him in public. The tying of the turban signifies that the responsibility for the family is now his and he has become the head of the family.

In the life of a Sikh, there are three domestic rites, namely, the birth of a child, marriage and cremation, which are socially and religiously of great significance, all of which began to be performed in the Sikh Temple. The Sikh Centre is heavily booked for wedding parties and birthday celebrations. The use of alcohol in the Sikh Centre has been permitted on these occasions to meet public demand, though drinking alcohol is against the Sikh ethos. Religious Sikhs use the Sikh Temple for these social occasions by taking *langar seva* and inviting their relatives and friends.

1. 3 Social festivals

Festivals in the Punjab mark the unfolding of the seasons, agricultural cycles and religious observances and rites. Sikhs in Britain celebrate many functions, which have both religious and social significance. The major summer festival is *Vaisakhi* named after the second lunar month, *Vaisakh*. *Vaisakhi* may be interpreted as a festival of renewal; the previous agricultural cycle has come to an end, a new one is about to begin. It is the most significant occasion for Sikhs as it marks the creation of *Khalsa Panth*. *Vaisakhi* is also significant as the New Year's Day for Sikhs. Technically, the first lunar month is *Chet*, but the New Year for Sikhs starts with *Vaisakhi*. It used to normally fall on 13th April. The date is fixed, being based on a solar calendar, though

Gurpurab **celebrations**

once in every thirty-six years it occurs on 14th April. Now, however, with the introduction of the *Nanakshahi* (Sikh) calendar, the date has been permanently fixed as 14th April. The Sikh Temple organizes social events on this occasion, such as parties for children and events involving the Sikh community. An *akhand path* or a series of *akhand paths* are organized in the Sikh Temple and *nagar kirtan* takes place on *Vaisakhi* day. The Sikh Temple also organizes special events involving the community such as competitions and children's programmes to mark the occasion. Sikhs also enjoy themselves by performing *bhangra* (folk dance) and singing and sometimes they book the Sikh Centre to hold *bhangra* gigs and parties.

Diwali is another festival widely celebrated by Sikhs. It is essentially a Hindu festival, and the principal ceremonial observance on the occasion of *Diwali* at the household level is the worship of the images of *Ganesh* and *Lakshmi*, the harbingers

Fireworks

of good fortune and prosperity. Sikhs celebrate *Diwali* to celebrate the release of the sixth *Guru*, Hargobind, from the Gwalior jail. The Sikh Temple in Leeds is lit up and a firework display is held in the evening. The sweet stalls are opened and *langar* is served all evening. This is a very well- organized event full of rejoicing and attracts huge gatherings of Sikhs and non-Sikhs.

Lohri and *Holi* are other popular seasonal festivals from the Punjab. Holi is seasonal in its significance and secular in its celebration. The festival marks the beginning of Spring and usually falls in the month of *Phagan* (February-March). There is a Hindu mythological legend attached to this festival about *Prahlad and Holika*, signifying the triumph of good over evil. The Sikh Temple holds a *diwan* in the evening to uphold the underlying principle of triumph of good over evil and this is well attended. The festival of *Lohri* falls on *Makar Sangrand*, which is normally on January 12th, 13th, or 14th. It is a day for almsgiving and for patching up differences. For Sikh families, *Lohri* is celebrated following the birth and marriage of a son. A fire is lit and corn, peanuts and sesame sweets are eaten around it. Foods eaten are rice pudding, *halwa,* cornmeal *chapatis* and mustard leaf *saag.* The Sikh Temple holds a special *diwan* on this day and *Lohri* is celebrated by lighting the fire. *Saag* and cornmeal *chapatis* are made for *langar.* Peanuts and sesame sweets are distributed in the congregation.

1. 4 Ladies' *Satsang*

Sohan Singh Kalsi suggested starting a ladies' *satsang* (gathering to sing religious hymns) and the Executive Committee considered this suggestion and gave their approval. A ladies' *satsang* was introduced in June 1969 and women met on Saturdays to do the *kirtan.* Sikh women from East Africa brought this tradition with them to Leeds. They used to hold such gatherings in East Africa and continued here in Leeds. This served many purposes such as providing social interaction for women, outings for women and learning *kirtan* (playing the harmonium and singing religious hymns) from one another. It also contributed to the *Gurdwara* fund as women raised money by generous offerings on special occasions. *Gurdwara* committees recognized this and this was pointed out in the Annual General Meeting on 23rd April 2000 when it was noted in the minutes that the ladies' *satsang* had raised a huge amount for this *Gurdwara* building.

Gian Kaur Syan was the founder member of this group. She gave the names of other women participants in her interview, and the names quoted were Niranjan Kaur Channa, Dalip Kaur, Jamuna Devi, Surjit Kaur Dhiman and Man Kaur Bahri. She also added that women met at her house in the beginning and later in the *Gurdwara* on Saturdays. It was normal for thirty to thirty-five women to attend the *satsang.* The *Gurdwara* offered them the opportunity to participate in the *kirtan* programme of *gurpurabs.* Gian Kaur Syan is very old now so the responsibility of running this group was offered to any volunteer who could manage it and do *seva.* Harbans Kaur Thandi together with other women runs this group now on every Wednesday afternoon but she also is getting old and wishes to delegate this work to another volunteer. In her interview she said that the *sangat* needed love, care and respect. Someone who could offer this to ladies should come forward to do this *seva.*

1. 5 *Sanjh* Group

It was decided by the Sikh Temple in May 1983 that an *Istri Sabha* (a women's association) should be organized. An announcement was made in the *sangat* that interested women should come forward and those women who participated in the work of the *Gurdwara* and the Sikh Centre were especially encouraged.

A group was formed by women, including myself, with the intention of making it an independent and secular group which would attempt to solve the growing problems of women which had come about as a result of social interaction with the indigenous community. I chaired the first meeting of this group in 1985 and it was well attended. The group was also given its name, the *Sanjh* group, in this meeting. The responsibility for running this group was given to the Executive Committee, as I had to be away from Leeds for a considerable time, and in my absence some women associated with the *Gurdwara* conveniently brought the group under the auspices of the Sikh Temple.

The *Sanjh* group celebrated the first International Women's Day on 8th March 1986, for which a grant of £250 was obtained from the City Council. The *Gurdwara* decided that any grant received by the group should be put into the *Gurdwara* account and that the group should work with the *Gurdwara* committee. The *Gurdwara* committee wanted to have a copy of all the correspondence conducted by this group. The *Sanjh* group celebrated *Diwali* in 1987 when the Sarao family paid for the food and Balbir Singh Lalli gave the prizes.

The *Gurdwara* laid down some conditions in 1987, which the *Sanjh* group accepted, that is to say:

a) The group committee is subordinate to the *Gurdwara* Management Committee.
b) It should be answerable to the *Gurdwara* sub-committee.
c) The group should keep a record of their expenditure and actions.
d) The auditors of the *Gurdwara* will audit their accounts.

e) Their accounts will be given to the *sangat* along with other accounts of the *Gurdwara*.
f) The *Gurdwara* Committee would also describe their other activities to the *sangat*.
g) Any correspondence with other groups or organizations should be copied to the General Secretary of the *Gurdwara*.
h) All groups should report their plans and other actions to the *Gurdwara* committee.
i) Groups holding their own accounts should have three signatories - President, Treasurer and Group Leader.
j) All their work should be according to *gurmat*.

This was agreed unanimously, but the group had lost its independence by accepting all the conditions imposed by the Sikh Temple and the *Gurdwara* Committee closely monitored the work of the group. It lost its impetus and encountered a number of problems in the years following. Finally constant tension between the *Gurdwara* Committee and the Group Leader in the end resulted in the *Sanjh* group's demise.

1. 6 Leeds Sikh Parents Association

The Leeds Sikh Parents Association was formed with the aim of combating social evils existing in the Sikh society and tackling the growing problems of the younger generation of Sikhs. The Sikh Temple received a letter from this organization in October 1992 asking them to nominate two representatives from the *Gurdwara* to participate in the work of this organization. It was decided by the *Gurdwara* committee that Baldev Singh Duggal and Beant Singh should represent the *Gurdwara*. This organization also requested the use of the *Gurdwara* hall for social evenings and the *Gurdwara* allowed them the free use of the hall. Unfortunately, the Association survived only for a short span of a couple of years.

1. 7 Radio Transmitter

The Leeds Sikh Temple wanted to have a radio transmitter in order to run religious programmes. Hardeep Singh Ahluwalia was given the responsibility of making inquiries. Later the responsibility was given to Gulzar Singh Thandi and he collected some leaflets. It was considered appropriate to have some advice from the Tong Road *Gurdwara* in Armley as they had been running a community radio programme for some time. A committee of five members was formed to find out more information. The President informed the committee that a radio transmitter would cost £60,000 annually, which was too expensive for the *Gurdwara* to install.

In the end, it was decided by the Committee that they would approach the BBC, Sunrise and Yorkshire TV to ask them to relay Sikh religious programmes and this responsibility was given to Hardeep Singh Ahluwalia and Kesar Singh Seehra. It was also suggested that the community radio run by the Armley *Gurdwara* should be persuaded to run only religious programmes and *kirtan*.

1. 8 Priests for hospitals and prisons

A suggestion was made in August 1976 that Sikh priests should visit prisons and hospitals in order to care for and fulfil the religious needs of sick patients and prisoners. The names suggested for this were Chetan Singh Marwaha, Ajit Singh Bansal, Kewal Singh, Sarwan Singh Cheema and Swaran Singh Panesar. Beant Singh was given the duty of visiting the prison in 1992. Inder Singh Ryatt suggested in July 2001 that one member of the Committee should be given the responsibility of visiting sick patients in hospitals and the Committee responded that it would not be possible to send one member regularly, due to a lack of volunteers.

1. 9 Vegetarian food for hospitals

Gurcharan Singh Kundi initiated this project to supply vegetarian food to Sikh or other Asian vegetarian patients in hospitals. He took responsibility for preparing the meals for hospitals and he had some support from the Sikh Temple. The authorities approved this for Asian patients for Leeds Infirmary, Roundhay Women's Hospital, the Maternity Hospital and Ida Hospital in Cookridge. The patients were told of this option but unfortunately this project did not last long because of the eventual lack of support from the Sikh Temple.

Gurdwaras are multifunctional institutions and fulfil many social obligations for the Sikh community. Some projects flourish and others disappear immaturely before coming to fruition. The reason is not that the committees are unwilling to support them, but that they also depend on human and financial resources and how these are managed. It has been observed that independent projects do not often get support or recognition from the *Gurdwara* and when they become part of the *Gurdwara* there is little chance of their healthy survival because of a lack of delegation skills and the ever-changing membership of the committees. Sharing information is not encouraged as *Gurdwara* policy and this can occasionally create tension between individuals and community members.

2. 0 Political Role

Gurdwaras are not only religious institutions but also perform many other functions for the welfare of the Sikhs and Sikh *Panth*. An All India Akali Conference was held in Jalandhar (Punjab) to discuss the issue of a Sikh homeland. During the meeting of 27th February 1966, the Management Committee of the Sikh Temple agreed that the Leeds *Gurdwara* would accept and support the resolutions passed at that conference. This was the first time that the *Gurdwara* committed to lending its support to the struggle for a Sikh homeland.

2. 1 Punjab

It is important to explain the historical background in order to comprehend the Punjab situation. Sikhs originate mainly from the Punjab, a state in northern India, where they form the majority of the population. Prior to the partition of India in 1947, Hindus, Muslims and Sikhs, encompassed by one generic term 'Punjabi', lived together in a united Punjab. The partition of 1947 was carried out on the basis of religion. East Punjab became a part of India and home to Sikhs and Hindus, and West Punjab formed part of Pakistan and was home to Muslims. East Punjab was further divided in three units on the basis of language in November 1966. The territory of the divided Punjab was split in three ways by the creation of two new states, Haryana and Himachal Pradesh, as Hindi speaking units which left the Punjab as a Panjabi-speaking state. Even Chandigarh, the city built as the new capital of Punjab after partition, was made a Union Territory to be directly administered by the Central Government. 'Partition of their homeland was nothing new. But whilst Punjab's 1947 division had taken place under the tutelage of an alien power, the second had been effected by the government of a free India' (Patwant Singh, 1999: 219).

Patwant Singh, a Sikh historian, stated that the Congress government had manipulated the media and public opinion to view the desire for a *Panjabi*-speaking state as a demand for a separate Sikh state, when it was a purely linguistic demand, which other language groups had also made and been granted. What the Congress Party had declared as its goal in 1929 was in the Punjab's case labelled a separatist demand. The Sikhs, without access to the media, were in no position to present their side of the case. They were disillusioned by the attitude of the Congress and felt discriminated against and bitter.

2. 2 Anandpur Sahib Resolution

The Akali Dal (a political party associated with Sikhs) at its General Session attended by over a hundred thousand persons at Ludhiana on 28th-29th October 1977 passed a resolution called Anandpur Sahib Resolution. According to Patwant Singh the main point of the resolution was to endorse the principle of state autonomy in keeping with the concept of federalism. The other points contained in the resolution concerned river waters, social structures, discrimination in jobs, refugee rehabilitation, abolition of duties on farm machinery, accelerated industrialisation and so on. There was nothing unconstitutional or secessionist in any of them (1999: 228-229).

The state of Punjab became India's breadbasket as a result of government investment in the development of irrigation schemes and rural infrastructure during the 1950s, combined with the robust input of the Sikh peasantry. Comparable interest was lacking when it came to funding Punjab's industrialization and hardly any large-scale state sector plant was located in the Punjab, in marked contrast to the extent to which these were allocated to other states in India. Lack of industrialization resulted in high unemployment amongst Sikh youths. There was also a territorial and river water dispute between Punjab and Haryana. Akali Dal also resisted the state of emergency declared in 1975, which was not liked by the Prime Minister Indira Gandhi.

In fact, the Resolution was attacked as a secessionist document, which would threaten the unity of the country and lead to an independent state. The Sikh Temple played a major role in disseminating information on the Anandpur Sahib Resolution. The following were the main points explained to the Leeds Sikh *sangat* though there were also other points in the resolution:

(1)   Amritsar should be granted the status of a holy city.
(2)   An all India *Gurdwara* Act should be constituted.
(3)   Permission should be requested to install a broadcasting station at the Golden Temple for the relay of *Gurbani* on air for nineteen hours a day.
(4)   Chandigarh should be returned to the Punjab.
(5)   The percentage of electricity and water given to the Punjab should be increased.
(6)   Sikhs should be accepted as a martial race and the percentage of their intake in the army should be increased.
(7)   The neighbouring states of the Punjab, including Delhi, should give 'second' language status to Panjabi.

A protest procession was organized in front of the Indian High Commission's office on 29th May 1983 to hand over the memorandum asking for these demands to be fulfilled.

2. 3 The Indian Army's attack on the Golden Temple and large-scale massacre

The government chose Jarnail Singh Bhindranwala, a seminary preacher with a considerable knowledge of the Sikh scripture, to undermine the Sikhs. He always claimed to be a religious man though he was built up without his knowledge as the voice of the Sikhs through the media and was given a high profile. He was portrayed to appear as if he represented Sikhs though millions of them had no interest in him or in Akalis. 'But after he had served the Congress purpose – of communalizing Punjab's politics – and had moved into its sacred precinct on 15 December 1983, the final gory scene was enacted in a carefully conceived political move which required the Indian army to unleash its firepower against the Golden Temple.' (Patwant Singh, 1999: 232) As a result, the Congress Party wanted to get rid of him. He was then portrayed as a Sikh extremist. The Indian army attacked *Harminder Sahib* - the holiest place of Sikhs - on 3rd June 1984. This stunned Sikhs the world over. Then the assassination of the Prime Minister, Indira Gandhi, at the hands of two Sikh bodyguards on 31st October 1984, resulted in the large-scale massacre of innocent Sikh men, women and children in Delhi, Kanpur, Bokaro and many other cities in Northern India. Encouraged by the Government, reprisal killing and plundering continued for four days in the capital city and Sikhs in Britain were able to watch all that brutal killing on BBC television, whereas the media were prevented in India from putting out any such news.

This was a very critical time for Sikhs living in India. The Management Committee felt it necessary to raise awareness of the atrocities committed on Sikhs and to highlight the Indian government's failure to respond to the legitimate demands of Sikhs. Sikhs felt that they were being treated unfairly in their own homeland and the Indian Army's attack on *Harminder Sahib* (the Golden Temple) was beyond their imagination. Sikhs living in Britain had families, relatives and friends in India and they were anxious to help them by raising their voices to stop the atrocities of the Indian government. An Emergency Executive Committee meeting was held on 7th June 1984 to discuss the attack on *Harmindar Sahib* by the Indian army. A demonstration was held in front of the Indian High Commission office in Liverpool at 1 pm on 8th June 1984 and Nishkam Sevak Jatha also held another demonstration in London. Gurdeep Singh Bhogal and Bakhshish Singh were the *Gurdwara* spokesmen. A case was prepared with the aim of getting it published in the newspapers and presenting it to the Human Rights Commission in the United Nations. In December 1984, it was decided that two committee members, Gurdeep Singh Bhogal and Harjit Singh Ryatt, would go to Strasbourg to present the case in the United Nations and the *Gurdwara* would pay their expenses. In January 1985, a committee of three members, Professor Bakhshish Singh, Gurdeep Singh Bhogal and Harjit Singh Ryatt, was formed to consider and attempt to solve the problems faced by the Sikh community. This committee received its correspondence at the *Gurdwara*'s address. The expenses were shared by three *gurdwaras* as follows: 50% paid by the Sikh Temple, 25% by the Ramgarhia Board and 25% by the Tong Road *Gurdwara*. Swaran Singh Panesar represented the Ramgarhia Board, Baldev Singh Duggal the Tong Road *Gurdwara* and Harbans Singh Sagoo the Nishkam Sevak Jatha. Two seminars were held to raise awareness of the Punjab situation, one when a *sangat* came from Canada and another for the indigenous community in 1987. A donation of £501 was sent to *Sri Akal Takht Sahib* (part of the Golden Temple in Amritsar) to be used for distressed families who had suffered in the 1984 *ghalughara* (struggle/attack) and £101 was given to Sikh Human Rights. A letter from Sikh Human Rights in 1988 was considered and £2,000 was sanctioned from the *Gurdwara* fund to support this project.

The *gurdwaras* in Leeds jointly set up the Leeds Sikh Council to look after the welfare of Sikhs. They participated in demonstrations, attended conferences and funded the International Youth Federation. They also raised a martyrdom fund to give financial help to the families of martyrs. The *Gurdwara* also brought out a magazine to raise awareness in the *panth* and *sangat*. It was stressed that Sikhs should follow *Sikh rahit maryada* in their day-to-day life, as the revival of religion and religious values becomes natural in times of crisis. The *Gurdwara*'s members attended the meeting of the International Youth Federation and donated £1,000. £500 was given in 1991 to the Council of *Khalistan*, a charitable organisation political in nature, based in the United States of America. The Sikh Temple continued to support and fund the activities of the Sikh Youth Federation.

2. 4 Turban

The turban is much more than a headdress for Sikhs. It has a particular religious significance. The turban is worn to cover the *'kes'* (uncut hair), which is one of the *'K's*. The legal question regarding the wearing of the turban first arose in the 1970s because of the law by which wearing a crash helmet while riding a motorcycle was made compulsory in England. After June 1973 controversy raged in the British press and in the minds of the public regarding the new Law. The law, though passed with good intentions, happened to be against the tenets of Sikhism that Sikhs were absolutely forbidden to wear any headgear other than the turban. On these grounds, practising Sikhs asked for exemption from wearing crash helmets and the Sikh Temple supported the meeting in favour of a turban campaign followed by demonstrations to be held in Birmingham. Funds were donated for the campaign and the *Gurdwara* organized a conference on *lohtop* (crash helmet) on 20th December 1972 in which many churches participated. The proceedings of this conference were notified for information to all the northern *gurdwaras*. As a result of the protest, a Bill to exempt the Sikhs was introduced in the House of Commons. There was a long debate on this subject in the House of Lords resulting in the passing of a law on 15th November 1976, which exempted the Sikhs from wearing crash helmets. It was also ruled that Sikh drivers and conductors of public vehicles were not to be compelled to wear caps.

Another controversy regarding the turban arose in the schools of England in 1982 when Gurinder Singh Mandela was refused admission to his school if he continued to wear a turban. This case was taken to court and Lord Denning rejected the right of Sikhs to wear a turban in the school on the grounds that Sikhs were neither a racial group nor a nation and their separate existence could not be accepted. Sikhs took this decision made on the 29th July 1982 as infringing their religious identity. They demonstrated against his decision on 10th October 1982 in a procession from Hyde Park to Downing Street to see the Prime Minister, Margaret Thatcher, and express their anger and displeasure, demanding that Sikhs should be accepted as a *qaum* (nation) and that the law should be amended. This demonstration was fully supported by the *Gurdwara* and the *Gurdwara* paid for the expense of hiring coaches for the participants. Four hundred and fifty-three Sikhs went to support the demonstration. After the October demonstration, it was decided to appeal against the decision and costs were to be paid by the Community Relations Council. The appeal was made to the House of Lords and letters were written to the Home Office, the Indian High Commission, members of Parliament and councillors about the importance of the turban for Sikhs. On appeal the House of Lords reversed the judgement of the Court of appeal, holding that: 'They are more than a religious sect, they are almost a nation. Therefore, their right to wear the turban is protected under the law'. The case for wearing a turban was won in March 1983. As a result, Sikh children were able to wear turbans in schools and also Sikhs were accepted as a separate nation.

2. 5 Local concerns

The *Gurdwara* also contributed to alleviating the problems faced by Sikhs living in Britain, by liaising with the appropriate authorities. An emergency meeting of the Executive Committee was called to discuss the meeting with Sir David Goodhall, the newly appointed British High Commissioner in India, to bring to his notice the problems faced by Sikhs living here in England. He was invited to visit the *Gurdwara* on 6th April 1987 at 10.45 am for fifty minutes. The committee suggested that:

a) The visa system should be improved.
b) There should be a sub-office in Jalandhar (Punjab).
c) A file should be made for any disputed case for later reference.

Sir David Goodhall could not come to the meeting because of an accident, but his secretary and some other members came. His secretary promised that the Committee's concerns would be addressed.

The *Gurdwara* has always been proactive in maintaining contacts with local politicians, dignitaries and relevant authorities. It is difficult to mention all the relevant occasions but, for example, the High Commissioner of India was honoured with a *saropa* on 2nd February 1968 and a dinner was arranged for him. Queen Elizabeth was sent a letter of congratulation on her Silver Jubilee. Prakash Singh Badal, the Chief Minister of the Punjab was invited to the Sikh Temple when he was on his visit to London.

3. 0 Conclusion

The *Gurdwara* has always taken a stand in support of Sikh religion and has promoted the welfare of the Sikh community not only by uniting Sikhs, but also by disseminating information to other organizations and the community. Sikhs raised a united voice when their *panth* seemed in danger and their religious values were undermined. The *Gurdwara* has also contributed to inter-faith relations.

Conclusion

Religion has always been a binding force for faith communities and plays an important part in the day-to-day lives of people. It is a symbol of solidarity, peace and harmony if interpreted correctly. Religion aims to create a peaceful and purposeful way of life where people support each other, exchange views and work collectively for the betterment of their neighbours, their community and society at large. By its very nature, religion can be seen as reinforcing social norms and values and prioritizing social solidarity. In order to promote, celebrate and continue religion and religious traditions, places of worship which provide a venue for dialogue are necessary. They help to sustain the faith. Sikhs believe in Sikhism and their place of worship is called *gurdwara*, also known as *gurughar* and Sikh temple. These are places where human beings imagine the invisible God and show their dedication to their creator by kneeling down, touching, listening and contemplating. In the case of Sikhs, they worship kneeling in front of their Holy book and listening to the *shabad* (words of the Holy book) while sitting in the *sangat* (congregation).

The present study has examined the historical development of the Sikh Temple in Leeds since its inception. The origin and development of the Sikh Temple is closely linked with the continuation of Sikh religious traditions in Leeds, which began with *shabad kirtan* sessions organized by a small group of Sikh male migrants. The study has also analysed the way in which the Sikh ethos and concepts (mainly *seva* and donation) played their part in the further development of the *Gurdwara*. The celebration of *gurpurabs* became the main focus of Sikh corporate identity and a unifying force behind the Yorkshire Sikhs. This unity resulted in the joint purchase by Yorkshire Sikhs of a small house at 3 Savile Road, Leeds in 1959, to serve as a *gurdwara*, originally named as the 'United Sikh Association', Yorks. Soon after, as a result of Africanization and the fear of restrictive immigration legislation, Sikh families came from East Africa and Punjab. This brought about a substantial change in the composition of the Sikh community in Leeds and an immediate effect of the growth of the Sikh community was the need to buy a bigger building for the *Gurdwara*. They bought the disused church building on Chapeltown Road, which was completely renovated to make it suitable for the needs of the Sikh Temple. Both the buildings purchased to serve as a *Gurdwara* were bought from donations and Sikh volunteers did most of the renovation work and the actual expense was only for materials. Sikhs donated generously to pay back the remaining balance of the cost over the next three years. They decided eventually to build a purpose-built *Gurdwara,* which cost them over a million pounds raised from the *Gurdwara* fund and donations. It took two years to build, and it was opened to the public on *Vaisakhi* day in 1999. The church building often mentioned as the old *Gurughar* was refurbished from the grants received from Leeds City Council and English Heritage. The Sikhs were also able to fulfil the social and cultural needs of the Sikh community by building the Sikh Centre adjoining the *Gurdwara*. These buildings are not only prestigious for the Sikh community but also an asset to the regeneration of the area as they created jobs for the long-term unemployed from run-down areas of Leeds.

The pattern of Sikh settlement in Leeds has been discussed here, as this was the determining factor for the location of the *Gurdwara* buildings. Initially the community lived in Chapeltown and Harehills and they subsequently attracted their relatives and friends to live near by. Many years later, a conscious decision was made to keep the same location on Chapeltown Road just on the opposite side for the new purpose-built *Gurdwara* and the Sikh Centre. Though the Sikh community had moved away from this area to settle in suburban and more affluent parts of Leeds, it was felt that this location was central and easily accessible for many.

The *Gurdwara* plays a most significant role in perpetuating the Sikh religious and cultural traditions among Sikh migrants and their children by providing Panjabi teaching and religious education. Panjabi is a prerequisite for religious education and music. The Sikh Temple from the very beginning laid emphasis on teaching Panjabi and also tried to persuade the local authority to introduce Panjabi as a modern language in the school curriculum. In spite of all the efforts the fact remains that children born and brought up in this country and speaking English most of the time, are able to acquire only a perfunctory knowledge of Panjabi and it has become a second language for them. The Sikh service is conducted in Panjabi, which makes it hard for them to understand the subtleties of their religion. Most children find the service incomprehensible, with the result that they lack any interest in the activities of the *Gurdwara*. This situation has made parents and leaders of the *Gurdwara* concerned about their children's inability to understand Panjabi and they are keen to find a way out. One suggestion is to use trained teachers and volunteers to teach Panjabi in parallel with other modern languages thus making learning more interesting. Panjabi should also be introduced at university level. Music, on the other hand, has become popular with Sikh children. In recent years, there have been qualified teachers teaching music in the *Gurdwara* and many children have taken advantage of this facility by learning to play musical instruments and singing *shabads*. Explaining the meanings of *shabads* in English would further increase their popularity.

There has been a major shift in the management structure of the *Gurdwara* since the mid-1970s. The first full-time paid *granthi* was appointed in 1978 and since then there have always been full-time paid *granthis* in post. The *Gurdwara* also invites many visiting *gianis* and *ragis*. These *granthis* and *ragis* have been brought over from the Punjab and usually they are proficient in Panjabi. They preach Sikh values and traditions by using episodes in Panjabi from Sikh history. This may be interesting for the older generation born and brought up in the Punjab but these methods do not attract younger generations of Sikhs towards taking advantage of the *granthis*' knowledge to learn about their religious roots. These days, in order to teach Sikh religious beliefs, the importance of Sikh identity and understanding of basic Sikh tenets, the Sikh Temple runs classes on the Sikh religion in which the younger generation of Sikhs is taught religion in English by baptized Sikhs using modern techniques. This approach has become popular with children and the number attending is growing every day. Learning from this approach, there is still a need to take such practical steps as training homegrown *granthis* instead of bringing them from the Punjab, producing religious literature in simple easy-to-read and jargon-free English and delivering part of the religious service in English. Recruiting and training *granthis* who have experience of life in England might also resolve other problems which exist in the relationship between *granthis* and management committees.

The presence of family units and the appointment of full-time *granthis* has enhanced the ceremonies of life cycle rituals. Life cycle rituals like birth, *naamkaran*, wedding and death are conducted according to the Sikh religion and religious traditions. The fusion of Sikh values with the social and cultural values of the Punjab, which stem usually from oral traditions, has had an enormous impact on the way in which Sikhs conduct their religious practices here in England. The overlapping boundaries between religion, *Punjabi* culture and caste have resulted in the development of practices not necessarily Sikh in essence. However, Sikhs in England are becoming increasingly conscious of their own religious values and Sikh culture with the preaching of Sikhism. It is nevertheless still important to discard those oral traditions which are not really religious in nature.

The Sikh Temple celebrates *gurpurabs* and religious festivals. Their significance lies not only in gathering for religious observance, but also in offering periods of re-evaluating and re-affirming one's religious beliefs and principles. They also allow the community an opportunity for collectively assessing just how faithfully it is adhering to and practising the fundamental tenets of its religious faith. In this regard, it becomes important for Sikhs to do self-assessment through introspection and evaluation of their beliefs. It is required from every Sikh that he or she should understand the words of the *Guru Granth Sahib* and act upon them faithfully in order to become *Khalsa* (pure ones). The Sikh Temple puts a heavy emphasis on Sikh identity and initiation in promoting Sikh religion. In order to be a complete Sikh it is important to be initiated and maintain a Sikh identity but it is equally important to put Sikh teachings into practice.

Sikhs believe in the universal brotherhood crossing the barrier of caste, class and status. This approach was adopted in the early days of Sikh settlement here but lost its impetus in the years to come with the growth of the Indian community. It is important to bring the Sikh ethos to the composition of management committees. It is also essential as a part of Sikh values to open the doors of the *Gurdwara* to all persons, irrespective of their caste, creed, colour, religion or nationality. They should be allowed to serve and contribute to the *Gurdwara* activities. In the future, the trend of marrying across caste, religion and culture in spite of the strong stigma against marrying someone outside the Sikh religion may well attract non-Sikhs towards Sikhism and its philosophy.

One of the main findings of this research concerns the strength of social and religious diversity among Sikhs in Leeds which has been discussed within the context of this book. Caste consciousness within the Sikh community has been very much alive since the arrival of East African Sikhs. The social structure of these Sikhs and the pattern of marriages followed by their families are based on caste. This has resulted in the reinforcement of traditional values and promotion of caste consciousness among Sikhs. The split in the Sikh community and the subsequent creation of several *gurdwaras* in the 1980s on the basis of caste and sect has badly affected the image of the Sikhs as being a homogeneous group. This has had a long-lasting effect and has caused irreparable damage to the community. It is true that there is a need for more than one *gurdwara* to fulfil the needs of the growing Sikh community and the community also needs easily accessible places of worship, but creating *gurdwaras* on the basis of caste and taking the caste line in the management of *gurdwaras* runs counter to the very basis of Sikh religion. The Sikh religion promotes equality and human dignity. It condemns the caste system and promotes the idea of valuing a person on the basis of his or her virtues and deeds. Many younger generation Sikhs are now marrying across caste and this is helping in a small way to overcome caste barriers.

Caste consciousness remains a persistent dividing factor among Sikhs. The division existing within the Sikh community and their inability to create a unified approach is certainly harmful and is affecting the image of Sikhs. The Leeds Sikhs, in spite of belonging to a reasonably well-educated and affluent community have made no collective approach towards taking the services or grants offered by Leeds City Council and at present lacking unity, they are unable to have any effective political voice at either local or national level. This is unfortunate as in the past they have made a united stand when their religion and religious values have been challenged, as for instance during the turban case and during the Indian Army's attack on the Golden Temple, 'Operation Blue Star', in 1984.

The projection of actual Sikh beliefs into actions and deeds is an essential criterion in the spread of the Sikh religion and its beliefs. Management of the *Gurdwara* should be in the hands of pious and committed Sikhs and the chance of serving on committees should be given to capable Sikhs rather than providing an opportunity for promoting one's family and relatives. The aim of *seva* is to provide free service without any self-gain and clinging to power using unfair means to retain the position negates its purpose. Such misuse of position often spoils the peaceful atmosphere of the *Gurdwara* and creates further dissensions in the community. Women and young Sikhs should be supported and encouraged to participate in the management of the *Gurdwara*. The *Gurdwara*, while maintaining its present policies, must also think carefully about alternative ways in which to retain the skills and expertise of those Sikhs who have not been initiated.

The *Gurdwara* is a busy place with many activities going on and volunteers do most of the work. It is important to acknowledge what they do and they should be given incentives in the form of appreciation or certificates of achievement. There is often a shortage of skilled volunteers, which affects the quality of work and sometimes it becomes difficult to maintain standards. The *Gurdwara* could gain by taking advantage of training, such as capacity building, constructive contribution to meetings and working in a team and many more, arranged by the voluntary sector.

The time has come to bring changes in the management of the *Gurdwara* because of the changing structure of service provisions in this country. The current situation is that most committed and dedicated volunteers prepared to give their time to the *Gurdwara* come from traditional backgrounds with little or no experience of bureaucratic ways and this creates problems of dissemination of information and effective liaison with other agencies and service providers. Community involvement and the contribution of faith communities have been emphasized in shaping service provisions and service delivery. The *Gurdwara* can play a pivotal role in this direction by liaising with Council departments, specialized agencies and service- providing bodies in order to benefit the Sikh community. Management committees should be able to respond to such demands by including experienced professionals and highly-skilled Sikhs equipped with the knowledge of service delivery and understanding of bureaucracy in order to take full advantage of existing facilities. It is also to the advantage of the *Gurdwara* to keep abreast of the changes in strategy of the local government and their policies towards service delivery.

The *Gurdwara* is a significant part of the Sikh way of life. It is a multipurpose institution, which fulfils the religious, social, educational and political needs of the Sikh community. The *Gurdwara* has contributed enormously towards enriching the religious life of Sikhs by enhancing their religion and religious traditions. The Sikh community enjoys religious activities and also conduct many of their social ceremonies in the Sikh Temple which have made an enormous impact on their life style. The aspiration of many Sikhs is to seeing in the *Gurdwara* a place of love, peace and harmony.

Bibliography

Books, Minutes books & Bulletins

Bhachu, Parminder. *Twice Migrants: East African Sikh settlers in Britain*. London: Tavistock, 1985.

Constitution. United Sikh Association. [1959].

Constitution. Leeds: The Sikh Temple, 2nd ed., 1965.

Constitution. Leeds: The Sikh Temple, 1988.

Kalsi, Sewa Singh. *The evolution of a Sikh community in Britain*. Leeds: University of Leeds. Community Religious Project, 1992.

Office for National Statistics. *Census 2001*. London: HMSO, 2003.

Paramjit Singh. *Vaisakhi: Celebrations and Birth of the Khalsa*. Birmingham: DTF, 2003.

Patwant Singh. *The Sikhs*. London: John Murray, 1999.

Rahit Maryada: A guide to the Sikh way of life. London: 1971. Amritsar: 1978.

Rait, Satwant Kaur. *Sikh women in England: Their religious and cultural beliefs and social practices*. London: Trentham Books, 2005.

'Ramgarhias in Leeds'. *Ramgarhia Sikh Bulletin*. Vol. 2, No 1. April 1985.

Registry of Deeds. 281A Chapeltown Road, Leeds. Vol. 106. Numbers 41 & 42. 97, 102 pp. Wakefield: West Yorkshire Archive Service.

Registry of Deeds. 3 Savile Road, Leeds. Vol. 229. Numbers 426 & 427. 922, 924pp. Wakefield: West Yorkshire Archive Service.

The Sikh Temple. Baisakhi Number 1985. Leeds: The Sikh Temple, 281A Chapeltown Road.

The Sikh Temple. Minute book. No. 1. 22.8.76 - 21.8.82. 350pp.

The Sikh Temple. Minute book. No.2. 18.9.82 - 9.5.99. 518pp.

The Sikh Temple. Minute book. No. 3. 23.5.99 -.

Sikh Temples in the UK and the people behind their management. London: Jan publications, 1976.

Newspaper Articles

'600 at opening of first Sikh Temple in Leeds', *Yorkshire Evening Post*, 23.4.1962, p. 7, col. 1.

'Eastern Worship', *Yorkshire Evening Post*, 30.5.1962, p. 6.

'Sunday service lasts 10 hours', *Yorkshire Post*, 7.1.1963, p. 7.

'The Sikh Temple: £44,000 extension plan turned down', *Yorkshire Evening Post*, 9.9.1975, p.7, col. 1.

'The Sikh Temple: Temple annexe opened', *Yorkshire Evening Post*, 28.11.1977, p. 8, 1/5.

'Sikh Temple cash aid' [£120,000 LCC grant to complete it], *Yorkshire Evening Post*, 7.1.1983, p.1, col. 8.

'Sikhs' ashes hope' [Wetherby an ideal site], *Wetherby News*, 3.4.1992, p.1.

'Ritual storm grows: Sikh's ashes plan stuns townsfolk': [Planning application to scatter cremated ashes on the Wharfe at Wetherby], *Wetherby News*, 10.4.1992, p. 1.

'Sikh Funeral Plan under fire' [Row over plan to build riverside platform for disposal of human ashes at Kirkstall], *Yorkshire Evening Post*, 9.11.1993, p.1, 10/1 and *Yorkshire Post*, 9.11.1993, p.1, 10/4.

'Sikh Platform not for ashes' [Plan rejected – another site sought], *Yorkshire Evening Post*, 24.11.1993, p. 5, 3/6.

'Work to start on new temple', *Yorkshire Evening Post*, 28.6.1997, p. 2.

APPENDIX 1
The Constitutions and Amendments

The under-mentioned are exact copies of the three Constitutions printed by the Sikh Temple and no corrections or alterations have been made either to the content or format. There are many words written in bold in the original document and they are kept as they were. Any comments added to the texts are given in square brackets. This Appendix covers the contents of three printed Constitutions and the drafts of major amendments.

Constitutions

There are three printed Constitutions: the first Constitution printed in 1959, the second in 1965 and the third in 1988. The exact wording and format is given below:

The first Constitution:

United Sikh Association
Yorks.
*
Constitution
*
3 SAVILE ROAD
LEEDS 7

CONSTITUTION
* *

1. NAME: -
This Society will be known by the name "United Sikh Association, Yorks."

2. AIMS AND OBJECTIVES: -
(a)   To build and manage a religious centre.
(b)   To celebrate the principal Sikh festivals.
(c)   To render the needy persons every possible assistance.

(d) To propagate the teachings of "Guru NANAK".
(e) To maintain a library and reading room (see section 40).
(f) To introduce adult education amongst its members.
(g) To encourage religious and social intercourse amongst its members.
(h) To do any other act coincidental or incidental to the above given aims and objects.

3. MEMBERSHIP AND RIGHT:-

Any person irrespective of cast, creed, colour, religion or nationality can become a member of the Society and the members shall be either:

(a) Ordinary full members. Those persons who pay an annual subscription of £1.0.0 by one or more instalments.
(b) Life members. The persons who pay a sum of £10.0.0 in one instalment.

4. (a) The membership of the Association shall be subject to the approval of the executive committee.
 (b) The right of vote for an election shall be restricted to the members enlisted one month prior to the date of election.
 (c) A membership card will be issued to all members, who shall produce it when required to do so.

Loss of the card shall be reported immediately to the General Secretary when a new card will be issued on payment of 1/-.

5. MANAGEMENT AND ELECTION:

The management of the Association shall be in the hands of an executive committee of twenty-three members including the office bearers. The executive committee will have the right to co-opt up to four members in which case the strength of the executive committee shall be twenty-seven.

6. ELECTION:

(a) All office bearers and the members of the executive committee shall be elected at the annual general meeting of the Association and shall hold office for a period of one year.

(b)   A retiring member or office-bearer shall be eligible for re-election.

(b)   The procedure of the election shall be decided by the executive committee.

7. BYE-ELECTION:

(a) A casual vacancy shall be filled at an ordinary general meeting of the Association within a reasonable time. The proceedings of the executive committee shall not be invalidated by reason of any vacancy so long as there is a quorum.

(b) The executive committee shall have the right to co-opt up to four members to the executive committee to fill up the vacancies in lieu of bye-elections. All such co-options shall be subject to ratification by next ordinary general meeting. In case of non-ratification fresh bye-election shall take place at the same general meeting. The notice convening this meeting shall inform the members of this contigency.

(c) In the event of President's, the General Secretary's or the Financial Secretary's office falling vacant, bye-election shall be held at the ordinary general meeting only.

8. Resolutions passed by the executive committee can be thrown out by the decision of an extra-ordinary general meeting.

9. Permission to celebrate any festivals will be given by the executive committee.

10. All office bearers of the Association shall be honorary.

11. THERE WILL BE FOLLOWING OFFICE BEARERS: -

(a)   PRESIDENT: shall have the general supervision of the affairs of the Association; shall preside at meetings; shall cause the rules of the Association to be put in force and will be responsible for the management of the affairs of the Association.

(b) VICE-PRESIDENT: shall assist the president and in his absence shall act for him.

(c) GENERAL SECRETARY: shall conduct general correspondence; shall convene meetings; shall give effect to the resolutions passed; shall have general supervision over the work of office bearers, sub committees and over the Granthi's affairs; shall be responsible for planning, programme organisation and discipline of the Association; shall call progress reports from other office-bearers and shall prepare the general report for presentation at and approval by the Annual General Meeting.

(d) ASSISTANT GENERAL SECRETARY: shall assist the General Secretary in the discharge of his duties and in his absence shall act for him; shall send notices and circulars of all meetings and shall be responsible for the maintenance of records of minutes and standing orders; shall keep records of all the correspondence.

(e) FINANCE SECRETARY: shall keep all the accounts and conduct correspondence regarding accounts; shall ensure that every sum is paid to the Association's Bankers; shall pay all the bills and shall prepare financial reports.

(f) ASSISTANT FINANCE SECRETARY: shall assist the Finance Secretary and in his absence shall act for him; shall collect the subscriptions with the help of group leaders.

(g) LITERATURE SECRETARY: shall be in charge of the Library; shall procure books, magazines and newspapers; shall be in charge of the educational activities; shall act as a missionary.

(h) PROPAGANDA SECRETARY: shall endeavour to popularise the ideals of the Association; shall be in charge of the public relations.

(i) AUDITORS: shall audit the accounts quarterly and submit their report to the executive committee; shall suggest the system of keeping proper books; shall prepare an annual report which shall be submitted along with the annual financial report in the annual general meeting.

12. If it is deemed necessary, additional office bearers shall be elected or sub-committees formed either at general meeting or at the executive meeting.

13. The executive committee shall have the power to re-define the duties of various office bearers.

14. EMPLOYERS.

(a) The executive committee shall have the right to employ a GRANTHI who shall work under the terms agreed between him and the executive committee.

(b) The executive committee has the right to employ such other personnel as may be considered necessary.

15. MEETINGS.

Meetings of the Association shall be convened by the General Secretary and shall be either: -

(a) Ordinary general meetings: held regularly not less than four times over a period of one year, or

(b) Extra-ordinary general meetings: to discuss matters of vital importance to the Association involving changes in the constitution, disciplinary action, etc., or

(c) Annual General Meetings: to be held once a year on or about the expiry of the term of the office bearers, or

(d) Ordinary executive committee meetings: held regularly not less than eight times over a period of one year, or

(e) Emergency meetings, Executive committee or General: to discuss matters needing urgent attention.

16. QUORUM.

(a) At all general meetings, twenty members or one fifth of the total strength of the Association, whichever is less, shall form a quorum.

(b) At Executive committee meetings half of its strength shall form a quorum.

17. NOTICE.

(a) A notice of every meeting shall be sent to every member concerned.

(b) A notice of seven days shall be necessary in case of ordinary meeting (executive or general) and annual general meetings, a notice of three days for emergency meetings and a notice of fourteen days for extra-ordinary general meetings.

18. (a) The decision of extra-ordinary general meetings will be valid only if a two-third majority of the members present vote for them. At all other meetings simple numerical majority of votes shall suffice.

(b) The President shall have a casting vote.

19. The chair shall be taken by the President, or in his absence by the Vice-President

20. The General Secretary shall call a meeting when requested (in writing) to do so by fifteen members. The requisitionists shall state specially the purpose of such request. In the event of the General Secretary's refusal to call a meeting, the President may be requested to do so.

21. The minutes of the proceedings of each meeting shall be read at the next meeting and when accepted as correct, shall be counter-signed by the chairman of the meeting.

22. No question of any kind other than that which either arises out of the minutes of the proceedings of the last meeting or appears on the agenda can be discussed except with the permission of the chairman of the meeting.

23. PUBLICITY.

The proceeding of the meeting of the Association shall not be open to the press except with the permission of the President.

24. The executive committee may decide to hold lectures, debates, discussions or other social functions concerning the ideals of the Association and invite outsiders to speak on such occasion.

25. ACCOUNTS. (Lloyds Bank Limited, Park Row, Leeds) or any other Banker decided by the executive committee will act as Association's Bankers.

26. All cheques issued by the Association shall be signed by two out of three: President, General Secretary, Finance Secretary.

27. Important papers and documents belonging to the Association may be deposited with the Bankers of the Association.

28. The Finance Secretary will not keep more than £20 in cash in hand without the special sanction of the executive committee.

29. The President and the General Secretary shall have the power to spend in case of urgency up to £10 and £5 at a time respectively and a total of £30 per year, and can sanction bills of the same amount.

30. The bills exceeding £10 shall be sanctioned by the executive committee.

31. The executive committee shall not invest any money or dispose of any property unless the approval is secured in a general meeting.

32. USES OF PREMISES. The Gurdwara or any part thereof cannot be converted into a place for business unless approved by a resolution passed in a general meeting.

33. The Granthi shall make a reasonable charge for the goods deposited in the store-room by any person.

34. Smoking, drinking and gambling on the Association's premises shall be strictly prohibited.

35. BREACH OF DICIPLINE, TERMINATION OF SERVICES, ETC.
Prompt disciplinary action shall be taken against any member guilty of a breach of discipline of the Association or any other misconduct.

36. The Association shall have the power to suspend and/or to punish (dun) any member of the Association and to terminate the services of any of its office bearers or members of the executive committee provided that:-
(a) An extra-ordinary general meeting of the Association is convened.
(b) The allegations are discussed in the presence of both the accuser and the accused. If one party is absent without valid reason the decision shall be given ex-party.
(c) Votes are taken by ballot.

37. Any member of the Association once discharged cannot hold office at any other time in future unless or otherwise decided to the contrary by an extra-ordinary general meeting.

38. The outgoing officers of Association shall be deemed to continue in office till the election of their successors.

39. Every member shall leave with the General Secretary his or her address and it shall be his or her responsibility to inform of any change.

40. LIBRARY.
(a) Library shall be for the use of its members.
(b) All the members of the United Sikh Association shall be the members of the Library.
(c) Non-member of the Association may become members of the Library on payment of an annual subscription of 2/6d.

41. VISITORS.
All visitors shall sign in the visitors' book kept at a conspicuous place.

42. AMEMDMENTS.
No proposal to alter, add to or amend the constitution shall be deemed to have been adopted unless passed at an extra-ordinary general meeting.

43. DISPLAYING THE CONSTITUTION.

Every member of the Association shall be entitled to a copy of the constitution of the Association at the nominal cost of 6d.

44. One copy of the constitution shall be displayed at an easily accessible place for the information of the members and the visitors.

45. This is a purely non-political Association.

46. RULES OF DEBATE.
Minutes passed as true record and signed by the President stand for six months and cannot be discussed or altered before the expiry of six months. No person may speak twice on the same subject, except the proposer in explanation to the opposition.

Signed by the President
(Mr. Balwant Singh)

3 Savile Road, Leeds 7.

The following amendments to the Constitution took care of the problems faced by Executive Committees in the past. The second revised edition of the Constitution was printed in 1965 in English. The exact wording of the Constitution is given and the original format of the wording is also retained.

The Revised Constitution

ੴ

THE SIKH TEMPLE
LEEDS

*

CONSTITUTION
2nd. Edition 1965

*

281a CHAPELTOWN ROAD
LEEDS 7, Yorks.

CONSTITUTION

1. NAME:-
This Society will be known by the name of "The Sikh Temple, Leeds" (hereinafter called "The Temple").

2. AIMS AND OBJECTS:-
(a) To advance the Sikh religion, and in furtherance of that object to

    (i) provide a building or buildings for use as a Temple for public worship.

    (ii) to celebrate the principal Sikh religious festivals.

(b) To advance education in the principles of the faith of the Sikh religion by:-

    (i) the propagation of the teaching of "Guru Nanak"

    (ii) maintaining a library and reading room (subject to the conditions of Section 40

(iii) encouraging and promoting the study of the Sikh religion amongst its members by religious and social intercourse.

(c) To relieve poverty by the provision of financial assistance to the needy members of the Temple.

The Temple may do any other act which is incidental to the attainment of these objects but nothing that would result in the use of the funds of the Temple for anything which is not legally charitable.

3. MEMBERSHIP AND RIGHT:-
Any person irrespective of cast, creed, colour, religion or nationality can become a member of the Society and the members shall be either:
(a) Ordinary full member. Those persons who pay an annual subscription of £1.0.0 by one or more instalments
(b) Life members. The persons who pay a sum of £10.0.0 in one instalment.

4. (a) The membership of the Temple shall be subject to the approval of the executive committee.
(b) The right of vote for an election shall be restricted to the members enlisted one month prior to the date of election.
(c) A membership card will be issued to all members, who shall produce it when required to do so.
Loss of the card shall be reported immediately to the General Secretary when a new card will be issued on payment of 1/-.

5. MANAGEMENT AND ELECTION.
The management of the Temple shall be in the hands of an executive committee of twenty-three members including the office bearers. The executive committee will have the right to co-opt up to four members in which case the strength of the executive committee shall be twenty-seven.

6. ELECTION.
(a) All office bearers and the members of the executive committee shall

be elected at the annual general meeting of the Temple and shall hold office for a period of one year. A retiring member or office-bearer shall be eligible for re-election.

(b) The procedure of the election shall be decided by the executive committee.

7. BYE-ELECTION.

(a) A casual vacancy shall be filled at an ordinary general meeting of the Temple within a reasonable time. The proceedings of the executive committee shall not be invalidated by reason of any vacancy so long as there is a quorum.

(b) The executive committee shall have the right to co-opt up to four members to the executive committee to fill up the vacancies in lieu of bye-elections. All such co-options shall be subject to ratification by next ordinary general meeting. In case of non-ratification fresh bye-election shall take place at the same general meeting. The notice convening this meeting shall inform the members of this contingency.

(c) In the event of President's, the General Secretary's or the Financial Secretary's office falling vacant, bye-election shall be held at the ordinary general meeting only.

8. **R**esolutions passed by the executive committee can be thrown out by the decision of an extra-ordinary general meeting.

9. **P**ermission to celebrate any festivals will be given by the executive committee.

10. **All** office bearers of the Temple shall be honorary.

11. THERE WILL BE FOLLOWING OFFICE BEARERS:-

(a) PRESIDENT: shall have the general supervision of the affairs of the Temple; shall preside at meetings; shall cause the rules of the Temple to be put in force and will be responsible for the management of the affairs of the Temple.

(b) VICE-PRESIDENT: shall assist the president and in his absence shall act for him.

(c) GENERAL SECRETARY: shall conduct general correspondence, shall convene meetings; shall give effect to the resolutions passed; shall have general supervision over the work of office bearers, sub-committees and over the Granthi's affairs; shall be responsible for planning, programme organisation and discipline of the Temple; shall call progress reports from other office bearers and shall prepare the general report for presentation at and approval by the Annual General Meeting.

(d) ASSISTANT GENERAL SECRETARY: shall assist the General Secretary in the discharge of his duties and in his absence shall act for him; shall send notices and circulars of all meetings and shall be responsible for the maintenance of records of minutes and standing orders; shall keep records of all the correspondence.

(e) FINANCE SECRETARY: shall keep all the accounts and conduct correspondence regarding accounts; shall ensure that every sum is paid to the Temple's Bankers; shall pay all the bills and shall prepare financial reports.

(f) ASSISTANT FINANCE SECRETARY: shall assist the Finance Secretary and in his absence shall act for him; shall collect the subscriptions with the help of group leaders.

(g) LITERATURE SECRETARY; shall be in charge of the Library, shall procure books, magazine and newspapers; shall be in charge of educational activities ; shall act as a missionary.

(h) PROPAGANDA SECRETARY: shall endeavour to popularise the ideals of the Temple; shall be in charge of the public relations.

(i) AUDITORS: shall audit the accounts quarterly and submit their report to the executive committee; shall suggest the system of keeping proper books; shall prepare an annual report which shall be submitted along with the annual financial report in the annual general meeting.

12. If it is deemed necessary, additional office bearers shall be elected or sub-committees formed either at general meeting or at the executive meeting.

13. The executive committee shall have power to re-define the duties of various office bearers.

14. EMPLOYERS.
(a) The executive committee shall have the right to employ a GRANTHI who shall work under the terms agreed between him and the executive committee.
(b) The executive committee has the right to employ such other personnel as may be considered necessary.

15. MEETINGS.
Meetings of the Temple shall be convened by the General Secretary and shall be either:-
(a) Ordinary general meetings: held regularly not less than four times over a period of one year, or
(b) Extra-ordinary general meetings: to discuss matters of vital importance to the Temple involving changes in the constitution, disciplinary action, etc., or
(c) Annual General Meetings: to be held once a year on or about the expiry of the term of the office bearers, or
(d) Ordinary executive committee meetings: held regularly not less than eight times over a period of one year, or
(e) Emergency meetings, Executive committee or General: to discuss matters needing urgent attention.

16. QUORUM.
(a) At all general meetings 45 members of the Temple shall form a quorum.
(b) At Executive committee meetings half of its strength shall form a quorum.

17. NOTICE.
(a) A notice of every meeting shall be sent to every member concerned.

(b) A notice of seven days shall be necessary in case of ordinary meeting (executive or general) and annual general meetings, a notice of three days for emergency meetings and a notice of fourteen days for extraordinary general meetings.

18. (a) The decisions of extra-ordinary general meetings will be valid only if a two-third majority of the members present vote for them. At all other meetings simple numerical majority of votes shall suffice.
(b) The president shall have a casting vote.

19. The chair shall be taken by the President, or in his absence by the Vice-President.

20. The General Secretary shall call a meeting when requested (in writing) to do so by fifteen members. The requisitionists shall state specially the purpose of such request. In the event of the General Secretary's refusal to call a meeting, the President may be requested to do so.

21. The minutes of the proceedings of each meeting shall be read at the next meeting and when accepted as correct, shall be counter-signed by the chairman of the meeting.

22. No question of any kind other than that which either arises out of the minutes of the proceedings of the last meeting or appears on the agenda can be discussed except with the permission of the chairman of the meeting.

23. PUBLICITY.
Proceedings of the meeting of the Temple shall not be open to the press except with the permission of the Executive Committee. In the case of a decision being required with insufficient time to call a meeting of the full Executive Committee at least 5 members of the Executive Committee may unanimously grant such permission.

24. The executive committee may decide to hold lectures, debates, discussions or other social functions concerning the ideals of the Temple and invite outsiders to speak on such occasion.

25. ACCOUNTS. (Lloyds Bank Limited, Park Road, Leeds) or any other Banker decided by the executive committee will act as Temple's Bankers.

26. All cheques issued by the Temple shall be signed by three: President, General Secretary, Finance Secretary.

27. Important papers and documents belonging to the Temple may be deposited with the Bankers of the Temple.

28. The Finance Secretary will not keep more than £20 in cash in hand without the special sanction of the executive committee.

29. The President and the General Secretary shall have the power to spend in case of urgency up to £10 and £5 at a time respectively and a total of £30 per year, and can sanction bills of the same amount.

30. The bills exceeding £10 shall be sanctioned by the executive committee.

31. The executive committee shall not invest any money or dispose of any property unless the approval is secured in a general meeting.

32. USE OF PREMISES. The Gurdwara or any part thereof cannot be converted into a place of business unless approved by a resolution passed in a general meeting.

33. Money collected by any member on behalf of the Temple must be deposited in the Temple's Bank Account through the Finance Secretary within 14 days of such money being collected.

34. Smoking, drinking and gambling on the Temple's premises shall be strictly prohibited.

35. BREACH OF DISCIPLINE, TERMINATION OF SERVICES, ETC.

Prompt disciplinary action shall be taken against any member guilty of a breach of discipline of the Temple or any other misconduct.

36. (i) **The** Temple shall have the power to suspend and /or to punish (dun) any member of the Temple and to terminate the services of any of its office bearers or members of the executive committee provided that:-

    (a) An extra-ordinary general meeting of the Temple is convened.
    (b) The allegations are discussed in the presence of both the accuser and the accused. If one party is absent without valid reason the decision shall be given ex-party.
    (c) Votes are taken by ballot.

(ii) Any executive member who fails to attend two consecutive meetings of the Executive Committee shall be asked by the Secretary for his explanation. If such member who fails to attend a third consecutive meeting and should not give reasonable explanation for his non-attendance, he shall thenceforth no longer be a member of the Executive Committee, and shall be replaced by a new member of the Executive Committee who shall be elected at a by-election to be held as soon thereafter as is possible.

37. Any member of the Temple once discharged cannot hold office at any other time in future unless or otherwise decided to the contrary by an extra-ordinary general meeting.

38. The outgoing officers of Temple shall be deemed to continue in office till the election of their successors.

39. Every member shall leave with the General Secretary his or her address and it shall be his or her responsibility to inform of any change.

40. LIBRARY.
(a) Library shall be for the use of its members.
(b) All the members of the Sikh Temple shall be the members of the Library.

(c) Non-members of the Temple may become members of the Library on payment of an annual subscription of 2/6d.

41. VISITORS.
All visitors shall sign in the visitors' book kept at a conspicuous place.

42. AMENDMENTS.
No proposals to alter, add to or amend the constitution shall be deemed to have been adopted unless passed at an extra-ordinary general meeting. Provided that no such amendment should result in the Temple applying its income for purposes which are not charitable.

43. DISPLAYING THE CONSTITUTION.
Every member of the Temple shall be entitled to a copy of the constitution of the Temple at the nominal cost of 6d.

44. One copy of the constitution shall be displayed at an easily accessible place for the information of the members and the visitors.

45. This is a purely non-political Temple.

46. RULES OF DEBATE.
Minutes passed as true record and signed by the President stand for six months and cannot be discussed or altered before the expiry of six months. No person may speak twice on the same subject, except the proposer in explanation to the opposition.

47. There shall be four trustees of the Temple who shall be ex-officio members of the committee. The first trustees shall be appointed by the committee and the property of the Temple (other than cash which shall be under the control of the treasurer) shall be vested in them to be dealt with by them as the committee shall from time to time direct by a resolution (of which an entry in the Minute Book shall be conclusive evidence). The trustees shall be indemnified against risk and expense out of the Temple property. The trustees shall hold office by a resolution of the committee who may for any reason which may seem sufficient to a majority of them present and voting at any meeting remove any trustee or trustees from the office of trustee. If by reason of such death resignation or removal it shall appear necessary to the committee that a new trustee or trustees shall be appointed or if the committee shall deem it expedient to appoint an additional trustee or additional trustees the committee shall by resolution nominate the person or persons to be appointed by the new trustee or trustees. For the purpose of giving effect to such nomination the president is hereby nominated as the person to appoint new trustees of the Temple and in the meaning of Section 36 of the Trustees Act 1925 and he shall by deed duly appoint the person or persons so nominated by the committee as the new trustee or trustees of the Temple and the provisions of the Trustee Act 1925 shall apply to any such appointment. Any statement of fact in any such deed of appointment shall in favour of a person dealing bona-fide and for value with the Temple or the committee be conclusive evidence of the facts so stated.

48. If at any time the Temple in general meeting shall pass a resolution authorising the committee to borrow money the committee shall thereupon be empowered to borrow for the purpose of the Temple such amount of money either at one time or from time to time and at such rate of interest and in such form and manner and upon such security as shall be specified in such resolution, and thereupon, the trustees shall at the discretion of the committee make all such dispositions of the Temple's property or any part thereof and enter into such agreements in relation thereto as the committee may deem proper for giving security for such loans and interest. All members of the Temple whether voting on such resolution or not, and all persons becoming members of the Temple after the passing of such resolution, shall be deemed to have assented to the same as if they had voted in favour of such resolution.

Signed by the Chairman
The Sikh Temple
281a, Chapeltown Road, Leeds 7

There were a number of discussions concerning this second edition of the Constitution and further suggestions were made. Some amendments were also unanimously agreed but it was not until 1988 that a final version of the Constitution was printed. There are some numbers missing in the Constitution which are added and put within brackets. The original form of the third edition of the Constitution is as follows:

The Constitution printed in 1988

CONSTITUTION

The
Sikh Temple

281A Chapeltown Road, Leeds 7. Tel. 629073

CONSTITUTION
The Sikh Temple, 28la Chapeltown Road, Leeds 7

Passed 15th January 1988

1. **NAME:**

This society will be known by the name of "The Sikh Temple" Leeds (hereafter called the "Gurdwara")

2. **AIMS AND OBJECT.**
2.1 To advance the Sikh religion in furtherance of that object to:–
2.1.1. Provide a building or buildings for use as a Gurdwara for public worship
2.1.2. To celebrate the principal Sikh religious festivals
2.2 To advance education in the principles of the Sikh religion by:-
2.2.1 Propagating the teaching of the Ten Gurus and Sri Guru Granth Sahib
2.2.2 Maintaining a library and reading room (subject to the conditions of section 11.2 hereof)
2.2.3 Encouraging and promoting the study of the Sikh religion amongst the public by religious and social cultural dialogue
2.3 To relieve poverty by the provision of financial assistance to needy members of the Gurdwara
2.4 The Gurdwara may do any other act which is incidental to the attainment of these objects but nothing that would result in the use of funds of the Gurdwara for anything which is not legally charitable

3. **MEMBERSHIP AND RIGHTS**

3.1 Any person aged eighteen or above irrespective of sex caste colour or nationality may become a member of the Gurdwara provided he believes in the teachings of the Ten Gurus and acknowledges the holy Guru Granth Sahib and he does not adhere to any other religion
3.2 Members shall be either a
3.2.1 Ordinary full member (who shall pay an annual subscription of one pound) or
3.2.2 Life member (who shall pay a sum of ten pounds in one instalment)
3.3 The rates of subscription mentioned in sub paragraph 3.2 here-

of may be altered or amended by an ordinary resolution of a General Meeting of the Gurdwara

3.4 Application for membership shall be made on an officially approved form and shall be subject to the approval of the Executive Committee

3.5 The right to vote in an election shall be restricted to those with approved and valid membership status at noon of Baisakhi day celebration in Leeds i.e Baisakhi celebration in the Gurdwara

3.6 Ordinary membership shall be for a year namely from 1st April to 31st of March and shall give the member the right to vote at general meetings held within that year.

3.7 A membership card will be issued to each member who shall produce it when required so to do

3.8 The loss of a membership card must be reported immediately to the General Secretary when a new card will be issued on payment of 50 pence

4. MANAGEMENT

The management of the Gurdwara shall be in the hands of an Executive Committee of 27 members including the office bearers. In the event of the total membership of the Executive Committee ceasing to hold office for any reason whatsoever at one time the Trustees shall be deemed to be the Executive Committee provided that they shall within two months of assuming office call an Extra-Ordinary General Meeting in order that a new Executive Committee may be elected.

5. ELECTION

5.1. All members of the Executive Committee shall be elected with in four weeks after the Annual General Meeting of the Gurdwara and shall hold office for a period of one year

5.2. The procedure of the election shall be proposed by the Executive Committee and presented for approval at the Annual General Meeting

5.3. Nominations for election to the Executive Committee shall be invited on an official form and shall be open for two weeks prior to the date of the election and shall close at twelve noon on the last day prior to the date of the election. The approved forms shall be serially numbered and at the time of the closing the list of nominations the names of the nominees shall be announced in the Sangat

5.4. The President, the General Secretary and the Treasurer shall not hold their respective offices for more than two consecutive years and any of the said officers who shall have completed two consecutive years' service as such may not, until the expiry of a further year, seek election to either of the offices. If the President, the General Secretary or the Treasurer shall fail to be re-elected to the Executive Committee they or any of them may be co-opted as ex-officio members of the Executive Committee without the right to vote

5.5. The Executive Committee shall have the right to fill any vacancy amongst its members including the Office Bearers.

6. **OFFICE BEARERS**

6.1 All Office Bearers of the Gurdwara shall be honorary.

6.2 There shall be the following Office Bearers who shall be elected from amongst and by a majority of the Executive Committee:–

6.2.1 The PRESIDENT who shall have the general supervision of the Gurdwara; shall preside at all meetings; shall cause the rules of the Gurdwara to be enforced and shall be responsible for the management of the affairs of the Gurdwara

6.2.2 The VICE PRESIDENT who shall assist the President and in his absence shall act for him

6.2.3 The GENERAL SECRETARY who shall conduct general correspondence; shall convene meetings; shall give effect to resolutions passed; shall have general supervision over the work of other Office Bearers and over the sub-committees and over the Granthi's affairs; shall be responsible for planning, programme organisation and discipline of the Gurdwara; shall call for progress reports from the Office Bearers and shall prepare the general reports for presentation at and approval by the Annual

General Meeting

6.2.4 The ASSISTANT GENERAL SECRETARIES. There shall be two assistant general secretaries who shall assist the general secretary in the discharge of his duties and in his absence shall jointly act for him; shall send notices and circulars of all meetings and be responsible for the maintenance of records, of minutes and standing orders; shall keep records of all the correspondence

6.2.5 The TREASURER who shall keep all the accounts; shall ensure that every sum is paid to the Gurdwara's Bankers; shall pay all the bills and prepare financial reports

6.2.6 The ASSISTANT TREASURERS: There shall be two assistant treasurers who shall assist the Treasurer and in his absence shall jointly act for him.

6.2.7 The RELIGIOUS SECRETARY who shall in co-operation with the General Secretary organise all religious debates and services in the Gurdwara

6.2.8 The LIBRARIAN who shall be in charge of the library, shall procure books, magazines and newspapers

6.2.9 The EDUCATION SECRETARY who shall be in charge of the educational needs of the Gurdwara

6.2.10 The ASSISTANT EDUCATION SECRETARY who shall assist the Education Secretary

6.2.11 The PUBLIC RELATIONS SECRETARY who shall endeavour to popularize the ideals of the Gurdwara and take charge of public relations

6.2.12 The AUDITOR who shall audit the accounts whenever he may wish (but no later than three months prior to the Annual General Meetings) in consultation with the Treasurer and submit reports thereon to the Executive Committee and to General Meetings

6.3 No person shall be elected as President, Treasurer or General Secretary unless such person shall have served for two years as a member of the Executive Committee which said period shall not necessarily be made up of two continuous or consecutive years services

6.4 There shall be following additional Office Bearers appointed by the Executive Committee:-

6.4.1 The EXTERNAL AUDITOR who shall be elected by the Executive Committee but who shall not be a member of the Executive Committee, shall audit the accounts of the Gurdwara independently and submit a report thereon to the Executive Committee prior to presenting the same to a General Meeting

6.4.2 Additional Office Bearers and Sub-Committees
If it is deemed necessary additional Office Bearers shall be elected from within the Executive Committee. Sub-Committees may be formed either at Executive or General Meetings. General Members shall be encouraged and invited to serve on the Sub-Committees

6.5 The President, General Secretary, Treasurer, Religious Secretary Public Relations Secretary and Trustees and all members of the Executive Committee must be Amrit- dhari Sikhs

7. GENERAL POWERS AND MATTERS RELATING TO THE EXECUTIVE COMMITTEE

7.1 Resolutions passed by the Executive Committee may be reversed or amended by the decision of an Extra-Ordinary General Meeting or by the Annual General Meeting

7.2 Permission to celebrate any festival may only be given by the Executive Committee

8. EMPLOYEES

The Executive shall have the right to employ or remove GRANTHI, RAAGIS and such other personnel as may be considered necessary

9. MEETINGS

9.1 Meetings of the Gurdwara or the Executive shall be convened by the General Secretary and shall be either:

9.1.1 Ordinary General Meetings which shall be held at mid term of the office of the Executive Committee, or

9.1.2 The Annual General Meeting which shall be held once a year on the second Sunday after the Baisakhi celebration day in the Gurdwara

9.1.3 An Extra-Ordinary General Meeting which may be called to discuss matters of vital importance to the Gurdwara involving changes in the constitutions, disciplinary actions etc.,

9.1.4 Ordinary Executive Committee Meetings which shall be held regularly and not less than eight times during a period of one year, or

9.1.5 Emergency Meetings (whether Executive or General) which shall be held to discuss matters needing urgent attention

9.2 The General Secretary shall call an Extra-Ordinary General Meeting when requested in writing to do so by the numbers equivalent to the quorum of the relevant body. The requisionists shall state specifically the purpose of such request. In the event of the General Secretary refusing or failing to call a meeting within one month of the date of the requisition the President may call such a meeting

9.3 Notice

9.3.1 Notice in writing of every meeting other than an Emergency Meeting shall be given to the members concerned

9.3.2 Seven days notice shall be necessary for an ordinary Executive or General Meeting and of the Annual General Meeting, Twenty four hours notice shall be given for Emergency Meetings and fourteen days notice shall be given for Extra Ordinary General Meetings.

9.4 Quorum

9.4.1 The Quorum for all General Meetings shall be fifty. In case the said quorum is not reached at the said General Meeting, the meeting shall be automatically adjourned to the same time fourteen days thereafter when the members present shall constitute a quorum

9.4.2 At an Executive Committee Meeting fourteen shall form a quorum

[9.5 Minutes]

9.5.1 Minutes of the proceedings of each meeting shall be kept and shall be read at the next meeting of that body and when accepted as correct shall be signed by the chairman of the meeting and countersigned by the secretary of the meeting

9.5.2 Minutes passed as a true record and signed by the President or chairman stand for six months and cannot be questioned or altered but this shall be without prejudice to the right of any member to re-raise the matter at a subsequent General Meeting thereafter

9.6 Rules of debate

9.6.1 No person may speak twice on any one item of the agenda except the proposer in winding up to answer the opposition

9.6.2 No matter other than that which either arises out of the minutes of the proceedings of the last meeting or appears on the agenda can be discussed except with the permission of the chairman of the meeting

9.7 Voting on Resolutions

9.7.1 Decisions of Extra-Ordinary General Meetings shall be valid only if passed by a two thirds majority of the members present and voting. At all other meetings a simple numerical majority of votes shall suffice

9.7.2 In the event of an equality of votes the President shall have a second and casting vote

9.8 AMENDMENTS: No proposals to alter, add to or amend the constitution shall be deemed to have been adopted unless passed at an Extra Ordinary General Meeting provided that no amendment shall be made which would cause the Gurdwara to cease to be a charity in law

[9.9 Press and Media]

9.9.1 Proceedings of the meetings of the Gurdwara shall not be open to the press or other media except with the permission of the Executive Committee

9.9.2 In case of an Office Bearer wishing to make a Press statement the permission of the Executive Committee shall first be obtained but if there is insufficient time to call a meeting of the full Executive Committee, at least five members of the Executive Committee including the President or Vice President and General Secretary may unanimously grant such permission

9.10 The Executive Committee may decide to hold lectures, debates, discussions or other social functions concerning the ideals of the Gurdwara and invite outsiders to speak on such occasions

10. FUNDS

10.1 The Bank Account of the Gurdwara shall be kept with such Bank or Banks as shall be decided by the Executive Committee from time to time

10.2 All cheques issued on behalf of the Gurdwara shall be signed by the President, General Secretary and the Treasurer

10.3 All important papers and documents belonging to the Gurdwara may be deposited with the Bank and/or Solicitors to the Gurdwara

10.4 The President and the General Secretary collectively shall have the power to spend in case or urgency up to two hundred pounds without the prior approval of the Executive Committee

10.5 The Executive Committee shall have the power to sanction payments of up to two thousand five hundred pounds on a single or combination of items of a non recurring nature in a committee year

10.6 The Treasurer may not retain more then one hundred pounds in cash in hand without the special sanction of the Executive Committee

10.7 The Executive Committee shall not invest any money or dispose of any property unless approval is first secured in general meeting

10.8 Money collected by an authorised member on behalf of the Gurdwara must be deposited in the Bank Account of the Gurdwara through the Treasurer within fourteen days of such money being collected.

11 **RULES GOVERNING THE USE OF THE PREMISES**

11.1 The Gurdwara or any part thereof cannot be converted into a place of busines unless approved by a resolution in a general meeting and unless the prior approval in writing of the Charity Commissioner has first been obtained

11.2 Library

11.2.1. All the members of the Gurdwara shall be the members of the library

11.2.2. Non-members of the Gurdwara may become a member of the library on payment of an annual subscription of one pound. Non-members of the Gurdwara may borrow one book at a time from the library on payment of a deposit of two pounds or the value of the book which ever is greater

11.3 Smoking, drinking, the consumption and preparation of meat, disorderly behaviour and gambling on the Gurdwara premises is strictly prohibited.

11.4 The premises shall only be used for the aims and objects set forth in Clause 2 hereof

11.5 Any Sikh whatever the degree of his religious observance shall be allowed to take part in all and every aspect of the work, practices and activities of the Gurdwara unless expressly prevented from so doing by the provisions of this Constitution

12. **BREACH OF DISCIPLINE TERMINATION OF SERVICES ETC**

12.1 Prompt disciplinary action shall be taken against any member guilty of a breach of discipline of the Gurdwara or any other misconduct. The Executive Committee shall have the power to suspend and/or punish (Dun) any member or a visitor to or congregant in the Gurdwara and to terminate the services of any of its Office Bearers or members of its Executive Committee provided that

12.1.1 An Extra Ordinary General Meeting of the Gurdwara is convened

12.1.2 The allegations are discussed in the presence of both the accuser and the accused. If one party is absent without valid reason the decision shall be given ex parte

12.1.3 Voting on the issue is taken by ballot

12.2 Any member of the Gurdwara once discharged, suspended or punished cannot become a member of the Gurdwara again unless decided to the contrary by an Extra Ordinary General Meeting

12.3 Any Executive Member who fails to attend two consecutive meetings of the Executive Committee shall be asked by the General Secretary for his explanation. If such a member fails to attend a third consecutive meeting and/or is unable to give a reasonable explanation for his non-attendance he shall thenceforth no longer be a member of the Executive Committee for that committee year and shall be replaced

13. **INFORMATION**

Every member shall leave with the General Secretary his address and it shall be his responsibility to inform the General Secretary of any change

14. **TRUSTEES:**

14.1 The property of the Gurdwara shall be held in the names of five individuals as trustees who shall administer the same in all respect in accordance with the direction of the Executive Committee given by way of resolution (of which an entry in the minute book shall be conclusive evidence). The trustee shall be indemnified against all the risk and expense out of the Gurdwara' property. The trustees shall hold office by resolution of the Executive Committee who may for any reason which may seem sufficient to a majority of them present and voting at any meeting remove any trustee or trustees from the office of trustee. If by reason such as death, resignation or removal it shall appear necessary to the Executive Committee that a new trustee should be appointed or if the Executive Committee shall deem it expedient to appoint an additional trustee or trustees the Executive Committee shall by resolution nominate a person or persons who may be appointed as a new trustee or trustees. For the purpose of giving effect to suchnomination the President is hereby nominated as the person to appoint new trustees of the Gurdwara within the meaning of Section 36 of the Trustees Act 1925 and shall by deed duly appoint the person or persons so nominated by the Executive Committee as the new trustee or trustees of the Gurdwara and the provisions of Section 40 of the Trustee Act 1925 shall apply to any such appointment. Any statement of fact in any such deed of appointment shall in favour of any person dealing bona fide and for value with the Gurdwara or the Executive Committee be conclusive of the facts so stated

14.2 Borrowing Powers

If at any time a General Meeting shall pass a resolution authorising the committee to borrow money the committee shall thereupon be empowered to borrow for the purpose of the Gurdwara such amount of money either at one time or from time totime and at such rate of interest and in such form and manner and upon such security as shall be specified in such resolution and thereupon the trustees shall at the discretion of the committee make all such dispositions of the Gurdwara's property or any part thereof and enter into such agreements in relation thereto as the committee may deem proper for giving security for such loans and interest. All members of the Gurdwara whether voting on such resolution or not, and all persons becoming members of the Gurdwara after the passing of such resolution shall be deemed to have assented to the same as if they had voted in favour of such resolution

14.3 The trustees shall be entitled to attend and speak at meetings of the Executive committee but shall not be entitled to vote

15. **OUTSIDE REPRESENTATION**

Any member of the Executive Committee or Office Bearer who is officially designated to represent the Gurdwara at any outside organisation must give a progress report to the Executive Committee in writing without delay. If he fails to report or ceases to represent the Gurdwara he shall be replaced. A non-Keshdhari Sikh may not be nominated by the Executive Committee to represent the Gurdwara at any outside organisation

16. **WINDING UP**

The Gurdwara may at any time be dissolved by a resolution passed by a two thirds majority of those present and voting at an Extra Ordinary General Meeting of which at least 21 days clear notice shall have been given to all members of the Gurdwara. Such resolution may give instructions for the disposal of any assets held by or in the name of the Trustees, provided that if any property remains after the satisfaction of all debts and liabilities, such property shall not be paid to or distributed amongst the members of the Gurdwara but shall be given or transferred to such charitable institution or institutions having objects similar to the Gurdwara as the Executive Committee may, with the approval of the Charity Commissioners, or other authority having charitable jurisdiction, determine

17. INTERPRETATION

In this constitution and where the context so admits the masculine shall include the feminine and the singular include the plural and vice versa

AMENDMENTS

Amendments to the Constitution were regularly discussed and approved though they were not always incorporated in the Constitution. Annotations translated from the Panjabi showing the degree of approval of these amendments are given in parentheses. The major amendments were as follows:

1. **The amendments suggested under the chairmanship of Pritam Singh Q.C. and presented on 27th February 1977 for the consideration of the committee.**

    1. This society will be known by the name 'The Sikh Temple' Leeds here after called (Gurdwara). (Passed unanimously)

    2. (b) (iv) To establish school for the teaching of Panjabi language and literature. (Passed unanimously)

    3. Any person above the age of 18 years may become a member of the Gurdwara provided that he/she believes in the teachings of the ten Gurus and acknowledges the Holy Guru Granth Sahib. (Passed unanimously after some discussion)

4. (a) Application for membership shall be made on the officially approved form and shall be subject to the approval of the Executive Committee.
(b) The right of vote for an election and at General meetings shall be restricted to the approved members.
(c) The ordinary membership shall be for a calendar year i.e. 1st of January to 31st December. (Passed unanimously)

5. The management of the Gurdwara shall be in the hands of the executive committee of 23 members including office bearers. The Executive Committee will have the right to co-opt up to four members whose presence and experience will facilitate the work of the Executive Committee in which case the strength of the Executive Committee shall be 27. All these 27 members shall have the right to vote. (There was a discussion on this and the clause was finally amended to 'The management of the Gurdwara shall be in the hands of an executive committee of 27 members including office bearers'. This was passed unanimously.)

6. (b) The nominations shall be invited on the official form and shall remain open from two weeks prior to the date of election and shall close at 12 noon on the last day.

The forms shall be serially numbered and at the time of closing the names of the applicants shall be announced in the sangat stating which of the forms have been handed in and which have not been handed in.

If the outgoing President, General Secretary and the Treasurer fail to be re-elected to the new Executive Committee they may be co-opted as ex-officio members of the Executive Committee without the right to vote.

The President, General Secretary and Treasurer shall not hold their respective offices for more than two years at a time and the exchange of portfolios shall not entitle them to hold any of the above mentioned offices for another year. (Passed unanimously)

11. (a) There shall be two Assistant General Secretaries.

(f) There shall be two Assistant Finance Secretaries

(h) [There shall be an] Education Secretary. (Passed unanimously)

16. The quorum of all General Meetings shall be determined by the number of members on the register on 31st January. It shall be 1/5 of such number of members. In case the said quorum is not reached at the said General Meeting, it shall be automatically adjourned to the same time 14 days hence when it shall be lawfully held with or without a quorum. (Passed unanimously after some discussion)

29. The President and the General Secretary, collectively, shall have the power to spend in case of urgency up to £20 and £10 at a time respectively, subject to a total of £60 per year and can sanction extraordinary bills of the same amount. (Passed unanimously)

30. (a) The bills exceeding £20 shall be sanctioned by the Executive Committee.
(b) An Executive Committee shall have the power to sanction new payments of up to £1,000 on a single or a combination of items of non-recurring nature in a calendar year. (Passed unanimously)

36. (a) The Executive Committee shall have the power to suspend any member of the Gurdwara with a two-third majority of the Executive members present for a specific period not more than 2 years.

The suspension shall be notified to the member by hand or recorded delivery post.

(b) A suspended member shall be entitled to appeal against the decision of the Executive Committee, within 14 days of the date of posting of the letter of suspension to the Board of Trustees. If such an appeal is not lodged within 14 days the decision of the Executive Committee will stand.

(c) The Board of Trustees shall consider any appeal lodged within 14 days. They may confirm, vary or remove the suspension and their majority decision shall be final and binding on the Executive Committee. (These clauses were not accepted)

40. Non-members of the Gurdwara may borrow one book at a time from the library on payment of a deposit of £2, or the value of the book borrowed, whichever is the greater. (Passed unanimously)

47. There shall be five trustees of the Gurdwara. The Trustee shall hold office by a resolution of the Executive Committee, who may appoint a trustee for any period not exceeding 5 years. Within such period the trustees shall hold office until death or resignation or until removed for good reason from office by a resolution of a majority of the Executive Committee. Such a Trustee shall not have any right of appeal whatsoever. Every year one Trustee shall be elected by the ex-committee [Executive Committee] and the retiring Trustee shall not be eligible for election for 3 years after retirement or removal. In the event of a trustee having been removed, the ex-committee [Executive Committee] shall fill the vacancy forthwith. The removal of a Trustee by the resolution of the majority of the Executive Committee or the death or the resignation of a Trustee during the period of a new Trustee shall be announced in the Sangat. (This was passed by a two-thirds majority)

Auditor shall be elected by the Executive Committee and will not be a member of the Executive Committee. (Passed unanimously)

Asst. Auditor can be elected from the Executive Committee. Shall check on taking office, the inventory of the effects of the Gurdwara and the stock of consumable stores and do the same one month before the next election and place his records thereof before the Executive Committee. (Passed unanimously)

If it is necessary additional office bearers shall be elected. This should be done at general meeting called for the purpose, but the Executive Committee may appoint sub-committees for any necessary purpose.

The President shall submit his draft budget for the year of his office to the Executive Committee for approval, in the first Executive Committee meeting. (Passed unanimously)

School - School shall be managed by a sub-committee, who shall appoint a suitable person as the Education Secretary to implement its policies, which shall be subject to approval by the Executive Committee.

Education Secretary shall report all matters including Budget concerning school to the sub-committee who shall obtain sanction on all financial matters. (Passed unanimously)

Any Sikh member or office bearer who is officially designated to represent the Gurdwara at any outside organisation must give a progress report to the Executive Committee in writing form without delay. If he omits to be the representative or fails to report, he shall be replaced. A non keshadhari Sikh cannot be nominated by the Executive Committee to represent at any outside organisation.

All office bearers and trustees elected shall be keshadhari Sikhs. A Non-keshadhari Sikh can be elected on Executive Committee as a member only. (Passed unanimously)

2. Amendments made at the Extraordinary General Meeting called on 6th October 1985:

3.1 Any person aged eighteen or above, irrespective of caste, colour or nationality, may become a member of the Gurdwara provided he/she believes in the teachings of the ten Gurus and acknowledges the holy Guru Granth Sahib and he/she does not believe in any other religion. (Unanimously agreed)

3.5 Ordinary membership for a year (1st of April to 31st of March) shall give the member the right to vote in general meetings.

3.7 The loss of the card shall be reported immediately to the General Secretary when a new card will be issued on payment of 50 pence.

5.4 The Executive committee shall have the right subject to the approval of Sangat, to fill any vacancy of the members or the office bearers.

6.2.9 There shall be an Assistant Education Secretary who shall assist the Education Secretary. (Unanimously agreed)

6.2.10 The Public Relations Officer shall be named as Public Relations Secretary. The Public Relations Secretary shall endeavour to popularise the ideals of the Gurdwara and take charge of public relations.

6.2.11 The Auditor shall audit the accounts whenever he may want in consultation with the treasurer and submit the reports thereof to the Executive Committee and for general meetings. (Passed with 24 votes for and 12 against)

6.4.1   An External Auditor shall be elected by the Executive Committee and shall not be a member of the Executive Committee, shall audit the accounts of the Gurdwara independently and submit a report to the Executive Committee before presenting it to the General Meeting. (Unanimously agreed)

6.5.   The President, General Secretary, Treasurer, Public Relations Secretary and Trustees shall be keshadhari Sikhs (not cutting their hairs and no trimming or shaving their beards). A non-keshadhari Sikh may be elected on the Executive Committee as a member only. (Passed with two-thirds majority of votes)

9.2   The General Secretary shall call a meeting when requested in writing to do so by the number of members equivalent to the quorum. The requirement shall state specifically the purpose of such requests. In the event of the General Secretary's refusal the President may be requested to call the meeting. (Passed unanimously)

9.9   The word media should be added after press. The proceedings of the meetings of the Gurdwara shall not be open to the press or media. (Passed unanimously)

10.5   The Executive Committee shall have the power to sanction new payment of up to two thousand and five hundred pounds on a single or a combination of items of a non-recurring nature in a committee year. (Passed unanimously)

10.6   The Finance Secretary may not keep more than one hundred pounds in cash in hand without the special sanction of the Executive Committee. (Passed unanimously)

Money collected by an authorised member on behalf of the Gurdwara must be deposited in the Bank account of the Gurdwara through the Treasurer within fourteen days of such money being collected. (Agreed unanimously)

14.3 The Trustees shall be ex-officio members of the Executive Committee. (Passed unanimously)

16. Transferred to SGPC Amritsar, Punjab, India. (Passed unanimously)

16 (i) The Constitution should be printed in Panjabi language. (Passed unanimously)

16 (ii) The Executive members who fail to attend three meetings consecutively should be relieved of their responsibilities and this is only to be applicable for that committee year.

3. The constitutional amendments considered at the meeting held on 17th January 1988:

2.1.2 To celebrate the principal religious festivals.

2.2 To advance the Sikh religion in furtherance of that object to:-
2.2.3 Encouraging and promoting the Sikh religion amongst the public by religious and social and cultural dialogue.

3.1 Any person aged 18 or above irrespective of sex, caste, colour or nationality may become a member of the Gurdwara provided he/she believes in the teachings of ten Gurus and acknowledges the holy Guru Granth Sahib and does not adhere to any other religion.

3.2 Member shall be either
3.2.1 Ordinary full member (who shall pay an annual subscription of £1)
or
3.2.2 Life member (who shall pay a sum of £10 in one instalment).

5.1 All members of the Executive Committee shall be elected within four weeks after the annual General Meeting of the Gurdwara and shall hold office for a period of one year.

5.2   The procedure of the election shall be proposed by the Executive Committee and presented for the approval of the Annual General Meeting.

5.3   The President, the General Secretary and the Treasurer shall not hold their respective offices for more than two consecutive years and any of the said officers who shall have completed two consecutive years service as such, may not until the expiry of a further year seek election to either of the other offices. If the President, the General Secretary or the Treasurer shall fail to be re-elected to the Executive Committee they or any of them may be co-opted as ex-officio members of the executive committee without the right to vote.

5.4   The Executive Committee shall have the right to fill any vacancy amongst its members including the office bearers.

6.2.7   The Religious Secretary shall in co-operation with the General Secretary organize all the religious debates and services in the Gurdwara.

6.5   The President, General Secretary, Treasurer, Religious Secretary, Public Relations Secretary, Trustees and all the members of the Executive Committee must be Amritdhari Sikhs.

9.1.1   Ordinary General Meetings shall be held at the mid-term of the office of the Executive Committee.

9.1.2   The Annual General Meeting which shall be held once a year on the second Sunday after the Vaisakhi celebrations day in the Gurdwara.

9.1.3   An extraordinary General meeting which may be called to discuss the matter of vital importance to the Gurdwara involving changes in the Constitution, disciplinary actions etc.

9.3.1. Notice in writing of every meeting other than an emergency meeting shall be given to the members concerned.

9.4.1   The quorum of all the General Meetings shall be 50. If the quorum is not reached at the said general meeting, the meeting shall automatically be adjourned to the same time 14 days thereafter when the members present constitute a quorum.

9.5.1   Minutes passed as a true record and signed by the President or Chairman stand for six months and cannot be questioned or altered but this shall be without prejudice to the right of any member to re-raise the matter at a subsequent general meeting thereafter.

9.6.1   No person may speak twice on any one item of the agenda except the proposer in winding up to answer the opposition.

9.7.2   In event of an equality of votes the president shall have a second and casting vote

9.8   Amendments: No proposal to alter, add to or amend the Constitution shall be deemed to have been adopted unless passed at an Extraordinary General meeting provided that no amendment shall be made which would cause the Gurdwara to cease to be a charity in law.

11.1   The Gurdwara or any part thereof cannot be converted into a place of business unless approved by a resolution in a general meeting and unless the prior approval in writing of the Charity Commissioner has first been obtained.

11.5   Any Sikh whatever the degree of his religious observance shall be allowed to take part in all and every aspect of the work, practices and activities of the Gurdwara unless expressly prevented from so doing by the provisions of this Constitution.

12.3 Any Executive member who fails to attend two consecutive meetings of the Executive Committee shall be asked by the General Secretary for his explanation. If such a member fails to attend a third consecutive meeting and/or is unable to give a reasonable explanation for his non-attendance he shall thenceforth no longer be a member of the Executive Committee for that committee year and shall be replaced.

14.1 The property of the Gurdwara shall be held in the names of five individuals as trustees who shall administer the same in all respect in accordance with the direction of the Executive Committee given by the way of resolution (of which an entry in the minute-book shall be conclusive evidence). The trustee shall be indemnified against all the risk and expense out of the Gurdwara property. The trustee shall hold the office by the resolution of the Executive Committee who may for any reason which may seem sufficient to a majority of them present and voting at any meeting remove any trustee or trustees from the office of trustee. If by reason such as death, resignation or removal it shall appear necessary to the Executive Committee that a new trustee shall be appointed or if the Executive Committee shall deem it expedient to appoint an additional trustee or trustees the Executive Committee shall by resolution nominate a person or persons who may be appointed as a new trustee or trustees. For the purpose of giving effect to such nominations the president is hereby nominated as the person to appoint new trustees of the Gurdwara within the meaning of section 36 of the Trustee Act 1925 and shall by deed duly appoint the person or persons so nominated by the Executive Committee as the new trustee or trustees of the Gurdwara and the provision of the Section 40 of the Trustee Act 1925 shall apply to any such appointment. Any statement of fact in any such deed of appointment shall in favour of any person dealing bona fide and for value with the Gurdwara or the Executive Committee be conclusive of the facts so stated.

14.3 A trustee shall be entitled to attend and speak at the meeting of the Executive Committee and shall not be entitled to vote.

16 The Gurdwara may at any time be dissolved by a resolution passed by a two-thirds majority of those present and voting at an extraordinary General meeting of which at least 21 days clear notice shall have been given to all members of the Gurdwara. Such resolution may give instructions for the disposal of any assets held by or in the name of the trustees, provided that if any property remains after the satisfaction of all debts and liabilities, such property shall not be paid to or distributed amongst the members of the Gurdwara but shall be given or transferred to such charitable institution or institutions having objects similar to the Gurdwara as the Executive Committee may with the approval of the Charity Commissioners, or other authority having charitable jurisdiction determine.

Appendix 2
Members of the Executive Committees

1957-1958
President	Balwant Singh Birdi known as *Mistry*
Vice-President	Narotam Dev Mishra (known as David)
General Secretary	Kirpal Singh Duggal
Secretary	Daljit Singh Sond
Finance Secretary	Inder Singh Ryatt and G. S. Chaudhary
Auditors	Dalip Singh Sohel and Sarwan Singh

1958-1959
President	Balwant Singh Birdi
Vice-President	Gurbaksh Singh Rai
General Secretary	Kirpal Singh Duggal
Secretary	Daljit Singh Sond
Publicity Secretary	Sarwan Singh Kang
Finance Secretary	Sohan Singh Virdi
Assistant Finance Secretary	Sarwan Singh Cheema
Auditors	Ranjit Singh Sahota and Gurdial Singh Virdi
Literature Secretary	Sarwan Singh Bahra

1959-1960
President	Balwant Singh Birdi
Vice-President	Gurbaksh Singh Rai
General Secretary	Ranjit Singh Sahota
Secretary	Lashkar Singh Azad
Finance Secretary	Sohan Singh Virdi
Assistant Finance Secretary	Ajit Singh
Auditor	Inder Singh Ryatt and Dalip Singh Sohel
Literature Secretary	Ranbir Singh Sahota
Propaganda Secretary	Rattan Singh Suman
Trustee	Tirath Singh Birdi

1960-1961

President	Sardara Singh
Vice-President	Tehal Singh
General Secretary	Jaswant Singh Mudhar
Assistant Secretary	Resham Singh Gill
Finance Secretary	Balwant Singh Birdi
Assistant Finance Secretary	Boota Tehal Singh generally known as B. T. Singh
Auditor	Ranjit Singh Sahota and Lashkar Singh Azad
Literature Secretary	Ranbir Singh Sahota
Propaganda Secretary	Nirmal Singh

1961-1962

President	Sardara Singh
Vice-President	Piara Singh Chaggar
General Secretary	Dalip Singh Sohel
Secretary	Resham Singh Gill
Cashier	Balwant Singh Birdi
Assistant Cashier	B. T. Singh and Sarwan Singh Cheema
Auditors	Lashkar Singh and Bhajan Singh
Literature Secretary	Mastan Singh
Propaganda Secretary	Sarwan Singh (from Bradford)
Trustees	Balwant Singh Birdi, Atma Singh Sood, Lashkar Singh Azad and Tehal Singh

1962-1963

President	Piara Singh Chaggar
Vice-President	Tehal Singh
General Secretary	Bhajan Singh Reehal
Assistant Secretary	Vishavmitar Chopra
Finance Secretary	Balwant Singh Birdi
Asst. Finance Secretary	Inder Singh Ryatt and Jaswant Singh
Literature Secretary	Sarwan Singh Cheema

Auditor	Dalip Singh Sohel
Propoganda Secretary	Ajit Singh Bansal and Sohan Singh (Doncaster)
Bhandari **(storekeeper) and *Granthi***	Sadhu Singh Sagoo
Jathedars **(In-charge)**	Kartar Singh, Niranjan Singh, Sohan Singh Seehra and Hari Singh

On 3rd March 1963 Tehal Singh became the Acting President. Dalip Singh Sohel was made General Secretary and Daljit Singh Sond became Auditor.

1963-1964

President	Kirpal Singh Duggal
Vice-President	Akali Balwant Singh
General Secretary	Dalip Singh Sohel
Assistant General Secretary	Resham Singh Gill
Treasurer	Sarwan Singh Cheema
Assistant Treasurer	Sampuran Singh
Auditor	Daljit Singh Sond and Gurbaksh Singh Rai
Literature Secretary	Ajit Singh Bansal and Rattan Singh
Jathedars	Kartar Singh, Niranjan Singh, Sohan Singh Seehra, Gurmeet Singh and Sarwan Singh
Trustees	Balwant Singh Birdi, Atma Singh Sood, Tehal Singh and Lashkar Singh Azad

1964-1965

President	Atma Singh Sood
Vice-President	Piara Singh Chaggar
General Secretary	Daljit Singh Sond
Assistant General Secretary	Resham Singh Gill
Financial Secretary	Sarwan Singh Cheema
Assistant Financial Secretary	Sohan Singh Seehra

Auditors	Bhajan Singh Reehal and Mohinder Singh Gill
Librarian In-charge	Ajit Singh Bansal
Assistant Librarian	Jagan Nath Bharat
Jathedars	Mota Singh, Jota Singh, Gurmeet Singh, Bachan Singh
Trustees	Balwant Singh Birdi, Atma Singh Sood, B. T. Singh and Lashkar Singh Azad

Atma Singh Sood resigned from the trusteeship and two trustees Gurmeet Singh and Gurbaksh Singh Rai were elected in the General Meeting held on 11th October 1963. Piara Singh Chaggar became the Acting President and Mohinder Singh Gill Acting Vice-President.

1965-1966

President	Piara Singh Chaggar
Vice-President	Bhajan Singh Reehal
General Secretary	Daljit Singh Sond
Assistant General Secretary	Dalip Singh Sohel
Finance Secretary	Sohan Singh Seehra
Assistant Finance Secretary	Karam Singh Matharu
Auditor	*Giani* Kesar Singh
Assistant Auditor	Hari Singh Lali
Literature Secretary	Kishan Singh Phull
Assistant Literature Secretary	Jagat Singh Chipra
Jathedars	Niranjan Singh Reehal, Jota Singh, Gurmeet Singh and Ranjit Singh
Bhandari	Sadhu Singh Sagoo
Trustees	Balwant Singh Birdi, Lashkar Singh Phull, B. T. Singh and Gurbaksh Singh Rai

1966-1967

President	Sarwan Singh Cheema
Vice-President	Bhajan Singh Reehal
General Secretary	Dalip Singh Sohel
Assistant General Secretary	Sewa Singh Kalsi
Finance Secretary	Resham Singh Gill
Assistant Finance Secretary	Kirpal Singh Jutla
Literature Secretary	Jagan Nath Bharat
Assistant Literature Secretary	Kewal Singh
Auditor	Satnam Singh Siddhu
Assistant Auditor	Gurdial Singh Sahota
Bhandari	Sadhu Singh Sagoo
Jathedars	Niranjan Singh Seehra, Gurdev Singh Cheema, Tarsem Singh and Gurbachan Singh Chaggar
Trustees	Balwant Singh Birdi, Lashkar Singh Phull, B. T. Singh and Gurbaksh Singh Rai

1967-1968

President	Piara Singh Sambhi
Vice-President	Sarwan Singh Cheema
General Secretary	Daljit Singh Sond
Assistant General Secretary	Sewa Singh Kalsi
Treasurer	Joginder Singh Channa
Assistant Treasurer	Harbhajan Singh Sond
Auditor	Bhajan Singh Reehal
Assistant Auditor	Udham Singh Syan
Librarian	Dalip Singh Sohel
Assistant Librarian	Mohan Singh Panesar
School In-charge	Sucha Singh Chahal and Tarsem Singh Bharat
Bhandari	Sadhu Singh Sagoo
Store keeper	Sarwan Singh Dandi

Jathedars	Niranjan Singh Seehra,
	Niranjan Singh Reehal,
	Amar Singh Sohanpal and
	Bhai Hari Singh
Co-options	Kulwant Singh Reehal, Kewal Singh,
	Harbans Singh Bhamra and
	Kewal Singh Matharu
Trustees	Balwant Singh Birdi,
	Lashkar Singh Phull, B. T. Singh
	and Gurbaksh Singh Rai

1968-1969

President	Piara Singh Sambhi
Vice-President	Sarwan Singh Cheema
General Secretary	Daljit Singh Sond
Assistant General Secretary	Sewa Singh Kalsi
Treasurer	Joginder Singh Channa
Assistant Treasurer	Harbhajan Singh Sond
Auditor	Bhajan Singh Reehal
Assistant Auditor	Udham Singh Syan
Librarian	Dalip Singh Sohel
Assistant Librarian	Mohan Singh Panesar
School In-charge	Sucha Singh Chahal
	and Tarsem Singh Bharat
Bhandari	Sadhu Singh Sagoo
Storekeeper	Sarwan Singh Dandi
Jathedars	Niranjan Singh Seehra,
	Niranjan Singh Reehal,
	Amar Singh Sohanpal and
	Bhai Hari Singh
Trustees	Balwant Singh Birdi,
	Lashkar Singh Phull,
	B. T. Singh and Gurbaksh Singh Rai

1969-1970

President	Piara Singh Sambhi
Vice-President	Sarwan Singh Dandi
General Secretary	Daljit Singh Sond
Assistant General Secretary	Sewa Singh Kalsi
Finance Secretary	Joginder Singh Channa
Assistant Finance Secretary	Sohan Singh Dhiman
Auditors	Sucha Singh Chahal and Bhajan Singh
Literature Secretary	Dalip Singh Sohel
Assistant Literature Secretary	Mohan Singh Panesar
Building Committee	Bakhshish Singh Channa, Balwant Singh Birdi and Gurbaksh Singh Rai
Storekeeper	Sohan Singh Seehra
Langar Jathedars	Jota Singh Nota, Amar Singh Sohanpal, Sohan Singh Kalsi and *Bhai* Hari Singh
Diwan Jathedars	Kewal Singh, Amrik Singh and Sarwan Singh Manota
Trustees	Balwant Singh Birdi, B. T. Singh, Gurbaksh Singh Rai and Lashkar Singh Phull
Election Board	Balwant Singh Birdi, B. T. Singh, Gurbaksh Singh Rai Lashkar Singh Phull and Piara Singh Sambhi

1970-1971

President	Bakhshish Singh Channa
Vice-President	Sarwan Singh Dandi
General Secretary	Dalip Singh Sohel
Assistant General Secretary	Sewa Singh Kalsi
Treasurer	Sucha Singh Chahal
Assistant Treasurer	Kirpal Singh Jutla

Auditor	Joginder Singh Channa
Assistant Auditor	Kesar Singh Panesar
Librarian	Gurcharan Singh Kundi
Assistant Librarian	Mohan Singh Panesar
Storekeeper	Amrik Singh Birdi
Jathedars	Piara Singh Channa, Jota Singh Nota Amar Singh Sohanpal, Amrik Singh and Kewal Singh Matharu
Assistant *Sevadars*	Mohan Singh Kalsi, Prakash Singh Dandi, Inderjit Singh, Sadhu Singh, Jagar Singh, Chanan Singh Fouji, Hari Singh Mann, Ajit Singh Bansal, Niranjan Singh Seehra, *Bibi* Dharam Kaur, Swaran Kaur and Jamuna Devi.
Cloakroom Attendants	Sarwan Singh Cheema and Resham Singh Gill
Caretaker	Sadhu Singh Sagoo
Trustees	Balwant Singh Birdi, Lashkar Singh Azad, B.T. Singh and Gurbaksh Singh Rai
Election Board	Balwant Singh Birdi, Lashkar Singh Azad, Gurbaksh Singh Rai, B. T. Singh and Piara Singh Sambhi. In the absence of Balwant Singh Birdi, Kesar Singh Reehal was nominated.

1971-1972

President	Bakhshish Singh Channa
Vice-President	Dalip Singh Sohel
General Secretary	Sarwan Singh Dandi
Assistant General Secretary	Sewa Singh Kalsi
Treasurer	Kirpal Singh Jutla

Assistant Treasurer	Jaswant Singh Phull
Auditors	Sucha Singh Chahal and Bhajan Singh Reehal
Literature Secretaries	Gurdeep Singh Bhogal and Satnam Singh Channa
Store keeper	Hari Singh Bhogal and Tara Singh Reehal
Jathedars	Jota Singh Nota, Piara Singh Channa, Amar Singh Sohanpal and Niranjan Singh Seehra
Trustees	Balwant Singh Birdi, Lashkar Singh Azad, B. T. Singh and Gurbaksh Singh Rai

1972-1973

President	Sarwan Singh Dandi
Vice-President	Resham Singh Gill
General Secretary	Sewa Singh Kalsi
Assistant General Secretary	Satnam Singh Channa
Treasurer	Kirpal Singh Jutla
Assistant Treasurer	Jaswant Singh Phull
Auditor	Sucha Singh Chahal
Assistant Auditor	Mohan Singh Saundh
Librarian	Dalip Singh Sohel
Assistant Librarian	Harjodh Singh Dandi
Storekeepers	Sadhu Singh Sandal and Piara Singh Chaggar
Assistant Storekeeper	Piara Singh Channa
Jathedars	Jota Singh Nota, Amar Singh Sohanpal, Niranjan Singh Reehal and Atma Singh Sood, Sarwan Singh Cheema, Piara Singh Channa, Piara Singh Chaggar, Lachman Singh Bharat,

	Sohan Singh *Giani*, Bir Singh Nangla and Chan Singh
Trustees	Gurbaksh Singh Rai, B. T. Singh, Balwant Singh Birdi and Lashkar Singh Azad

1973-1974

President	Dalip Singh Sohel
Vice-President	Resham Singh Gill
General Secretary	Sewa Singh Kalsi
Assistant General Secretary	Jaswant Singh Phull
Treasurer	Sucha Singh Chahal
Assistant Treasurer	Hari Singh Mann
Auditor	Mohan Singh Sond
Assistant Auditor	Satnam Singh Channa
Librarian	Harjodh Singh Dandi
Assistant Librarians	Avtar Singh Ghataura and Rabinder Singh Jutla
Storekeeper	Sadhu Singh Sandal
Assistant Storekeeper	Piara Singh Channa
Jathedars	Niranjan Singh Reehal, Jota Singh Nota, Hari Singh Bhogal, Sarwan Singh Channa, Piara Singh Chaggar and Bir Singh Nangla
Trustees	B. T. Singh, Gurbaksh Singh Rai, Lashkar Singh Azad and Balwant Singh Birdi

1974-1975

President	Dalip Singh Sohel
Vice-President	Sarwan Singh Dandi
General Secretary	Resham Singh Gill
Assistant General Secretary	Kirpal Singh Jutla
Treasurer	Sucha Singh Chahal

Assistant Treasurer	Ravinder Singh Jutla
Auditor	Mohan Singh Panesar
Assistant Auditors	Ravinder Singh Jutla and Hari Singh Mann
Librarian	Mohan Singh Jutla
Assistant Librarian	Avtar Singh Ghataura
Store keeper	Harbans Singh Shahid
Assistant Storekeeper	Sadhu Singh *Bhandari*
Jathedars	Niranjan Singh Reehal, Piara Singh Chaggar, Piara Singh Channa, Mohinder Singh Virdee and Hari Singh Bhogal
Trustees	Balwant Singh Birdi, B. T. Singh, Lashkar Singh Azad and Gurbaksh Singh Rai

1975-1976

President	Resham Singh Gill
Vice-President	Sucha Singh Chahal
General Secretary	Dalip Singh Sohel
Assistant General Secretary	Kirpal Singh Jutla
Treasurer	Sarwan Singh Dandi
Assistant Treasurers	Rabinder Singh Jutla and Amroa Singh
Auditor	Mohan Singh Saundh
Assistant Auditor	Satnam Singh Channa
In charge of School and Library	Sewa Singh Kalsi
Storekeepers	Lacchman Singh Rall and Lacchman Singh Bharat
Jathedars	Piara Singh Chaggar, Piara Singh Channa, Niranjan Singh Reehal, Mohinder Singh Birdi, and Hari Singh Bhogal
Trustees	Balwant Singh Birdi, B. T. Singh, Lashkar Singh Azad and Gurbaksh Singh Rai

1976-1977

President	Sarwan Singh Cheema
Vice-President	Chetan Singh Marwaha
General Secretary	Sohan Singh Kalsi
Assistant Secretary	Dalip Singh Sohel
Treasurer	Joginder Singh Channa
Assistant Treasurers	Gurdev Singh and Harbans Singh Sagoo
Auditor	Bhajan Singh Reehal
Assistant Auditor	Satnam Singh Channa
Building Chairman	Bakhshish Singh Channa
In-charge of School	Gurdeep Singh Bhogal
Librarians	Kewal Singh and Kesar Singh Panesar
Storekeeper	Swaran Singh Panesar
Assistant Storekeeper	Buta Singh Rattan
Langar Jathedars	Niranjan Singh Reehal, Piara Singh Channa, Amar Singh Sohanpal, Khushwant Singh Chodha and Mohan Singh Panesar
Trustees	Balwant Singh Birdi, B. T. Singh, Lashkar Singh Azad and Gurbaksh Singh Rai

1977-1978

President	Sarwan Singh Cheema
Vice-President	Chetan Singh Marwaha
General Secretary	Sohan Singh Kalsi
Assistant General Secretaries	Dalip Singh Sohel and Gurdeep Singh Bhogal,
Treasurer	Joginder Singh Channa
Assistant Treasurers	Gurdev Singh Dahele and Surjit Singh Bhogal
Education Secretary	Jagdish Singh Saundh
Librarian	Kewal Singh
Assistant Librarian	Kesar Singh Panesar

Auditor	Surinder Singh
Assistant Auditor	Harbans Singh Sagoo
Storekeeper	Balbir Singh Bains
Assistant Storekeeper	Ujjagar Singh Sahota
Bhandari	Sadhu Singh Sagoo
Representative to the CRC	Bakhshish Singh Channa
Langar Jathedars	Piara Singh Channa, Mohinder Singh Birdi, Amar Singh Sohanpal, Niranjan Singh Seehra, Niranjan Singh Reehal and Sohan Singh Seehra
Path (*gurbani* recitation) **organiser**	Malia Singh Rathor
Sub-Committees	
Education Sub-committee	Ajit Singh Bansal, Bakhshish Singh Channa and Swaran Singh Panesar
Building Sub-committee	Bakhshish Singh Channa (chairman), Sarwan Singh Cheema, Chetan Singh Marwaha, Jagdish Singh Saundh, Sohan Singh Kalsi, Amrik Singh Sohel, Ajit Singh Nijjar and Chain Singh Bhachu
Trustees	Balwant Singh Birdi, Lashkar Singh Azad, B. T. Singh and Pritam Singh QC

1978-1979

President	Chetan Singh Marwaha
Vice-President	Sarwan Singh Cheema
General Secretary	Gurdeep Singh Bhogal
Assistant General Secretaries	Ajit Singh Bansal and Surinder Singh Saimbhi
Treasurer	Gurdev Singh Dahele
Assistant Treasurers	Surjit Singh Bhogal and Ravinder Singh Bharaj

Auditor	Avtar Singh Matharu
Assistant Auditor	Joginder Singh Channa
Education Secretary	Jagdish Singh Saundh,
Literature Secretary	Kesar Singh Panesar
Assistant Literature Secretary	Pritam Singh Sagoo
Building Secretary	Bakhshish Singh Channa
Storekeepers	Hari Singh Syan and Harbans Singh Saimbhi
Bhandari	Sadhu Singh Sagoo

Sub-committees

Education sub-committee	Jagdish Singh Saundh (Chairman), Ajit Singh Bansal, Gurdeep Singh Bhogal, Harvinder Singh Saimbhi, Kulwant Singh Rayit and Pritam Singh Sagoo
Building sub-committee	Bakhshish Singh Channa (Chairman), Jagdish Singh Saundh, Amrik Singh Sohel, Chain Singh Bhachu, Ajit Singh Nijjar, Joginder Singh Channa, Kesar Singh Panesar, Hari Singh Bhogal, Trustees, President, Secretary and Assistant Secretary
Jathedars	Piara Singh Channa, Niranjan Singh Reehal, Mohinder Singh Virdee, Mohan Singh Panesar, Hari Singh Bhogal and Niranjan Singh Seehra
Religious Preaching	Bakhshish Singh Channa, Harbans Singh Sagoo, Sohan Singh Kalsi, Gurdeep Singh Bhogal, Piara Singh Sambhi and Pritam Singh Sagoo
Path **Organisers**	Malia Singh Rathor (Chairman), Hari Singh Bhogal, Hari Singh Syan, Sarwan Singh Cheema, Balwant Singh Birdi, Amar Singh Sohanpal, Darshan Singh Channa, Sohan Singh Kalsi, Gajjan

Singh, Bhagat Singh Kalsi and Harbans Singh Saimbhi

1979-1980

President	Chetan Singh Marwaha
Vice-President	Bakhshish Singh Channa
General Secretary	Ajit Singh Bansal
Assistant General Secretaries	Pritpal Singh Manku and Swaran Singh Panesar
Treasurer	Gurdev Singh Dahele
Assistant Treasurers	Mohinder Singh Mudhar and Ravinder Singh Bharaj
Auditor	Harbans Singh Sagoo
Assistant Auditor	Avtar Singh Matharu
Education Secretary	Jagdish Singh Saundh
Literature Secretaries	Pritam Singh Sagoo and Niranjan Singh Bansal
Assistant Literature Secretary	Kesar Singh Panesar
Storekeeper	Hari Singh Syan
Assistant Storekeeper	Harbans Singh Shahid
Jathedars (food-stuff)	Gajjan Singh and Amar Singh Sohanpal
Bhandari	Sadhu Singh Sagoo

1980-1981

President	Ajit Singh Bansal
Vice-President	Gurdev Singh Dahele
General Secretary	Gurdeep Singh Bhogal
Assistant General Secretaries	Pritpal Singh Manku and Swaran Singh Panesar
Treasurer	Ravinder Singh Bharaj
Assistant Treasurers	Surinder Singh Saimbhi and Kewal Singh Badesha
Auditor	Harbans Singh Sagoo
Assistant Auditor	Gurcharan Singh Kundi
Librarian	Niranjan Singh Bansal

Assistant Librarians	Pritam Singh Sagoo and Paramjit Singh Mudhar
Storekeeper	Hari Singh Syan
Assistant store keepers	Pritpal Singh Plaha and Avtar Singh
In-charge of the School	Jagdish Singh Saundh
Assistant In-charge	Harjinder Singh Sagoo
Building- Improvement and Maintenance	Bakhshish Singh Channa
Assistant- Building Improvement and Maintenance	Inder Singh Mudhar and Gian Singh Rayit
***Path* Organiser**	Malia Singh Rathor
Langar Jethedars	Piara Singh Channa, Mohan Singh Panesar, Niranjan Singh Reehal, Bhagat Singh Kalsi and Niranjan Singh Seehra
***Jathedars* (food-stuff)**	Amar Singh Sohanpal, Gajjan Singh, Sarwan Singh Bahra and Puran Singh
Bhandari	Sadhu Singh Sagoo

Sub-committee

School sub-committee	Jagdish Singh Saundh (Chairman), Harjinder Singh Sagoo, Gurdev Singh Dahele, Gurdeep Singh Bhogal, Pritpal Singh Manku, Pritpal Singh Sagoo and Sarwan Singh Panesar

1981-1982

President	Gurdev Singh Dahele
Vice-President	Gurdeep Singh Bhogal
General Secretary	Pritpal Singh Manku

Assistant General Secretaries	Gurcharan Singh Kundi and Swaran Singh Panesar
Treasurer	Kewal Singh Badesha
Assistant Treasurers	Paramjit Singh Mudhar and Gian Singh Rayit
Auditor	Harbans Singh Sagoo
Assistant Auditor	Kamaljit Singh Ryatt
School Secretary	Pritam Singh Sagoo
Assistant School Secretary	Harjinder Singh Sagoo
Librarian	Niranjan Singh Bansal
Assistant Librarian	Kuldip Singh Lall
Storekeeper	Pritpal Singh Plaha
Assistant Storekeepers	Gurmel Singh Sahota and Mohinder Singh Virdee
Building Chairman	Bakhshish Singh Channa
Assistant Building Chairman	Niranjan Singh Seehra
Path and Religious Functions Organiser	Malia Singh Rathor
Jathedars	Niranjan Singh Reehal, Amar Singh Sohanpal, Punna Singh, Bhagat Singh Kalsi and Mohan Singh Panesar
Langar Jathedars	Hari Singh Syan and Gajjan Singh
Bhandari	Sadhu Singh Sagoo

1982-1983

President	Gurdev Singh Dahele
Vice-President	Gurdeep Singh Bhogal
General Secretary	Gurcharan Singh Kundi
Assistant General Secretaries	Pritpal Singh Manku and Paramjit Singh Mudhar
Treasurer	Gian Singh Rayit

Assistant Treasurers	Swaran Singh Bharaj and Amrik Singh Sahota and later a new appointment of Kirpal Singh Bhui was made
Auditors	Kewal Singh Badesha and Hardeep Singh Ahluwalia
School Secretaries	Dr. Kamaljit Singh Ryatt and Pritam Singh Sagoo

(Dr. Ryatt resigned in August 1982 and Kewal Singh Badesha became Asst. School Secretary)

Librarian	Pritpal Singh Plaha
Assistant Librarian	Kirpal Singh Bhui
Storekeeper	Gurmel Singh Sahota
Assistant Storekeepers	Mohinder Singh Virdee and Santokh Singh Dhillon
Building Chairman	Ajit Singh Nijjar
Assistant Building Chairman	Ajit Singh Bansal
***Path* and Religious Functions Organiser**	Malia Singh Rathor
Jathedars	Shiv Singh Johal, Piara Singh Virdee, Bhagat Singh Kalsi, Pritpal Kaur Shahid, Gurbakhash Singh Chaggar and Hazara Singh Ghatore
Langar Jathedars	Hari Singh Syan and Amar Singh Sohanpal
Bhandari	Sadhu Singh Sagoo

Sub-committees

Education Sub-committee	Kamaljit Singh Ryatt, Gurdeep Singh Bhogal, Pritpal Singh Manku, Inderjit Manrai, President and Secretary

Building Sub-committee	Ajit Singh Nijjar, Ajit Singh Bansal, Dr. Gurdev Singh, Buta Singh Mudhar, Niranjan Singh Seehra, President and Secretary
Policy and Planning Sub-committee	Gurcharan Singh Kundi, Gurdev Singh Dahele, Gurdeep Singh Bhogal, Pritpal Singh Manku, Paramjit Singh Mudhar, Kamaljit Singh Ryatt, Ajit Singh Nijjar, Gian Singh. Rayit, Piara Singh Sambhi, Ajit Singh Bansal and Malia Singh Rathor

(Later three more names were added to this sub-committee in order to combine the work of the Social and Welfare Committee)

Religious Education Sub-committee	Piara Singh Sambhi, Harbans Singh Sagoo, Ajit Singh Bansal and Chamkaur Singh Dhaliwal
Selection Board for appointing teachers	Gurdeep Singh Bhogal, Kamaljit Singh Ryatt, Gurcharan Singh Kundi and Sarwan Singh Rai
Sikh Youth Club	Gurdeep Singh Bhogal (Chairman), Paramjit Singh Mudhar, Kewal Singh Badesha, Pritpal Singh Manku, Paramjit Singh Bhogal, Malia Singh Rathor, Ajit Singh Nijjar, Piara Singh Bains, President and Secretary

Community Relations Council Representatives	Gurdeep Singh Bhogal (Chair), Kamaljit Singh Ryatt, Rughvir Singh and Bakhshish Singh Channa

1983-1984

President	Gurdeep Singh Bhogal
Vice-President	Kamaljit Singh Ryatt
General Secretary	Pritpal Singh Manku
Assistant General Secretaries	Bakhshish Singh (Professor) and Paramjit Singh Mudhar
Treasurer	Kewal Singh Badesha
Assistant Treasurers	Surjit Singh Bhogal and Kirpal Singh Bhui
Auditor	Mohinderpal Singh Sarang
External Auditor	Jagjit Singh Bansal
Education Secretary	Tarlochan Singh Duggal
Assistant Education Secretary	Harjit Singh Ryatt
Librarian	Gurmeet Singh Sohel
Assistant Librarian	Harjodh Singh Rai
Building Secretary	Ajit Singh Nijjar
Assistant Building Secretary	Ranjit Singh Sahota
Sports Secretary	Paramjit Singh Bhogal
Storekeeper (foodstuff)	Gurdial Singh Gill
Assistant Storekeeper	Avtar Singh Patara
Storekeeper (utensils)	Piara Singh Birdi
Assistant Storekeepers (utensils)	Swaran Singh Suryabansi and Harbans Singh Ghatora
Path and Religious Functions Organiser	Malia Singh Rathor
Jathedars	Shiv Singh Johal, Hari Singh Syan, Sher Singh Sathi, Santokh Singh Dhillon and Pritpal Singh Plaha
Bhandari	Sadhu Singh Sagoo

1984-1985
President	Kewal Singh Badesha
Vice-President	Pritpal Singh Manku
General Secretary	Paramjit Singh Mudhar
Assistant General Secretaries	Bakhshish Singh and Mohinderpal Singh Sarang
Treasurer	Kirpal Singh Bhui
Assistant Treasurers	Harbans Singh Shahid and Gulzara Singh Thandi
Auditors	Surjit Singh Bhogal and Gurmel Singh
Education Secretary	Harjit Singh Ryatt
Assistant Education Secretary	Santokh Singh Dhillon
Librarian	Harjodh Singh Rai
Assistant Librarian	Manjit Singh Hunjan
Building Chairman	Ajit Singh Nijjar
Assistant Building Chairman	Ujjal Singh Ryatt
Sports Secretary	Gurdeep Singh Bhogal
Religious Secretaries	Malia Singh Rathor and Hari Singh
Langar Jathedars	Avtar Singh Toor, Balbir Singh Lalli, Shiv Singh Johal and Gurbachan Singh Chhokar
Bhandari	Sadhu Singh Sagoo
CRC representative	Harjit Singh Ryatt
Police Forum representative	Ujjal Singh Ryatt

1985-1986
President	Bakhshish Singh (Professor)
Vice-President	Gulzar Singh Thandi
General Secretary	Tarlochan Singh Duggal
Assistant General Secretaries	Satvinder Kaur Matharu and Santokh Singh Dhillon
Treasurer	Harbans Singh Shahid
Assistant Treasurers	Prithipal Singh Sahota

Auditor	and Gurmel Singh
External Auditor	Kewal Singh Badesha
Education Secretary	Jaspal Singh Gakhal
Assistant Education & Sports Secretary	Harjit Singh Ryatt
Librarian	Gurdeep Singh Bhogal
Assistant Librarian	Ranjit Singh Hunjan
Storekeepers	Amritpal Singh
	Tarlochan Singh Bahia, Avtar Singh Aujula and Niranjan Singh Jheeta
Building Chairman	Ajit Singh Nijjar
Assistant Building Chairmen	Mohinder Singh Virdee and Inder Singh Bahth
Path and Religious Functions Organiser	Malia Singh Rathor
Jathedars	Ujjal Singh Ryatt, Shiv Singh Johal, Bhagat Singh Kalsi, Avtar Singh Toor and Harbans Singh Guntali
Langar Jathedars	Gurdial Singh Gill and Pritpal Kaur Shahid
Spokesman of the *Gurdwara*	Gurdeep Singh Bhogal
Leeds Sikh Council	Tarlochan Singh Duggal
Police Forum	Ujjal Singh Ryatt
CRC representatives	Tarlochan Singh Duggal, Gurmel Singh and Amritpal Singh but CRC took two representatives from the *Gurdwara*, i.e. Ajit Singh Nijjar and Harbans Singh Shahid
Representative on Elderly Centre	Gulzar Singh Thandi
Representation to other meetings	Gurdeep Singh Bhogal, Gurmel Singh and Amritpal Singh
Leeds Careers Association	Ujjal Singh Ryatt

Buta Singh Mudhar was included on the Building committee. Tarlochan Singh Duggal and Santokh Singh Dhillon resigned on 7th December 1985. The Committee was dissolved and the new Committee was formed:

President	Harjit Singh Ryatt
Vice-President	Gulzar Singh Thandi
General Secretary	Bakhshish Singh (Prof)
Assistant General Secretaries	Harjodh Singh Rai and Nirmal Singh Sangha
Treasurer	Harbans Singh Shahid
Assistant Treasurers	Gurmel Singh and Kewal Singh
Auditor	Ujjal Singh Ryatt
Education Secretary	Prem Singh Duggal
Assistant Education Secretary	Tarlochan Singh Hunjan
Librarian	Ranjit Singh Hunjan
Assistant Librarian	Amritpal Singh
Building Committee	Ajit Singh Nijjar (chairman), Kulwant Singh Bhamra and Mohinder Singh Virdee
Public Relations Secretary	Gurdev Singh
Religious Secretary	Malia Singh Rathor
Sports Secretary	Gurdeep Singh Bhogal
Jathedars	Bhagat Singh Kalsi, Jasvir Singh Gill and Hari Singh Syan
Storekeepers (foodstuff)	Shiv Singh and *Bibi* Pritpal Kaur
Storekeepers (utensils)	Avtar Singh and Niranjan Singh Jheeta
Co-option	Kirpal Singh Rayit

1986-1987

President	Kewal Singh Badesha
Vice-President	Nirmal Singh Sangha

General Secretary	Paramjit Singh Mudhar
Assistant General Secretaries	Mohinderpal Singh and Kashmir Singh
Treasurer	Gulzar Singh
Assistant Treasurers	Prithipal Singh and Jagjiwan Singh
Auditor	Jaspal Singh
Education Secretary	Vacant
Assistant Education Secretary	Surinder Singh
Public Relations Secretary	Tarlochan Singh
Building Chairman	Ajit Singh Nijjar
Assistant Building Chairman	Kulwant Singh
Sports Secretary	Gurdeep Singh Bhogal
Religious Secretary	Prem Singh Duggal
Librarian	Ranjit Singh
Storekeepers (foodstuff)	Tarlok Singh and Satnam Singh
Storekeepers (utensils)	Avtar Singh, Santokh Singh and Gurmel Singh
Jathedars	Harbans Singh, Pritpal Singh, Harjodh Singh and Avtar Singh
Police Forum Representative	Harbans Singh
CRC Representative	Pritpal Singh
Law Centre Representative	Paramjit Singh
<u>**Sub-committees**</u>	
Education Sub-committee	Tarlochan Singh, Gurdeep Singh, Pritpal Singh, Prem Singh and Surinder Singh
Sikh Centre	Ajit Singh Nijjar, Kulwant Singh, Mohinderpal Singh, Tarlochan Singh, Gurdeep Singh, Jaspal Singh, Kewal Singh, Paramjit Singh and Santokh Singh

Swaran Singh Suryavansi, Amar Singh, Pritpal Kaur Shahid, Niranjan Singh Kang and Roop Singh were elected as new members on the committee.

Kewal Singh Badesha, Avtar Singh and Surinder Singh resigned. Paramjit Singh and Mohinderpal Singh Sarang resigned on 7th September 1986 in the Sunday *diwan*. Gurmel Singh also mentioned he wished to resign because of his domestic problems. Piara Singh Sambhi indicated he would resign and he was asked to give his resignation in writing. These vacant places were filled with the under-mentioned:

General Secretary	Prem Singh Duggal
Assistant Secretary	Harjodh Singh Rai
Treasurer	Prithipal Singh
Assistant Treasurer	Swaran Singh
Education Secretary	Santokh Singh Dhillon
Trustee	Harbans Singh Shahid

1987-1988

President	Gulzar Singh Thandi
Vice-President	Nirmal Singh Sangha
General Secretary	Prem Singh Duggal
Assistant General Secretary	Manmohan Singh
Treasurer	Kewal Singh Kular
Assistant Treasurers	Kirpal Singh Bhui
	and Avtar Singh Patal
Auditor	Parminder Singh Sethi
External Auditor	Hardeep Singh Ahluwalia
Education Secretary	Baljinder Kaur Ranu
Assistant Education Secretary	Surinder Kaur
Librarian	Ranjit Singh Hunjan
Assistant Librarian	Gurmeet Singh Sohanpal
Religious Secretary	Pritpal Kaur Shahid
Public Relations Secretary	Kirpal Singh Rayit
Storekeeper (foodstuffs)	Tarlok Singh
Assistant Storekeeper	Amar Singh

Storekeeper (utensils)	Avtar Singh Aujula
Assistant Storekeepers (utensils)	Lachhman Singh and Hazara Singh
Building Chairman	Kulwant Singh Bhamra

Sub-committees

Education Sub-committee	Baljinder Kaur Ranu (Chairperson), Surinder Kaur, Inderjit Kaur, Ranjit Singh Hunjan and Mrs Sagoo
Building and Sports Centre	Kulwant Sing Bhamra (Chairman), Harbans Singh Dogra, Tara Singh, Dharam Singh and Gurdeep Singh Bhogal
Policy and Resources Sub-committee	Gulzar Singh Thandi (Chairman), Prem Singh Duggal, Nirmal Singh Sangha, Kulwant Singh, Tarlok Singh Kewal Singh and Avtar Singh Aujula
Sports Sub-committee	Paramjit Singh Channa (Chairman), Kirpal Singh Bhui, Paramjit Singh Mudhar and Gurdeep Singh Bhogal
Religious Sub-committee	Hari Singh Syan, Jagdish Kaur and Mukhtiar Kaur
Public Relations Sub-committee	Kirpal Singh Rayit (Chairman), Pritpal Singh Manku, Ujjal Singh Ryatt, Paramjit Singh Mudhar and Harcharan Singh Siddhu

New members appointed were Ajit Singh Nijjar, Kirpal Singh Bhui, Parminder Singh Sethi, Paramjit Singh Channa, Harcharan Singh Siddhu, Dalvinder Singh, Hardeep Singh Ahluwalia and Roop Singh.

New members appointed and approved by the committee in place of those who resigned:

Assistant Secretary	Harjodh Singh Rai
Public Relations Secretary	Darshan Singh
Religious Secretary	Hari Singh Syan
Building Vice-Chairman	Ujjal Singh Ryatt
Librarian	Sewa Singh Bhamra
Education Secretary	Manmohan Singh Brah

(There was a lot of friction and disagreement in the course of this year)

1988-1989

President	Nirmal Singh Sangha
Vice-President	Gulzar Singh Thandi
General Secretary	Tarlok Singh Toor
Assistant General Secretaries	Prem Singh Duggal and Hari Singh Mann
Treasurer	Kewal Singh Kular
Assistant Treasurers	Joginder Singh Ral and Mohinder Singh Sanghera
Auditor	Hardeep Singh Ahluwalia
External Auditor	Kirpal Singh Rayit
Education Secretary	Manmohan Singh Brah
Assistant Education Secretary	Roop Singh
Librarian	Surinder Singh Bansal
Assistant Librarians	Kesar Singh Seehra and Mohinderpal Singh Sarang
Religious Secretary	Avtar Singh Aujula
Public Relations Secretary	Paramjit Singh Mudhar
Building Secretaries	Gulzar Singh Thandi and Mahan Singh
Sports Secretary	Beant Singh
Storekeepers (foodstuff)	Amar Singh, Niranjan Singh and Harbans Singh Thandi

Storekeepers (utensils)	Bakhshish Singh Kang, Sukhpal Singh and Hazara Singh
Langar Jathedars	Inder Singh Bahth, *Bibi* Punna Kaur, *Bibi* Surinder Kaur, Hari Singh Syan, *Bibi* Kashmir Kaur and Gurnam Singh
Trustees	Those trustees who were not initiated resigned including: Arminder Singh, Sarao, Buta Singh Mudhar, Bahadur Singh Landa. In their place, initiated Sikhs were appointed: Inder Singh Ryatt, Sarwan Singh Rai and Kesar Singh Seehra

Avtar Singh Aujula and Surinder Kaur resigned and the following were co-opted:

Co-option	Gurnam Singh *(langar)* and Mohinderpal Singh Sarang (to assist in the library work)

1989-1990

President	Gulzar Singh Thandi
Vice-President	Tarlok Singh Toor
General Secretary	Nirmal Singh Sangha
Assistant General Secretaries	Hari Singh Mann and Gurnam Singh
Treasurer	Mohinder Singh Sanghera
Assistant Treasurers	Kewal Singh Kular and Joginder Singh Ral
External Auditor	Kewal Singh
Education Secretary	Manmohan Singh Brah,
Librarian	Surinder Singh Bansal

Religious and Public Relations	Paramjit Singh Mudhar
Building Repairs	Maha Singh Bhogal
Sikh Youth Group - Leaders	Gurdeep Singh Bhogal and Parminder Singh
Jathedar – Darbar **Hall**	Hazara Singh
Jathedars **- Store**	Amar Singh and Niranjan Singh
Jathedars - Langar	Bakhshish Singh, Inder Singh Bahth and Tarlok Singh
Jathedarnis	*Bibi* Punna Kaur and *Bibi* Harbans Kaur
Co-options	Prem Singh Duggal to work as Secretary, Roop Singh to help to manage the stage and Gurnam Singh as Assistant Treasurer

1990-1991

President	Gulzar Singh Thandi
Vice-President	Prem Singh Duggal
General Secretary	Hari Singh Mann
Assistant General Secretaries	Tarlok Singh Toor and Gurnam Singh
Treasurer	Manmohan Singh Brah
Assistant Treasurers	Beant Singh and Hari Singh Syan
Auditor	Nirmal Singh Sangha
Religious Secretary	Roop Singh
Education Secretary	Surinder Singh Bansal
Assistant Education Secretary	Gurdev Singh
Librarian	Kewal Singh Kular
Assistant Librarian	Jatinder Singh Mehmi
Public Relations Secretary	Gurcharan Singh Kundi
Building Secretary	Inder Singh Bahth
Storekeepers	Niranjan Singh

Jathedar - Diwan Hall Langar *Jathedars*	and Amar Singh Hazara Singh Bakhshish Singh Kang, Paramjit Singh Mudhar, Joginder Singh Ral, Maha Singh Bhogal, Darshan Singh Cheema

Sub-committees

School Sub-committee	Paramjit Singh Mudhar, Professor Bakhshish Singh, Gurcharan Singh Kundi, Prem Singh and Gulzar Singh Thandi
Sub-committee to prepare the syllabus for teaching Panjabi	Professor Bakhshish Singh, Gurcharan Singh Kundi, Paramjit Singh Mudhar, Surinder Singh Bansal, Pritpal Singh Manku and Gurdeep Singh Bhogal
***Gurdwara* Management sub-committee**	Amar Singh, Gulzar Singh Thandi, Hari Singh Syan, Professor Bakhshish Singh and Kesar Singh Seehra
Changes in the committee	Manmohan Singh Brah resigned and Hari Singh Syan took his place as Treasurer. Hari Singh Mann became an ordinary committee member because of his illness. In his

place Nirmal Singh Sangha became General Secretary and Darshan Singh Cheema Assistant Treasurer. Joginder Singh Saimbhi became Internal Auditor and Kewal Singh Badesha External Auditor.

1991-1992

President	Prem Singh Duggal
Vice-President	Hari Singh Mann
General Secretary	Tarlok Singh Toor
Assistant General Secretaries	Paramjit Singh and Nirmal Singh
Treasurer	Beant Singh Bhamra
Assistant Treasurers	Hardeep Singh and Kewal Singh
Auditor	Gurdev Singh
External Auditor	Mohinderpal Singh Sarang
Education Secretary	Surinder Singh Bansal
Librarian	Manmohan Singh
Assistant Librarian	Joginder Singh
Public Relations Secretary	Gulzar Singh Thandi
Building Chairmen	Darshan Singh and Inder Singh
Storekeepers (utensils)	Niranjan Singh and Amar Singh
Jathedar - Darbar Sahib	Hazara Singh
Langar Jathedars	Bakhshish Singh Kang, Gurnam Singh, Maha Singh, Hari Singh, Dharam Singh, Resham Kaur and Harbans Kaur

Later in the year in June Gulzar Singh Thandi became a Trustee and

Hardeep Singh Ahluwalia became Public Relations Secretary. Certain members had to withdraw their names as they had off-licence shops selling alcohol and cigarettes, namely, Nirmal Singh Sangha, Balbir Singh Sindhar and Darshan Singh Cheema.

In November Roop Singh became Assistant Librarian, Bakhshish Singh represented *Gurdwara Sahib* on the Law Centre Committee and Hardeep Singh Ahluwalia represented the *Gurdwara* on the Chapeltown and Harehills Committee.

In December two members were co-opted, namely Ujjal Singh and Harpal Singh. Gulzar Singh resigned from the trusteeship. In January Manmohan Singh Brah became Internal Auditor. In February, Beant Singh went into hospital and Sarabjit Singh replaced him.

1992-1993

President	Prem Singh Duggal
Vice-President	Paramjit Singh Mudhar
General Secretary	Tarlok Singh Toor
Assistant General Secretaries	Harpal Singh
	and Baldev Singh
Treasurer	Kewal Singh Kular
Assistant Treasurer	Manmohan Singh Brah
Auditor	Hardeep Singh Ahluwalia
External Auditor	Pritpal Singh Manku
Education Secretary	Surinder Singh Bansal
Librarian	Hari Singh Syan
Assistant Librarian	Amar Singh Nahal
Religious Secretary	Roop Singh
Building Secretary	Inder Singh
Jathedar - Darbar **Hall**	Hazara Singh
Langar Sevadars	Harbans Kaur Thandi,
	Daljit Kaur Duggal,
	Devinder Kaur,
	Paramjit Kaur,
	Kashmir Kaur, Jatinder Kaur,

Simarjit Kaur,
Maha Singh Bhogal,
Gurnam Singh and
Jatinder Singh

Sub-committees

Building Sub-committee Prem Singh, Tarlok Singh, Inder Singh, Beant Singh and Kesar Singh Seehra

***Nagar-kirtan* Ad-hoc Committee** Kesar Singh Seehra, Tarlok Singh, Prem Singh Duggal, Professor Bakhshish Singh, Inder Singh Ryatt, Hardeep Singh Ahluwalia and Manmohan Singh

1993-1994

President	Nirmal Singh Sangha
Vice-President	Tarlok Singh
General Secretary	Professor Bakhshish Singh
Assistant General Secretaries	Baldev Singh Duggal and Harpal Singh
Treasurer	Kewal Singh Kular
Assistant Treasurer	Manmohan Singh Brah
Auditor	Hardeep Singh Ahluwalia
Education Secretary	Surinder Singh Bansal
Librarian	Hari Singh Syan
Assistant Librarian	Amar Singh Nahal
Public Relations Secretary	Prem Singh Duggal
Building Secretary	Darshan Singh Cheema
Police Forum	Paramjit Singh Mudhar
***Jathedar - Darbar* Hall**	Hazara Singh Sindhar
***Jathedar* (utensils)**	Inder Singh Bahth
Langar Jathedars	Bakhshish Singh Kang, Balbir Singh Nahal, Harbans Kaur

Thandi, Resham Kaur Kang, Daljit Kaur Duggal, Kashmir Kaur and Paramjit Kaur Boye

Sub-Committee

Gurdwara **Sub-committee** Professor Bakhshish Singh, Prem Singh Duggal, Tarlok Singh Toor, Kesar Singh Seehra, Nirmal Singh Sangha, Manohar Singh, Hardeep Singh Ahluwalia and Inder Singh Bhakhar

Trustees Piara Singh Bains and Balbir Singh Sindhar

It was decided at the meeting of 5th September 1993 that another Assistant Treasurer was needed and Manohar Singh was appointed.

1994-1995
President Nirmal Singh Sangha
Vice-President Kewal Singh Kular
General Secretary Bakhshish Singh
Assistant General Secretaries Paramjit Singh Mudhar and Harpal Singh

Treasurers Tarlok Singh Toor and Surinder Singh Bansal

Education Secretary Hardeep Singh Ahluwalia
Librarians Jatinder Singh Mehmi and Roop Singh Khalsa

Public Relations Secretaries Prem Singh Duggal and Ujjal Singh Ryatt

Building Secretaries Manohar Singh Bhakhar and Maha Singh Bhogal

Jathedar - Darbar **Hall**	Hazara Singh
Langar Jathedars	Joginder Singh Patara,
	Bakhshish Singh Kang,
	Baldev Singh Duggal,
	Harbans Kaur Thandi,
	Simranjit Kaur Toor,
	Kashmir Kaur,
	Daljit Kaur Duggal,
	Resham Kaur Kang,
	Amrit Kaur Bhakhar,
	Rani Kaur and Santosh Kaur

1995-1996

President	Tarlok Singh Toor
Vice-President	Nirmal Singh Sangha
General Secretary	Harpal Singh
Assistant General Secretaries	Baldev Singh Duggal
	and Paramjit Singh Mudhar
Treasurer	Kewal Singh Kular
Assistant Treasurers	Surinder Singh Bansal
	and Manohar Singh Bhakhar
Education Secretary	Hardeep Singh Ahluwalia
Librarian	Jatinder Singh
Public Relations Secretary	Ujjal Singh Ryatt
Building Secretary	Inder Singh Bahth
Law Centre Representative	Manohar Singh
Jathedars - Darbar **Hall**	Hazara Singh
	and Gurmit Singh
Langar Jathedars	Avtar Singh,
	Joginder Singh Patara,
	Bakhshish Singh,
	Harbans Kaur Thandi,
	Resham Kaur,
	Daljit Kaur Duggal,
	Kashmir Kaur,
	Rani Kaur, Amrit Kaur
	and Simranjit Kaur.

Co-opted Members Roop Singh Khalsa,
Darshan Singh Cheema,
Kartar Kaur

Sub-Committee

School Sub-committee Professor Bakhshish Singh,
Manohar Singh, Paramjit
Singh Mudhar,
Ujjal Singh Ryatt,
Surinder Singh Bansal,
Hardeep Singh Ahluwalia,
Tarlok Singh Toor,
Kewal Singh Kular

Avtar Singh Toor resigned on 27th May 1995 because of lack of time.

1996-1997

President Kewal Singh Kular
Vice-President Prem Singh Duggal
General Secretary Harpal Singh
Assistant General Secretaries Tarlok Singh Toor
and Baldev Singh Duggal

Treasurer Surinder Singh Bansal
Assistant Treasurers Hardeep Singh Ahluwalia
and Manohar Singh Bhakhar

Auditor Joginder Singh Patara
External Auditor Pritpal Singh Manku
Education Secretaries Jatinder Singh Mehmi
and Ujjal Singh Ryatt

Librarian Rupinder Kaur
Public Relations Secretaries Ujjal Singh Ryatt
and Jatinder Singh Mehmi

Building Secretary Inder Singh Bahth
(he resigned and Manohar
Singh Bhakhar became the

Jathedars - Darbar **Hall**	Building Secretary) Bakhshish Singh Kang and Nirmal Singh
Langar Jathedars	Simarjit Kaur Toor, Harbans Kaur Thandi, Daljit Kaur Duggal, Kashmir Kaur, Amrit Kaur, Surinder Kaur Khalsa, Resham Kaur and Jasvinder Kaur
New *Gurughar* Committee	Ujjal Singh Ryatt, Prem Singh Duggal, Tarlok Singh Toor, Professor Bakhshish Singh and Manohar Singh Bhakhar (Later three members, Kewal Singh Kular, Nirmal Singh and Surinder Singh Bansal were added to the Committee.
Marriage Registrars	Hardeep Singh Ahluwalia, Ujjal Singh Ryatt and later Paramjit Singh Mudhar
Co-opted Members	Hari Singh Syan and later Avtar Singh Toor

There had been a problem in electing the President. Three names were proposed. One was withdrawn immediately and the other two remained. As the decision between these two could not be made amicably, the member who had withdrawn was appointed President.

1997-1998
President	Joginder Singh Patara
Vice-President	Paramjit Singh Mudhar
General Secretary	Tarlok Singh Toor
Assistant General Secretaries	Prem Singh Duggal and Nirmal Singh Sangha

Treasurer	Surinder Singh Bansal
Assistant Treasurers	Kewal Singh Kular and Baldev Singh Duggal
Auditor	Hardeep Singh Ahluwalia
Education Secretary	Ujjal Singh Ryatt
Librarian	Rupinder Kaur
Public Relations Secretary	Jatinder Singh Mehmi
Building Secretaries	Manohar Singh Bhakhar and Gurmit Singh Sohanpal
Storekeepers	Gurmeet Singh and Bakhshish Singh Kang
Langar Jathedars	Simran Kaur Toor, Amrit Kaur, Harbans Kaur Thandi, Daljit Kaur Duggal, Kashmir Kaur, Prakash Kaur Hunjan, Devinder Kaur and Jasvinder Kaur
Co-opted Members	Hazara Singh, Avtar Singh Toor, Inder Singh Bahth and Nirmal Singh Sangha
Resignation	Devinder Kaur resigned on 7th September 1997.

Nirmal Singh Sangha became General Secretary on 14th December 1997.

1998-1999

President	Joginder Singh Patara
Vice-President	Jatinder Singh Mehmi
General Secretary	Avtar Singh Toor
Assistant General Secretaries	Nirmal Singh Sangha and Harbans Singh
Treasurers	Ujjal Singh Ryatt, Gurmeet Singh Nahal and

	Harjodh Singh Rai
Auditor	Harbans Singh
External Auditor	Bakhshish Singh
Education Secretaries	Sarabjit Kaur
	and Ujjal Singh Ryatt
Librarian	Rupinder Kaur
Public Relations Secretary	Jatinder Singh Mehmi
Building Secretary	Manohar Singh Bhakhar
Jathedar **(foodstuff)**	Gurmeet Singh Nahal
Jathedar **(shopping)**	Hazara Singh
Langar Jathedars	Harbans Kaur Thandi,
	Simranjit Kaur Toor,
	Kashmir Kaur
	and Prakash Kaur Hayer
Co-option	Tajinder Singh Bal
Resignation	Avtar Singh Toor resigned as General Secretary on 6th September 1998.
Replacements	Nirmal Singh Sangha became General Secretary and Harjodh Singh Rai Assistant Secretary on 11th November 1998
Trustee	Manmohan Singh Bal.

1999-2000

President	Nirmal Singh Sangha
Vice-President	Daljit Singh Bhamra
General Secretary	Harjodh Singh Rai
Assistant General Secretaries	Tejinder Singh Bal
	and Harbans Singh
Treasurer	Ujjal Singh Ryatt
Assistant Treasurers	Gurmeet Singh Nahal
	and Gurmeet Singh
Auditor	Surinder Singh Sagoo

External Auditor	Kalyan Singh
Education Secretary	Sukhraj Singh Gill
Religious Secretary	Gurdev Singh Sandhu
Librarian	Rupinder Kaur
Assistant Librarian	Surjit Kaur
Public Relations Secretary	Jetinder Singh Mehmi
Building Secretary	Joginder Singh Patara
Assistant Building Secretary	Niranjan Singh Kalirai
Stall In-charge	Hazara Singh Sindhar
Langar Jathedars	Bakhshish Singh Kang, Sohan Singh Khaira and Hari Singh Syan
Langar Sevadars	Kashmir Kaur, Jasvinder Kaur, Simarjit Kaur Kamaljit Kaur Phull, Santosh Kaur, Kulbir Kaur and Harbans Kaur Thandi
Co-options	Harjodh Singh Rai and Surinder Singh Sagoo
Marriage Registrars	Kanwarpal Singh, Amarjit Singh Uppal and Kalyan Singh Aulakh
Trustee	Sukhchain Singh

Two members had resigned, so Harjodh Singh Rai was co-opted and was made General Secretary. Surinder Singh Sagoo was co-opted as a new member and was appointed Internal Auditor. Harpal Singh left in March 2000.

2000-2001

President	Harpal Singh
Vice-President	Gurmeet Singh Nahal
General Secretary	Harbans Singh
Assistant General Secretaries	Tejinder Singh and Inderjit Singh
Treasurer	Joginder Singh Patara

Assistant Treasurers	Daljit Singh and Gurmeet Singh
Education Secretary	Nirmal Singh
Librarian	Surinder Singh Sagoo
Assistant Librarian	Santosh Kaur
Public Relations Secretary	Jatinder Singh Mehmi
Building Secretary	Ujjal Singh Ryatt
Assistant Building Secretary	Inder Singh Bahth
Langar **In-charge**	Bakhshish Singh Kang
Langar **and** *Darbar* **Sevadars**	Inderjit Singh Gill, Jasvinder Kaur, Sarabjit Kaur, Mohinder Singh Seehra, Kashmir Kaur, Gurmeet Kaur, Simranjit Kaur Toor and Rupinder Kaur Mehmi
Co-options	Harbans Kaur Thandi, Kulbir Kaur Teja, Hazara Singh Sindhar and on 8th October 2000 Bhagat Singh

Sub-committees

Gurughar **committee for the old Church building**	Bakhshish Singh, Ujjal Singh Ryatt, Kalyan Singh Nirmal Singh Sangha and President

2001-2002

President	Harpal Singh
Vice-President	Daljit Singh Bhamra
General Secretary	Harbans Singh
Assistant General Secretary	Nirmal Singh Sangha
Treasurer	Tejinder Singh Bal

Assistant Treasurers	Gurmeet Singh Nahal and Balraj Singh Gill
Auditor	Kalyan Singh
Education Secretaries	Ujjal Singh Ryatt and Inderjit Singh Gill
Librarians	Sarabjit Kaur and Rupinder Kaur
Public Relations Secretary	Jatinder Singh Mehmi
Building Secretary	Inder Singh Bahth
Assistant Building Secretary	Sukhraj Singh Gill
Stall *Jathedars*	Hazara Singh and Harbans Singh Saimbhi
Storekeeper	Bakhshish Singh Kang
Langar Jathedars	Gurmeet Singh, Harbans Kaur Thandi, Simarjit Kaur, Kashmir Kaur, Santosh Kaur, Kulbir Kaur and Jasvinder Kaur
Co-options	Joginder Singh Patara, Sukhraj Singh Gill and Bhagat Singh Kular

Later in the year Joginder Singh Patara became Treasurer in place of Tejinderpal Singh Bal and Tejinderpal Singh Bal became Assistant Treasurer.

2002-2003

President	Daljit Singh Bhamra
Vice-President	Harpal Singh
General Secretary	Tejinder Singh Bal
Assistant General Secretaries	Joginder Singh Patara and Harbans Singh
Treasurer	Nirmal Singh Sangha
Assistant Treasurers	Gurmeet Singh and Gurmukh Singh
Auditor	Harbans Singh Saimbhi

External Auditor	Kalyan Singh
Education Secretary	Ujjal Singh Ryatt
Assistant Education Secretary	Sukhraj Singh
Assistant Public Relations Secretary	Rupinder Kaur
Building Secretary	Gurmeet Singh Nahal
Assistant Building Secretary	Balraj Singh Gill
Stall *Jathedar*	Harbans Singh Saimbhi
Assistant Stall *Jathedar*	Gurbakhash Singh
Jathedars - Darbar Sahib	Bhagat Singh Kular and Prithipal Singh
Langar Jathedar	Bakhshish Singh Kang
Langar Sevadars	Kashmir Kaur, Jasvinder Kaur, Simranjit Kaur Toor, Santosh Kaur Ryatt, Kalbir Kaur Teja and Harbans Kaur Thandi
Co-options	Inderjit Singh Gill and Jatinder Singh Mehmi
Resignation	Inder Singh Ryatt
Trustee	Niranjan Singh Kalrai

2003-2004

President	Daljit Singh Bhamra
Vice-President	Nirmal Singh Sangha
General Secretary	Tejinder Singh Bal
Assistant General Secretaries	Amarjit Singh Uppal and Pakhar Singh
Treasurer	Harpal Singh
Assistant Treasurers	Gurmeet Singh and Harpal Singh Nijjar
Education Secretary	Sukhraj Singh
Assistant Education Secretary	Baljinder Singh Sangha
Sports and Library	Inderjit Singh Gill and Surjit Singh Bahth
Public Relations Secretaries	Jatinder Singh Mehmi and Balraj Singh

Building Secretary	Joginder Singh Patara
Stall - *Jathedars*	Harbans Singh Saimbhi and Hazara Singh
Jathedar (foodstuff)	Gurbakhash Singh
Langar *Jathedar*	Bakhshish Singh Kang
Members	Jasvinder Kaur, Balvinder Kaur Toor, Balbir Kaur, Rajesh Singh, Harbans Kaur Thandi, Simarjit Kaur Toor, Kulbir Kaur Teja and Paramjit Kaur.

2004-2005

President	Nirmal Singh Sangha
Vice-President	Daljit Singh Bhamra
General Secretary	Joginder Singh Patara
Assistant General Secretaries	Faqir Singh and Amarjit Singh Uppal
Treasurer	Harpal Singh Nijjar
Assistant Treasurers	Baljinder Singh Sangha and Charanjit Singh Reehal
Religious and Education Secretary	Sukhraj Singh Gill
Assistant Religious and Education Secretary	Jaspal Kaur Toor
Librarian	Surjit Singh Bahth
Public Relations Secretary	Jatinder Singh Mehmi
Sports Secretary	Balraj Singh Gill
Assistant Sports Secretary	Inder Singh Gill
Building Secretary	Tejinder Singh Bal
Assistant Building Secretary	Gurbax Singh
Stall In-charge	Harbans Singh Saimbhi
Assistant Stall In-charge	Hazara Singh
Langar *Jathedar*	Bakhshish Singh Kang
Langar *Sevadars*	Jasvinder Kaur,

Trustees Simarjit Kaur Toor, Ratan Kaur. Harbans Kaur, Jaswant Kaur Bahth, Prabhjot Kaur Gill, Harpal Singh and Gururaj Singh Gill Sarwan Singh Rai, Bakhshish Singh, Manmohan Singh Bal, Niranjan Singh Kalrai and Gujjar Singh

Marriage Registrars Bakhshish Singh, Ujjal Singh Ryatt, Kalyan Singh, Kanwarpal Singh Gill and Amarjit Singh Uppal

APPENDIX 3
Biographical Information

Short biographical notes on the pioneer Sikhs and those Sikhs who served as presidents of the Sikh Temple are given here, which will give an idea of their backgrounds and experience. The choice of names was made because of the scope of this book. This does not mean that other *sevadars* have not contributed or their contributions are in any way belittled. Details of their many contributions are found in the main body of the book and are, therefore, not repeated here. Committee members are listed in Appendix 2. The information given here is based on personal interviews, details given by families or friends and written evidence, such as minutes or other published material. The authors have tried to be fair to all those involved, without any bias or prejudice, and apologise if they have missed any names which deserve mention. In some instances it was impossible, in spite of enormous efforts being made, to locate certain persons and their details and we regret that. The details of some of the Presidents are missing, either because they did not want to offer the information or preferred not to be included. Their wishes have been honoured. The details given below are concise and names are alphabetically arranged according to their given name. Some abbreviations have been used, such as, in the second line of each entry, 'm' for mother and 'f ' for father.

Ajit Singh Bansal (1929-2004)
m. Harbans Kaur f. Puran Singh

He was born in Hadiabad near Phagwara in the Punjab. He matriculated from Punjab University. He was twenty when he married Harbans Kaur in 1948. He migrated to the UK in 1962 and settled in Leeds. He worked in Kirkstall Forge and also in the building trade. Later he bought a grocery shop and combined this business with his wife's business selling fabric, mainly Punjabi suit material. He had three sons and two daughters. He was President of the Sikh Temple in 1980-1981.

Ajit Singh Bansal

Ajit Singh Nijjar (5.2.1942 -)
m. Chanan Kaur f. Gurcharan Singh

He was born in the village of Bhar Singh Pur in the district of Jalandhar in the Punjab. He did his matriculation at Punjab University and City and Guilds in Motor Engineering at Huddersfield College. He married Rashpal Kaur in 1960 and migrated to the UK in February 1961. He lived in Huddersfield from 1961-1966 and then settled in Leeds. He has five children, four girls and one boy. For some years he owned a garage in Leeds. He is very committed to his family as his father died at an early age and he took on the responsibility of looking after the family. He has devoted a lot of his time for the welfare of the Sikh community. The Sikh Centre is his creation and he played a major role in acquiring most of the site of the purpose-built *gurdwara*.

Ajit Singh Nijjar

Atma Singh Sood (1921-1978)
m. Basant Kaur f. Deva Singh

He was born in the village of Amargarh in the district of Jalandhar in the Punjab. He had no formal qualification but had schooling in Urdu. He married Rattan Kaur in 1934 and had seven children, four boys and three girls. Prior to migrating to Leeds in 1953 he was a master tailor in Poona. In Leeds he worked in a foundry and then became a face worker in a mine near Temple Newsam in Leeds. He took keen interest in the work of the *Gurdwara*. He was a Trustee for many years and was also one of the trustees who signed the *Gurdwara* deed for the church building. He served as a President of the Sikh Temple for a year in 1964.

Atma Singh Sood

Bakhshish Singh Channa (1934-1991)
m. Rattan Kaur f. Jagat Singh

He was born in the village of Chachari in the district of Phagwara in the Punjab. He graduated in Civil Engineering and migrated to Kenya in East Africa. He settled in Nairobi and worked as a civil engineer for the Ministry of Works. He came to the United Kingdom in 1965 and settled in Leeds. He worked in Leeds City Council's Works Department. He married Gurmeet Kaur in 1950 and had two sons and two daughters. He was an influential member of the community and was President of the Sikh Temple from 1970 to 1972.

Bakhshish Singh Channa

Bakhshish Singh, Professor (25.5.1935 -)
m. Kartar Kaur f. Katha Singh

He was born in the village of Kartarpur in the district of Jalandhar in the Punjab. He did his M.Sc in Physics at the University of Sagar, now known as Dr Hari Singh Gaur University (Madhya Pradesh). He migrated to the United Kingdom in 1966. He settled in Leeds and worked in telecommunications and in Leeds Education Department as a Panjabi language teacher. He married Kashmir Kaur in 1964 and had two girls and one boy. He became involved in the Sikh Temple and held executive positions. He was President of the *Gurdwara* from 1985 to 1986. He also became a Marriage registrar and trustee. He still spends a lot of time with school parties taking them around the Sikh Temple and explaining to them about Sikh religion.

Prof. Bakhshish Singh

Balwant Singh (Akali) (1908-1988)
m. Rukmani Kaur f. Gushal Singh

He was born in Lahore which is now in Pakistan. He had primary education and started his own business. He married Tej Kaur in 1928 and had four children, two boys and two girls. He came to this country in 1951 and went into the drapery business. He was a very religious man and keen to promote Sikh identity. He encouraged Sikhs to keep their hair uncut and wear a turban. He was a good reciter of the *Guru Granth Sahib*.

Akali Balwant Singh

Balwant Singh Birdi (1912-1984)
m. Lakshman Kaur   f. Ganga Singh

He was born in the village of Kote-Badal Khan in the district of Jalandhar in the Punjab. He had very little education as he had to work with his father from an early age. He came to the UK in 1938. He always maintained his Sikh identity and never felt embarrassed about it,

Balwant Singh Birdi

even in the early days when there were not many Sikhs in Yorkshire. He was a hardworking man who started his business as a pedlar (door-to-door selling), then owned a market stall and eventually became one of the richest Asians in Leeds by owning wholesale and retail businesses. His constant *seva* in *gurdwaras* and for his own community made him well known in the Sikh community. He married Balwant Kaur who was also devoted to her religion and community. He had one son and two daughters. He was a founder member of the first *Gurdwara* in Leeds and devoted his life to *gurdwaras* and often made donations. He held executive positions and was President of the Sikh Temple from 1957 to 1960. He remained a trustee of the *Gurdwara* for many years.

Bhajan Singh Reehal (3.3.1929 -)
m. Laaj Kaur   f. Bhagat Singh

He was born in the village of Gaunachor in the district of Jalandhar in the Punjab. He did his Matriculation in 1946 and was married in 1948 to Joginder Kaur and had two girls and one boy. He migrated to Uganda after the marriage and worked there as a civil draughtsman. In 1956 he came to Leeds and worked as

Bhajan Singh Reehal

a draughtsman. From time to time he also worked as a bus conductor and a turner and did building work. There was no *gurdwara* in Leeds when he came so he encouraged other Sikhs to think in this direction. He was a pioneer Sikh and his religious zeal made him serve *gurdwaras* in Leeds and contribute to their management (see Appendix 2).

Boota Tehal Singh (1925-2001)
m. Harnam Kaur   f. Boota Singh Rathor

He was born in Lahore which is now in Pakistan. He had primary education. After the partition of India he moved to Bombay. He married Agya Kaur in 1949 and migrated to this country in the same year. He had seven children, five boys and two girls. He worked as a pedlar selling drapery from door-to-door. He opened the first Indian grocery shop on Roundhay Road, Leeds in 1950. He was honoured with a trophy for his services towards the Sikh Temple. He was a founder member of the Sikh Temple. He was generally known as B.T. Singh.

Boota Tehal Singh

Dalip Singh Sohel (1924-1978)
m. Harjinder Kaur f. Gurbachan Singh

He was born in the village of Virka in the district of Jalandhar in the Punjab. He passed the Intermediate F.A.(Faculty of Arts) Examination at Punjab University. He worked in a dairy-farm in Poona before migrating to Leeds in 1948. He married Harbhajan Kaur in 1945 and had six children, five daughters and one son. He set up his own business of knitwear and jewellery in Castleford and later worked as a Railway Guard. He was very devoted to the Sikh religion and was a founder member of the Sikh Temple. He held many executive posts and served as the President of the *Gurdwara* in 1973 to 1975. He was a noble and affectionate man.

Dalip Singh Sohel

Daljit Singh (3.3.1956 -)
m. Rattan Kaur   f. Mehanga Singh

He was born in the village of Ramgarh in the district of Kapurthala in the Punjab. He came to Leeds in 1970 and did his GCSE. He studied Motor Engineering at Kitson College and also did many specialist courses in this field. He did an apprenticeship with KD Brothers in Leeds and is now a director of this firm. He married Karamjit Kaur in 1985 and had three children, two boys and a girl. He is a kind and soft-spoken man. He is generous in making donations to the Sikh Temple and served as President in 2002-2004.

Daljit Singh

Daljit Singh Sond (1.5.1924 -)
m. Sundar Kaur   f. Mehar Singh

He was born in the village of Boparai Kalan in the district of Jalandhar in the Punjab. He passed his Matriculation examination at Punjab University and in 1944 married Gurbachan Kaur. He has five daughters and one son. He migrated to the UK in 1949. He worked in Catton foundry and then as a press operator with Langham & Company. He also worked as a spinner in textile mills. His passion for the Sikh religion made him contribute to the creation and development of this *Gurdwara*. He was one of the founder members of this *Gurdwara* and his religious zeal led him to continue serving the *gurdwaras* with commitment. He has been teaching *gurbani* for many years.

Daljit Singh Sond

Gulzar Singh Thandi (1925-1990)
m. Charan Kaur f. Kartar Singh

He was born in Lahore which is now in Pakistan. He passed his Matriculation at Punjab University. He worked as a ticket collector in India. He married Harbans Kaur in 1947 and had five children, four girls and one boy. He came to England in 1965 and worked in a foundry in Doncaster. He moved to Leeds and became a market trader and later set up a clothing factory in Meanwood, manufacturing ladies' wear. He had a good personality and was devoted to Sikh religion and the Sikh Temple. He spent a lot of his time working for the advancement of the Sikh religion in spite of his personal commitments. He served as President in the years 1987-1988 and 1989-1991.

Gulzar Singh Thandi

Gurbaksh Singh Rai (1918-1976)
m. Dhan Kaur   f. Hari Singh

He was born in the village of Jeenpur in the district of Hoshiarpur in the Punjab. He did his matriculation and was a good sportsman. He came from a farming background but joined the army. He soon left his army job and went to Bombay where he worked on the building site. He married Kartar Kaur in 1932. He had no children. He moved to Kenya and stayed there for a year and migrated to the UK in 1937. He settled in Doncaster where he worked as a labourer in a steel factory. He began his business of door-to-door selling and bought his house in 1939 and car in 1940. He was very ambitious and also devoted to his religion. He played a major role in collecting donations for building the Sikh Temple. He spent his last days in Boston in Lancashire.

Gurbakhash Singh Rai

Gurdeep Singh Bhogal (1934-2004)
m. Basant Kaur f. Fauja Singh

He was born in the district of Lyallpur now in Pakistan. He did his B.A. (Bachelor of Arts) and acquired his teaching qualification B.T. (Bachelor of Teaching) at the Government College, Ludhiana affiliated to Punjab University. He married Pavanjit Kaur in 1957 and married Paramjit Kaur in 1969 after the death of his first wife in 1959. He had four children, two boys and two girls. He went to Kenya in 1957 and then migrated to England in 1962. He worked in different capacities such as an interpreter in Nairobi and as a teacher in Leeds. For a brief period he worked in the Weight and Measurements Department of the Government of India and also as a labourer in construction work in London. He took an enormous interest in the development of the Sikh Temple and made valuable contributions. He held many executive positions and also served as President for a year in 1983-1984.

Gurdev Singh Dahele (2.4.1942 -)
m. Bhan Kaur f. Gajjan Singh

He was born in Nairobi, Kenya in East Africa. He acquired an ONC in Business studies from Park Lane College in Leeds. He married Swaran Kaur in 1968 and has two children, a boy and a girl. He came to the UK in 1970 and settled in Leeds. He works for the Economic and Social Regeneration of Inner Cities. He was awarded an MBE by the Queen in 1996 for his outstanding services to the Department of Employment in the Government Office for Yorkshire and the Humber and to the community. He comes from a religious family and contributed towards *gurdwaras* in Leeds. He held executive positions and served as President of the Sikh Temple in the years 1981-1983. He is a well-respected member of the Sikh community.

Gurmeet Singh Nahal (10.3.1931 -)
m. Harnam Kaur f. Thakar Singh

He was born in Adi Kalan in the district of Kapurthala in the Punjab. He studied up to sixth class at the village school. He came to Coventry in 1951 and worked there in Singer Motors as a labourer. After seven months, he came to Leeds and got a job in Catton Foundry. He went back to India in 1957 to get married and his wife joined him in 1958. He has three boys and three girls. He bought his first house in 1953. Surain Singh Bhambra was his lodger and very fond of doing *kirtan*. In the absence of a *gurdwara*, Sikhs gathered in his house on a weekly basis to join in the *kirtan*. Gurmeet is a pioneer Sikh whose passion and dedication in the service of the *Gurdwara* still remain even today. He helped by collecting donations for the Sikh Temple. He is not keen to be on Management Committees. He works for the unity of Sikhs and wants to see all Sikhs united.

Gurmeet Singh Nahal

Harbans Singh Bhambra (1925-1985)
m. Dhan Kaur f. Pritam Singh

He was born in the village of Ramgarh in the district of Kapurthala in the Punjab. He had his formal and religious education at the village school. He was a skilled carpenter. He married Mohinder Kaur in 1943 and had four children, two boys and two girls. He migrated to the UK in 1957 and settled in Leeds. He was very committed to religion and had contributed to the building work of the Sikh Temple. His *seva* (voluntary service) towards the Sikh community was invaluable.

Harbans Singh Bhamra

Harjit Singh Ryatt (31.7.1958 -)
m. Daljit Kaur f. Inder Singh

He was born in the district of Jalandhar in the Punjab. He came to Leeds in 1965 and studied Engineering and Law in this country. He is in the legal profession. He married Rabinder Kaur in 1984 and has four children, three girls and one boy. He took a keen interest in the *Gurdwara* and its activities at a very young age and played a prominent role in the events of 1984, when he was very concerned about the atrocities committed on Sikhs and took this case to the Human Rights Commission at Strasbourg. He also encouraged Sikh youths to learn about their heritage and taught Sikh history in English. He is shy by nature and a very reserved person but committed to the Sikh religion and religious traditions.

Harjit Singh Ryatt

Harpal Singh (7.5.1961 -)
m. Gurmej Kaur   f. Resham Singh

He was born in the village of Soos in the district of Hoshiarpur in the Punjab. He passed Higher Secondary Examination and worked in different capacities in the Punjab. He came to this country in 1990 and worked as a supervisor in a warehouse and as the *granthi* of the Sikh Temple. He married Jasvinder Kaur in 1988 and had two children, one boy and one girl. He became involved in the Sikh Temple and held executive positions. He served as President in 2000-2002.

Harpal Singh

Inder Singh Ryatt (1922- 2002)
m. [not known]   f. Gurditt Singh

He was born in Rawalpindi, which is now in Pakistan. He studied up to Matriculation and came to Leeds in 1956. He did a City and Guilds electrical course in Leeds and worked as an electrician with the firm Lu-

Lucas. He also had a market stall in Leeds. He married Daljit Kaur in 1938 and had six children, three boys and three girls. He chaired the first recorded meeting held on 2nd February 1958 and after that served the Sikh Temple in different capacities.

Inder Singh Ryatt

Joginder Singh Patara (28.9.1949 -)
m. Banti Kaur f. Thakur Singh

He was born in the village of Mohaddipur Ryaan in the district of Jalandhar in the Punjab. He studied up to eighth class at the village school. He came to Leeds in 1966 where he worked in Textile Mills and later in Catton Foundry. He married Paramjit Kaur in 1976 and has five girls and two boys. He became *amritdhari* in 1992 and after that took an active part in the *Gurdwara*. He became the President of the Sikh Temple in 1997-1999 and played a major role in building the purpose-built *gurdwara*.

Joginder Singh Patara

Kesar Singh Reehal (1920-1971)
m. Lajo f. Bhagat Singh

He was born in the village of Gunachor in the district of Jalandhar in the Punjab. He had his basic education in the village school and later went to study in Khankhana village. He was keen to keep the company of saints from his early life and became interested in *gurbani*. He enjoyed doing *kirtan* and had a good voice. He

Kesar Singh Reehal

married Pritam Kaur in 1936 and had three children, two boys and one girl. He was a skilled carpenter and worked as bricklayer in India. He migrated to East Africa in 1943 and settled in Kampala where he worked as a building supervisor with Hunts Motor Ltd for 20 years. He came to the UK in 1962 and settled in Leeds. He served *gurdwaras* devotedly and did *kirtan* in the Sunday *diwan* regularly.

Kewal Singh Badesha (4.9.1944 -)
m. Bant Kaur f. Narang Singh

He was born in the village of Budhiana in the district of Jalandhar in the Punjab. He passed his Matriculation at Punjab University. He migrated to the UK in 1963 and did various jobs such as crane driver and heat treatment worker in the foundry. He married Surinder Kaur in 1966 and has three children, one boy and two girls. He has served the Sikh Temple in various capacities and was President in 1984-1985 and 1986-1987.

Kewal Singh Badesha

Kewal Singh Kular (17.3.1959 -)
m. Surjit Kaur f. Dharam Singh

He was born in the village of Kular in the district of Jalandhar in the Punjab. He did his Matriculation at Punjab University. He married Jitender Kaur in 1978 and has five children, three boys and two girls. He came to Leeds in 1978 and is at present working as a general operator in a factory. He is interested in the Sikh religion and participated in the *Gurdwara* activities and eventually became President in 1996-1997.

Kewal Singh Kular

Kirpal Singh Duggal (1924-2006)
m. Kartar Kaur f. Teja Singh

He was born in the village of Jamsher Khas in the district of Jalandhar in the Punjab. He gained an F.A. (Faculty of Arts, equivalent to A level) from Punjab University. He worked as a printing master in India and became the supervisor in Calico Mills in Ahmedabad. He was the General Secretary of Singh Sabha *Gurdwara* in Ahmedabad and President of the Young Men's Association for 4-5 years. He married Gurbachan Kaur in 1942 and had three sons and two daughters. He came to London to study Automobile Engineering in 1956. Within a year, he moved to Leeds where he worked as a spinner in a textile mill on night shifts. He lived in rented accommodation and later bought his house at 3 Ebberston Terrace, Leeds 6. His family joined him in 1966. His background made him interested in participating in the *Gurdwara* and he had made enormous contributions to the development of the Sikh Temple. He was the one who came up with the idea of building a *gurdwara*, which could fulfil the religious and social needs of the Sikh families in future.

Kirpal Singh Duggal

Lashkar Singh Phull (2.4.1926 -)
m. Swaran Kaur f. Kishan Singh

He was born in the village of Nadela in the district of Kapurthala in the Punjab. He studied up to Intermediate level (Faculty of Arts equivalent to A level) at Punjab University. In 1944, he married Joginder Kaur and he has seven children, six sons and one daughter. He has travelled widely. He went first to Iran and in 1951 went to Africa and then migrated to the United Kingdom in 1957 and finally to Canada in 1980. In the UK, he worked as bus conductor and motor binder. He was associated with the Sikh Temple in one capacity or another while he lived in this country. He made enormous contributions to the development of the Sikh Temple.

Lashkar Singh Phull

Malia Singh Rathor (1922-1997)
m. Harnam Kaur f. Boota Singh

He was born in Lahore which is now in Pakistan. He had primary education at his village school. He married Maan Kaur in 1945 and had eight children, four boys and four girls. He migrated to this country in 1948 after the partition of India. He worked as a weaver in textile mills. Later he had a market stall and also a shop on Roundhay Road, Leeds selling mens' wear. He served the Sikh Temple devotedly in many capacities. He was truly and sincerely a religious man.

Malia Singh Rathor

Mota Singh Bhamra (1921-1997)
m. Dhan Kaur f. Pritam Singh

He was born in the village of Ramgarh in the district of Kapurthala in the Punjab. He did not have formal education but learnt Panjabi, *path* and *shabad kirtan* from the local village school situated in a *gurdwara*. He was a skilled carpenter and joiner. He married Gurbachan Kaur in 1939 and had four children, two boys and two girls. He went to East Africa in 1950 and stayed in Kampala, Uganda and Kenya. He migrated to this country in 1956 and made valuable contributions towards the renovation of the Sikh Temple. He was an excellent bonesetter which also made him popular in the Sikh community.

Mota Singh Bhamra

Narotam Dev Mishra (1924-1985)
m. Karam Devi f. Amar Nath

He was born in Nikodar town in the district of Jalandhar. He passed his Matriculation at Punjab University and joined his father's business. He married Kamla Devi and had three children, one boy and two girls. He came to Leeds in 1950 and like other early immigrants did door-to-door selling. Later he had a market stall in Barnsley. He was very broad-minded, social and generous. He was generally known as David. He was a founder member of the Sikh Temple and did a lot of voluntary work in promoting religion and retaining religious traditions.

Narotam Dev Mishra

Niranjan Singh Bhatra (1930-1979)
m. Tej Kaur f. Balwant Singh Akali

He was born in Lahore, which is now in Pakistan. He acquired formal education up to Primary level. He married Charan Kaur in 1946 and had seven children, three boys and four girls. He migrated to the UK in 1948 just after the partition of India. He settled in Leeds and first worked in the drapery business and then went into the property business. He was a religious man and did voluntary service in the *Gurdwara*.

Niranjan Singh Bhatra

Nirmal Singh Sangha (1.1.1951 -)
m. Kartar Kaur   f. Resham Singh

He was born in the village of Sindhran in the district of Jalandhar in the Punjab. He did his Matriculation at Punjab University and he tried to improve his English when he came to Leeds in 1966. He married Balbir Kaur in 1968 and has two sons and a daughter. In this country, he worked in a foundry, as a bus conductor and in the ICL making computer bodies. Eventually he bought an off-licence shop. His life was changed when he came in

Nirmal Singh Sangha

contact with Bhindrawala in 1984. He gave up drinking and took an interest in religious studies. Since then he has served the Sikh Temple devotedly. He was President of the *Gurdwara* in 1988-89, 1993-94, 1994-95, 1999-2000, and 2004-2006.

Piara Singh Chaggar (30.11.1915 -)
m. Basant Kaur f. Jiwan Singh

He was born in the village of Banga in the district of Nawan Sehar in the Punjab. He had no formal education. He married Rattan Kaur in 1931 and his second marriage was to Harbans Kaur in 1969 with whom he had one son. He came to England in 1956 and worked as a bricklayer with Trevor Thorpe Construction Company. He was passionate about a *gurdwara* and was involved from the very beginning. He became the President of the Indian Workers Association in 1966 and stayed in this position for 4-5 years. He has had a record of *gurseva* since his migration and served as President of the Sikh Temple in 1962-63 and 1965-66.

Piara Singh Sambhi (1929-1992)
m. Puna Kaur f. Shere Singh

He was born in the village of Mahatpur in the district of Jalandhar in the Punjab. He did an MA in English at Punjab University in 1956. He married Avtar Kaur in 1956 and had two children, one boy and one girl. He was a ration inspector before migrating to the UK in 1963. He settled in Leeds and took a job on night shifts as textile worker. He was a prolific writer and an internationally respected Sikh scholar. He wrote many books and took a keen interest in the *Gurdwara*. He served as President from 1967 to 1970.

Prem Singh Duggal (4.5.1943 -)
m. Kartar Kaur f. Teja Singh

He was born in the village of Jamsher Khas, in the district of Jalandhar in the Punjab. He passed his Matriculation examination at Punjab University and migrated to Britain in 1963. He worked as a conductor, a weaver in textile mills and in engineering fittings. He married Daljit Kaur and had three boys. At present he is a financial advisor. He has always been involved in voluntary work and has done some useful work for the Sikh community, for example, a survey of Panjabi. He regularly attends the Sikh Temple and takes a keen interest in the work of the Temple. He served as President from 1991 to 1993.

Prem Singh Duggal

Resham Singh Gill (1935 -)
m. Dhanti f. Gurditt Singh

He was born in the village of Gillan in the district of Jalandhar in the Punjab. He did his Matriculation at Punjab University. He worked as an Assistant Panchayat Officer before his migration to Britain in 1954. He married Rajinder Kaur in 1962 and has three sons and one daughter. He worked in Catton foundry and also did building work in Leeds. He contributed to the development of the *Gurdwara* and held the executive posts of President, Secretary and Treasurer (see Appendix 2). In addition to his voluntary service towards the Sikh Temple he has served on the Racial Equality Council, the CRC and Police Committees. He became the President of the Congress Party in Leeds and Vice President of the UK Congress Party.

Resham Singh Gill

Sadhu Singh Bhandari (1917-1992)
m. [not known] f. Dal Singh

He was born in the village of Loharian in the district of Jalandhar in the Punjab. He had no formal education, but was a skilled carpenter. He married Rattan Kaur and had four children, three girls and one boy. He came to Leeds in 1960 and worked as a joiner. He was keen to serve the *Gurdwara* and made an enormous contribution to the building work. He lived in the *Gurdwara* and served as a caretaker on a voluntary basis until he retired.

Sadhu Singh Bhandari

Sardara Singh (10.3.1929)
m. Kishan Kaur f. Ujjagar Singh

He was born in the village of Mathada Kalan in the district of Jalandhar in the Punjab. He did his Matriculation in Phillour. He married Surjit Kaur in 1945 and had five children, three boys and two girls. He came to Bradford in November 1950. He worked as a spinner in a wool mill for a year and then set up his own clothing business. He was among the early pioneers to set up a *gurdwara* in Leeds and also became President of the Sikh Temple in 1960-1962 and served for two years.

Sardara Singh

Sarwan Singh Cheema (1924-2003)
m. Pratap Kaur f. Gurdial Singh

He was born in the village of Cheema Khurd in the district of Jalandhar in the Punjab. He had only a primary education but his inclination towards religion and the company of saints from an early age made him much more knowledgeable.

Sarwan Singh Cheema

He was married at the early age of eleven to Bishan Kaur in 1935. He had four sons and two daughters. He came to England in 1955 and worked as a crane driver in Carltons Foundry. He took a keen interest in the Sikh Temple and was President in 1966-67 and 1976-78.

Sarwan Singh Dandi (6.5.1937 -)
m. Sada Kaur f. Lala Bant Lal

He was born in the village of Dandiyan in the district of Hoshiarpur in the Punjab. He had only a primary education from his village school and was more inclined towards music. He learned music at an early age, which proved very useful in his later life here in Britain. He married Balwant Kaur in 1958 and had six children, five boys and one girl. He migrated to Britain in 1964 and worked in textile mills and in the building trade. He is devoted to the *gurdwara seva* and has been involved in *gurdwaras* since his migration to this country mainly as a *kirtaniya*, though he served as President for a year in 1972-1973.

Sarwan Singh Dandi

Sohan Singh Seehra (1.1.1931 -)
m. Amar Kaur   f. Bawa Singh

He was born in the village of Hakimpur, in the district of Jalandhar in the Punjab. He studied up to the fifth class in the village school and then learned carpentry and worked as a carpenter. In 1949, at the age of 18, he married Surinder Kaur. He has three sons and three daughters. He migrated to East Africa in June 1951 and subsequently to England in 1958. From the very beginning, he was inclined to do *seva* in the *Gurdwara* in whatsoever capacity he was asked to take on.

Sohan Singh Seehra

Tarlok Singh Toor (1947-1997)
m. Pritam Kaur f. Punna Singh

He was born in the village of Kang Sahbo near Nakodar in the Punjab. He studied up to Middle class and migrated to this country in 1962. He married Simarjit Kaur in 1965 and had four children, two boys and two girls. He worked in a glass factory and later as a plumber. He bought an off-licence shop and sold it after two years. He was very involved with the Sikh Temple and spent most of his later years in *gurdwara seva*. He was President of the Sikh Temple in 1995-1996.

Tarlok Singh Toor

Tehal Singh (1911-1963)
m. Sada Kaur   f. Barkat Singh

He was born in the village of Galotia Kalan in the district of Gujranwala which is now in Pakistan. He did his Matriculation and after the partition moved to Amritsar in India. He married Swaran Kaur in 1930 and had five children, four girls and one boy. He came to Britain for the first time in 1935, then in 1937 and finally came to live here in 1949. He worked as a pedlar in the beginning and then had a market stall and eventually managed to go into the wholesale business. He took a keen interest in the work of the Sikh Temple and remained very active until his death.

Tehal Singh

Vir Singh Rayat (1917- 2006)
m. Dhan Kaur f. Basant Singh

He was born in the village of Bhulla Rai in the district of Kapurthala in the Punjab. He did his Matriculation in Lahore in 1936. He married Chanan Kaur in 1933 and had four boys and one girl. He migrated to Kampala (East Africa) in 1955 and subsequently came to the UK in 1960, where he worked as a bricklayer for 25 years. He contributed towards the building work of the Sikh Temple, being an experienced bricklayer. He also participated in the weekly *kirtan diwan* in the early years when the Sikh Temple could not afford to employ *kirtaniya*.

Vir Singh Rayat

Appendix 4
Glossary

Akal Takht	ਅਕਾਲ ਤਖਤ	a) Supreme Sikh Authority b) a building in the Golden Temple, Amritsar
Akal Purakh	ਅਕਾਲ ਪੁਰਖ	God, not affected by death or time
Akhand path	ਅਖੰਡ ਪਾਠ	Continuous reading of the *Guru Granth Sahib* taking 48 hours
Amrit	ਅੰਮ੍ਰਿਤ	Nectar, solution of water and sugar used at the Sikh ceremony of initiation
Amrit chhakna	ਅੰਮ੍ਰਿਤ ਛਕਣਾ	To undergo initiation ceremony
Amritdhari	ਅੰਮ੍ਰਿਤਧਾਰੀ	An initiated Sikh
Amrit Pahul	ਅੰਮ੍ਰਿਤ ਪਾਹੁਲ	A Sikh initiation ceremony
Amrit Prachar	ਅੰਮ੍ਰਿਤ ਪ੍ਰਚਾਰ	Administering Sikh initiation ceremony.
Anand Karaj	ਆਨੰਦ ਕਾਰਜ	Sikh marriage ceremony
Anandpur Sahib	ਆਨੰਦਪੁਰ ਸਾਹਿਬ	Holy city of Sikhs
Ardas	ਅਰਦਾਸ	Sikh prayer recited at the conclusion of a service
Baba	ਬਾਬਾ	a) A term used for paternal grandfather b) A term used for a respected and religious man

Baisakhi	ਬੈਸਾਖੀ	<u>See</u> *Vaisakhi*
Bani	ਬਾਣੀ	Hymns - a term collectively used for the compositions of the *Gurus* and the saints included in the *Guru Granth Sahib*.
Barahmaha	ਬਾਰਹਮਾਹ	Hymns relating to the twelve months
Besan	ਬੇਸਨ	Gram Flour
Betaba	ਬੇਤਾਬਾ	Disclaimer
Bhagat	ਭਗਤ	A devotee
Bhangra	ਭੰਗੜਾ	*Punjabi* folk dance
Bhai	ਭਾਈ	a) A term used for a brother b) A respectful term used to address a man c) the custodian of a *gurdwara*
Bhajiya	ਭਜੀਆ	Savoury snacks made of vegetables wrapped in *besan*
Bhana manana	ਭਾਣਾ ਮੰਨਣਾ	Accepting the will of God
Bhatra	ਭਾਟੜਾ	Name of a caste
Bhog	ਭੋਗ	Finishing ceremony of the reciting of *Guru Granth Sahib*
Bibi	ਬੀਬੀ	A respectful term used for a woman
Biradari	ਬਰਾਦਰੀ	Refers both to brotherhood and caste group; the term is used by Sikhs, Muslims and *Punjabi* Hindus
Chamar	ਚਮਾਰ	a) A leather worker

		b) A term used for the *Chamar* caste
Chapati	ਚਪਾਤੀ/ ਰੋਟੀ	Flat bread
Chaubedar	ਚੋਬੇਦਾਰ	A carrier of *Nishan Sahib* in front of the *palki* in which the Holy scripture is carried
Chaubedara di seva	ਚੋਬੇਦਾਰ ਦੀ ਸੇਵਾ	Volunteering to carry *Nishan Sahib* in the procession
Chaur	ਚੌਰ	a) Ritual fan made of yak hair waved over the *Guru Granth Sahib* b) Symbol of authority
Chaur di seva	ਚੌਰ ਦੀ ਸੇਵਾ	Volunteering to wave *chaur*
Chet	ਚੇਤ	Name of Indian lunar month corresponding to March-April
Daan	ਦਾਨ	Charitable gifts or donations
Dal	ਦਾਲ	Pulses
Darbar Hall	ਦਰਬਾਰ ਹਾਲ	A hall where the Holy book is kept
Darshan	ਦਰਸ਼ਨ	Visiting religious person or places
Dastar	ਦਸਤਾਰ	Turban
Daswandh	ਦਸਵੰਦ	Donating one tenth of the earning for religious purposes
Degh	ਦੇਗ਼	Sacred sweet made of a mixture of sugar, semolina and butter
Dhadi Jatha	ਢਾਡੀ ਜਥਾ	Bards - a group who sing warrior songs

Dharam	ਧਰਮ	a) Social and religious obligations b) Panjabi term for religion
Dhup	ਧੂਪ	Incense
Diwali	ਦਿਵਾਲੀ	Festival of lights celebrated by Hindus and Sikhs, which usually fall in the months of October or November
Diwan	ਦੀਵਾਨ	A term used for the Sikh act of worship as in Sunday *diwan*
Dun	ਡਨ	Religious punishment
Five K's	ਪੰਜ ਕਕਾਰ	Sikh symbols of identity
Ganesh	ਗਣੇਸ਼	A Hindu god
Gatka	ਗਟਕਾ	Martial art
Ghalughara	ਘਾਲੂਘਾਰਾ	Struggle
Giani	ਗਿਆਨੀ	a) Religious Sikh b) Qualification in Panjabi
Golak	ਗੋਲਕ	Money-box
Granth	ਗ੍ਰੰਥ	a) A book b) Literary composition
Granth Sahib	ਗ੍ਰੰਥ ਸਾਹਿਬ	<u>See</u> *Guru Granth Sahib*
Granthi	ਗ੍ਰੰਥੀ	a) One who looks after the *Granth Sahib* b) A reader of the *Granth Sahib*. c) Custodian of the *Gurdwara*
Gur maryada	ਗੁਰਮਰਯਾਦਾ	According to Sikh religion
Gurbani	ਗੁਰਬਾਣੀ	Religious hymns

Gurbani Sikhya	ਗੁਰਬਾਣੀ ਸਿਖਿਆ	Teaching to read *Guru Granth Sahib*
Gurdwara	ਗੁਰਦੁਵਾਰਾ	Literally the house of the God or doorway to God
Gurmat	ਗੁਰਮਤ	*Gurus*' teaching
Gurmukhi	ਗੁਰਮੁੱਖੀ	Script used for writing Panjabi
Gurpurab	ਗੁਰਪੁਰਬ	Anniversary of the birth or death of Sikh *Gurus*
Gursikh	ਗੁਰਸਿਖ	One who leads his life according to the principles of the Sikh religion
Guru	ਗੁਰੂ	Religious teacher or a preceptor
Guru Granth Sahib	ਗੁਰੂ ਗ੍ਰੰਥ ਸਾਹਿਬ	The Sikh Holy scripture
Guru Maryada	ਗੁਰੂ ਮਰਿਆਦਾ	Compulsory rituals in the presence of the *Guru Granth Sahib*
Gurughar	ਗੁਰੂਘਰ	Another Panjabi term for a *Gurdwara*
Gutka	ਗੁਟਕਾ	Handbook of prayers
Halal	ਹਲਾਲ	Slaughtered by the process of slow and ritual killing
Halwa	ਹਲਵਾ	A sweet made of butter, sugar and semolina
Hankar	ਹੰਕਾਰ	Pride
Harminder Sahib	ਹਰਿਮੰਦਰ ਸਾਹਿਬ	The Golden Temple
Haumen	ਹੌਮੈਂ	Individualism or self-centredness

Hola Mohalla	ਹੋਲਾ ਮਹੱਲਾ	Mock battles held by *Nihang* warriors at Anandpur Sahib
Holi	ਹੋਲੀ	Hindu festival held at the full moon in February-March
Istri sabha	ਇਸਤ੍ਰੀ ਸਭਾ	An organization for women
Japuji	ਜਪੁਜੀ	Morning prayer hymns
Jat	ਜੱਟ	Land-owning caste
Jatha	ਜਥਾ	Organization
Jathedar	ਜਥੇਦਾਰ	A leader of an organization
Jhir	ਝੀਰ	Male person belonging to the water-carrier caste
Jore seva	ਜੋੜੇ ਸੇਵਾ	Looking after the shoes in the *Gurdwara*
Jyot	ਜੋਤ	Flame lit with cotton bud
Julaha	ਜੁਲਾਹਾ	Male person belonging to the weaver caste
Kaccha	ਕੱਛ/ਕੱਛਾ	Loose fitting underwear - one of the five *K*'s
Kam	ਕਾਮ	Lust
Kangha	ਕੰਘਾ	Comb - one of the five *K*'s
Kara	ਕੜਾ	Bangle - one of the five *K*'s
Karma	ਕਰਮ	Action
Katha	ਕਥਾ	Story
Kathakar	ਕਥਾਕਾਰ	Story-teller
Kaur	ਕੌਰ	Name assumed by all female Sikhs - literally it means 'princess'

Kavi darbar	ਕਵੀ ਦਰਬਾਰ	Programme given by poets collectively
Kes	ਕੇਸ	Uncut hair - one of the five *K*'s
Kesadhari	ਕੇਸਾਧਾਰੀ	One who keeps uncut hair
Keshadhari	ਕੇਸ਼ਾਧਾਰੀ	See *Kesadhhari*
Kesri	ਕੇਸਰੀ	Saffron colour
Khalistan	ਖਾਲਿਸਤਾਨ	Sikh State
Khalsa	ਖਾਲਸਾ	a) The Sikh order, brotherhood, instituted by the 10th Sikh *Guru* in 1699 b) The pure ones
Khalsa Panth	ਖਾਲਸਾ ਪੰਥ	Sikh religious order
Khanda	ਖੰਡਾ	Double-edged sword - one of the emblems of Sikhism
Khatri	ਖਤੱਰੀ	A mercantile caste
Kirpan	ਕਿਰਪਾਨ	Sword - one of the five *K*'s
Kirt karo	ਕਿਰਤ ਕਰੋ	Earn a living by honest and approved means
Kirtan	ਕੀਰਤਨ	Hymn singing
Kirtiniya	ਕੀਰਤਨੀਆਂ	Hymn singer
Krodh	ਕ੍ਰੋਧ	Anger
Kurahit	ਕੁਰਹਿਤ	Breach of the (Sikh) Code of Conduct
Ladoos	ਲੱਡੂ	Indian sweets distributed on auspicious occasions
Lakshmi	ਲਕਸ਼ਮੀ	Hindu goddess of wealth

Langar	ਲੰਗਰ	Communal food served in *gurdwaras* free of charge
Langar seva	ਲੰਗਰ ਸੇਵਾ	Undertaking or volunteering to serve communal food
Lavan	ਲਾਵਾਂ	a) Walking around the *Guru Granth Sahib* at the marriage ceremony b) The recitation of four stanzas from the *Guru Granth Sahib*
Lobh	ਲੋਭ	Greed
Lohri	ਲੋਹੜੀ	Harvest festival
Lohtop	ਲੋਹਟੋਪ	Crash helmet
Maghi	ਮਾਘੀ	Harvest festival
Majha	ਮਾਝਾ	Region in the Punjab
Maryada	ਮਰਜਾਦਾ	Religious tradition
Mela	ਮੇਲਾ	Fair or festival
Milni	ਮਿਲਣੀ	Ritual meeting of the family members of both sides before the marriage ceremony
Mukti	ਮੁਕਤੀ	a) Liberation b) Transmigration of soul and its union with God
Naam	ਨਾਮ	God's name
Naam Japo	ਨਾਮ ਜਪੋ	The reciting of God's name
Naamkaran	ਨਾਮਕਰਨ	Naming ceremony
Nagar Kirtan	ਨਗਰ ਕੀਰਤਨ	Religious procession
Nai	ਨਾਈ	Barber

Namdharis	ਨਾਮਧਾਰੀ	A Sikh movement following *Baba* Ram Singh - *Namdharis* believe in a living *guru*
Namsimran	ਨਾਮ ਸਿਮਰਨ	Meditation on God's name
Nanakshahi	ਨਾਨਕਸਾਹੀ	A Sikh calendar
Nirankar	ਨਿਰੰਕਾਰ	Without form - used for God
Nirankari	ਨਿਰੰਕਾਰੀ	A religious sect
Nishan Sahib	ਨਿਸ਼ਾਨ ਸਾਹਿਬ	Sikh flag
Nishkam Sevak Jatha	ਨਿਸਕਾਮ ਸੇਵਕ ਜਥਾ	Association of Sikh Volunteers
Pali	ਪਾਲੀ	Language of Buddhist scriptures
Palki	ਪਾਲਕੀ	A palanquin
Pandit	ਪੰਡਤ	a) Knowledgeable person b) Brahman caste
Pangat	ਪੰਗਤ	Sitting together without caste and class distinction
Panj	ਪੰਜ	Five
Panjabi	ਪੰਜਾਬੀ	The language of the Punjab and also of Sikh scripture
Panj granthi	ਪੰਜ ਗ੍ਰੰਥੀ	A religious book containing five prayers
Panj pyare	ਪੰਜ ਪਿਆਰੇ	Five beloved Sikhs
Panth	ਪੰਥ	Sikh religious order
Path	ਪਾਠ	Recitation of the *Granth Sahib* or *gurbani*
Path bhaitan	ਪਾਠ ਭੇਟਾਂ	Money given to a *granthi* to recite *Guru Granth Sahib*

Path-bhog	ਪਾਠ-ਭੋਗ	Finishing ceremony of the recitation of the *Granth Sahib*
Phagun	ਫਗਣ	An Indian lunar month corresponding to February - March
Phulka	ਫੁਲਕਾ	a) Soft chapati bigger in size b) Another term used for a chapati
Prasad	ਪ੍ਰਸ਼ਾਦ	Mixture of semolina, sugar and butter - sacramental food shared at the end of Sikh service
Punjabi	ਪੰਜਾਬੀ	People of the Punjab
Qaum	ਕੌਮ	Nation
Radhasoami	ਰਾਧਾ ਸੁਵਾਮੀ	A sect which believes in the living *Guru*
Ragan	ਰਾਗਣ	A female singer
Ragas	ਰਾਗਾ	Musical rhythms or metres
Ragi	ਰਾਗੀ	Hymn-singers
Rahit Maryada	ਰਹਿਤ ਮਰਯਾਦਾ	Sikh Code of Conduct
Ramgarhia	ਰਾਮਗੜੀਆ	A Sikh artisan caste comprising carpenters, blacksmiths, masons, or village artisans
Ravidasi	ਰਵੀਦਾਸੀ	Untouchables
Rein swayi	ਰੈਣ ਸਵਾਈ	Continuous *kirtan* during the night
Romalla/ Rumallas	ਰੁਮਾਲਾ	Expensive cloth to cover the *Guru Granth Sahib*

Saag	ਸਾਗ਼	A kind of cooked mixed vegetable puree made mainly of green mustard and spinach
Sadharan/sehaj path	ਸਧਾਰਨ/ ਸਹਿਜ ਪਾਠ	A non-continuous *path* of the *Granth Sahib*
Sagan	ਸਗਨ	Auspicious gift or act
Sahibjada	ਸਾਹਿਬਜ਼ਾਦਾ	a) Prince b) an affectionate term for a son
Sainchi	ਸੈਂਚੀ	*Guru Granth Sahib* in two volumes
Samagam	ਸਮਾਗਮ	Celebration
Samosas	ਸਮੋਸਾ	An Indian snack made of flour pastry stuffed with potatoes and peas
Sampuran	ਸੰਪੂਰਨ	Complete
Sangat	ਸੰਗਤ	Congregation
Sangharash	ਸੰਘਰਸ	Struggle
Sangrand	ਸੰਗਰਾਂਦ	First day of Lunar month
Sant	ਸੰਤ	A pious man
Sant Maryada	ਸੰਤ ਮਰਜਾਦਾ	Traditions founded by saints
Santmat	ਸੰਤ ਮਤ	Principles and traditions set by saints
Saropa	ਸਰੋਪਾ	Honoured with a *dastar*
Satguru	ਸਤਿਗੁਰੂ	A true teacher
Satsang	ਸਤਸੰਗ	*Kirtan* sessions
Sehajdhari	ਸਹਿਜਧਾਰੀ	Sikh who believes in the

		teachings of Sikhism but not in Sikh identity
Seva	ਸੇਵਾ	Voluntary service to the community
Sevadar	ਸੇਵਾਦਾਰ	Volunteers
Shabad	ਸ਼ਬਦ	a) Hymns b) Words of the Holy book
Shabad kirtan	ਸ਼ਬਦ ਕੀਰਤਨ	Hymn singing
Shahid	ਸ਼ਹੀਦ	Martyr
Shigligar	ਸਿਗਲੀਗਰ	Gypsies
Shromani Gurdwara Parbandhak Committee (SGPC)	ਸ਼ਰੋਮਣੀ ਗੁਰਦੁਆਰਾ ਪ੍ਰਬੰਧਕ ਕਮੇਟੀ	An authoritative religious committee based in Amritsar, Punjab
Singh	ਸਿੰਘ	Literally meaning lion - added to the name of Sikh males
Tabla	ਤਬਲਾ	Drums
Tavya bahina	ਤਾਬਿਆ ਬਹਿਣਾ	To sit in attendance behind *Guru Granth Sahib*
Thal/Thali	ਥਾਲ/ਥਾਲੀ	A metal plate
Vaisakhi	ਵੈਸਾਖੀ	a) The Sikh festival associated with the birth of *Khalsa*. b) New year for Sikhs c) Harvest festival
Vak	ਵਾਕ	Opening sentence from a page of the *Guru Granth Sahib*
Viakhia	ਵਿਆਖਿਆ	Explaining the religious traditions
Wand chhako/chhakna	ਵੰਡ ਛਕੋ /ਛਕਣਾ	Share with the less fortunate

About the Authors

Bibi Satwant Kaur Rait & ***Sardar*** Harbhajan Singh Rait

Dr. Satwant Kaur Rait was born in India in the village of Lambra in the district of Hoshiarpur in the Punjab. She did an MA in history at Delhi University in 1967 and came to Leeds in 1968 to join her husband after their marriage.

Dr Rait had worked as a Librarian in a school with the Directorate of Education in Delhi and wanted to pursue the same career here in England. She took the Post-graduate Diploma in Librarianship in Leeds and an MA in Librarianship from Sheffield University in order to qualify for a professional library post. She got her first job in Leeds in 1974 as a library assistant but by 1986 she had become a Principal Officer and had also been appointed a Justice of the Peace on the Bradford Bench. She gained a PhD from Loughborough University in 1993. She has been on the executive committees of many associations and had enjoyed working at grass root level. Over the years she has combined a close commitment to her family with her career and research, and has many books, reports and research articles to her name.

Dr. Rait has kept her religious and cultural values very close to her heart. Her deep attachment to the Sikh religion and culture has inspired her to write books closely associated with the Sikh community and related themes. Among her publications those specifically related to the Punjabi culture are: *Bibliography on Ethnic minorities* (1981), *Dictionary of Punjabi name elements* (1984), *Acquisition and cataloguing of Punjabi language literature in British public libraries* (1985), *Punjabi Rasoi kala* (1989), *Sikh women in Leeds* (2003), *Breaking the barrier: the voice of Asian women* (2004) and *Sikh women in England* (2005). Her retirement in 2001 gave her more time to concentrate on research in the areas of her interest and passion. She has been fortunate in being funded by small grants for her community-related publications.

Sardar Harbhajan Singh Rait was born in India in the village of Bham in the district of Hoshiarpur in the Punjab. He graduated from Punjab University and acquired qualifications in Mechanical Engineering from Delhi Polytechnic in India and worked in a government post in the Seismology Department in Delhi before migrating to Leeds. He came to Leeds in 1963 and worked in private engineering firms. After obtaining qualifications in Electrical Engineering from the University of Leeds, he worked at the University as Technician-in-charge of the Textile Engineering workshop until his retirement.